Entertaining Entrepreneurs

Entertaining Entrepreneurs

REALITY TV'S *Shark Tank* AND THE

AMERICAN DREAM IN UNCERTAIN

TIMES

DANIEL HOROWITZ

THE
UNIVERSITY OF
NORTH CAROLINA
PRESS
Chapel Hill

Publication of this book was supported by a generous gift from VICKI & PORTER DURHAM.

© 2020 Daniel Horowitz
All rights reserved
Designed by Richard Hendel
Set in Utopia and TheSans
by Tseng Information Systems, Inc.
Manufactured in the United States of America

The University of North Carolina Press has been a member of the Green Press Initiative since 2003.

Cover images: swimming pool background © iStockphoto/ Nastco, money pile © iStockphoto/choness, sharks © iStockphoto/MediaProduction and © iStockphoto/ Nerthuz, and diver © shutterstock/Sergey Nivens

Interior shark image © iStockphoto/Nerthuz

Library of Congress Cataloging-in-Publication Data
Names: Horowitz, Daniel, 1938– author.
Title: Entertaining entrepreneurs : reality TV's Shark Tank and the American dream in uncertain times / Daniel Horowitz.
Description: Chapel Hill : The University of North Carolina Press, 2020. | Includes bibliographical references and index.
Identifiers: LCCN 2020013191 | ISBN 978-1-4696-5943-5 (cloth: alk. paper) | ISBN 978-1-4696-6260-2 (pbk.: alk. paper) | ISBN 978-1-4696-5944-2 (ebook)
Subjects: LCSH: Shark tank (Television program) | Entrepreneurship—United States. | American Dream. | Reality television programs—United States.
Classification: LCC HB615.H67 2020 | DDC 791.45/72—dc23
LC record available at https://lccn.loc.gov/2020013191

To the editors who made
it all possible: Peter Agree,
Chris Appy, Lew Bateman,
Tom Bender, Clark Dougan,
Lynn Dumenil, Abby Gross,
Helen L. Horowitz,
Robert Lockhart, Lucy Maddox,
Mark Simpson-Vos, and
Judy Smith

Contents

Illustrations

Preface

When I first watched the reality TV show *Shark Tank*, supposedly to take my mind off work, I was struck by its dramatic stories and captivating characters. However, when I set out to write this book, I came to feel that the muted skepticism I had often deployed in the past when encountering popular culture was not up to the task of assessing contemporary American entrepreneurship. To be sure, as a historian I believe that it is my obligation to comprehend the worldviews of those I write about on their own terms. Yet, as fascinated as I am with this television show, I find it highly problematic. *Shark Tank* presents a distorted picture of the world and relies on a skewed vision of American entrepreneurship. It hides the roles of workers, who help make so many enterprises possible. It minimizes and even obliterates the crucial role that the federal government plays in undergirding the success of so many corporations. It celebrates the American dream even as it leaves vague its nature. It treats matters of race, class, gender, and sexuality as little more than theatrical fodder. It hoists individualism and even ruthlessness to honored positions neither deserves.

As I delved into other representations of American entrepreneurship—in school competitions, university programs, other television shows, how-to books, memoirs—I found many of them similarly problematic. Preparing students as early as the third grade to become entrepreneurs strikes me as inappropriate indoctrination. High school and college competitions too often take place in a vacuum that blocks out the many troubling elements that shape our society. The proliferation of entrepreneurial programs within universities—supported by interlocking corporate, nonprofit, and government organizations—represents the more practical dimensions of STEM's increasing power in the curriculum. Though some scholarly writing on entrepreneurship is critical, that criticism usually appears within a naively celebratory framework that accepts the basic premises of contemporary American capitalism.

In researching and writing this book, I had to think about a series of fundamental changes I have witnessed in my lifetime: from the organization man to the entrepreneur; from the language of free enterprise to that of entrepreneurship; from the New Deal Keynesian order that dominated American life from the mid-1930s until the late 1960s to a newer neoliberal one. The former, whatever its imperfections, at its best entailed commitments by the federal government, corporations, and labor unions to provide many Americans a measure of economic security via wage growth and a robust social safety net that might even narrow the gap between rich and poor. On the other hand, neoliberalism rests on individual self-governance instead of communitarian obligations. In the world *Shark Tank* presents, creative disruption brings economic growth and social entrepreneurship takes the place of social welfare programs. In the pages that follow, I juxtapose this entrepreneurial vision with what I consider to be the accurate picture of American life that many social scientists and journalists have recently offered—one where insecurity, inequality, incarceration, racism, and the breakdown of communities play prominent roles.

Some might think that I am trying to provide information that will enable readers to become successful entrepreneurs. Although that is hardly my intent, I suspect that this book will teach not only the basics of entrepreneurship but also what pitfalls to avoid, practically but also, more importantly, ethically. Moreover, I hope that what one astute observer has called my "performed neutrality" does not hide my belief that *Shark Tank* and, more generally, contemporary American entrepreneurship cannot be allowed to obscure the very real problems tens of millions Americans face daily.[1] There is much that is admirable in specific and transformative entrepreneurial enterprises. However, embracing entrepreneurship as the centerpiece of a social vision of what America is at present and can be in the future means forgetting alternative choices, ones that focus less on creative destruction and more on social justice.

Introduction

On October 23, 2015, during season seven of the reality
TV show *Shark Tank*, more than 6 million viewers
watched J. D. Claridge, an aerospace engineer, and
Charles Manning, a businessman with extensive experience managing software enterprises, offer five celebrity
investors—the Sharks for whom the show is named—
a stake in xCraft.[1] Founded in 2014, xCraft produces
drones that can operate with more flexibility than those
of many of its competitors. Claridge and Manning already had orders from a Kickstarter campaign. During
the episode several Sharks clearly seemed taken with
the xCraft pitch. Promising to invest their own money,
they quickly bid up the value of the proposed deal to
$6 million, three times the original ask. Sensing victory,

J. D. Claridge and Charles Manning pitch xCraft on October 23, 2015.
Well before this, the seventh season of *Shark Tank*, producers and
contestants began enhancing their pitches with elaborate displays,
in this case one that included dramatic signage and a sample drone.

Manning suggested a syndicate involving all five Sharks and asked for an even higher figure, $10 million. "I smell greedy people," remarked Daymond John, an African American businessman whose empire began with the clothing line FUBU.

Claridge and Manning left the stage briefly. Upon returning, they said they would accept an offer of $6 million, with each of the Sharks getting a 5 percent equity stake. As often happens, Mark Cuban, the billionaire owner of the Dallas Mavericks and the wealthiest of the Sharks, was the silent holdout, a situation that changed when, after the contestants (a.k.a. "pitchers") answered questions about other possible investors, he joined the other four Sharks. It turned out that venture capitalists had expressed considerable interest. However, to Claridge and Manning, these investors lacked the range of "operational execution experience" that they felt the Sharks would bring to the table. Another Shark, Robert Herjavec, a Canadian technology entrepreneur, made it clear that he and his colleagues all had experience with "VC guys" who were "super smart" when it came to "theory" but "rarely got their hands dirty in running businesses." A little over two years later, a reporter talked of "a meteoric rise" in xCraft's revenues, helped by added depth to the management team, sales on Amazon, and the development of a range of drones that cost from just under $500 to just over $2,000.[2] "By and large, *Shark Tank* is pet food and potty training products," remarked another writer, with more wit than accuracy. "To be sure, there's plenty of variety in *Shark Tank* pitches, but it's rare that an idea checks all the boxes for 'cool.' XCraft is the exception."[3]

Rick Hopper's offer of ReadeREST, which aired on February 24, 2012, during season three, stands in sharp contrast to Claridge and Manning's xCraft presentation. Hopper, a handyman and inveterate inventor who had never attended college and had been hit hard by the Great Recession, was tired of losing his glasses and had invented a simple product that used magnets to connect them to his shirt. He literally stumbled onto the *Shark Tank* set, deliberately tripping over the edge of the carpet—as if he couldn't see it without his glasses—and falling down. Cuban gasped, and Herjavec said, "Oh no." Their reactions seemed to confirm the cleverness of Hopper's stagecraft, but not all the Sharks bought the gag. Kevin O'Leary, another Canadian who had made it big in technology, labeled Hopper's tactic "bad theater."

Hopper had hand-glued 100,000 of his devices in a small shop at a cost per unit of $1.05 and sold them for at least $9.99 to friends and at trade shows and farmers markets, grossing $65,000. Having secured a patent

On February 24, 2012, Rick Hopper offered the Sharks the opportunity to invest in ReadeREST, a device that helps people avoid losing their eyeglasses. Hopper's invention, its uses illustrated by the images behind him, typifies the low-tech but often lucrative products developed by inveterate tinkerers.

and trademark but still needing capital to produce inventory and a strategic partner to help expand the market, he appeared on the show and handed a sample to each Shark. "Oh, mine has diamonds," remarked Lori Greiner, a serial inventor of small conveniences and the "Queen of QVC," the television shopping network. "So now you want us to give you the money, work, and then pass off our connections," said John sarcastically. He quickly declared, "I'm out," one of the show's frequent catchphrases. O'Leary likewise mocked a $1 million valuation for "a little piece of metal with two magnets on it" as "sheer insanity."

Only Greiner made an offer, expecting she could earn Hopper and herself gobs of money by featuring ReadeREST on her TV show, *Clever and Unique Creations*. Sensing (perhaps incorrectly but nonetheless strategically) that Hopper was skilled at neither sales nor business management, she told him that he needed someone to "take over and make this work for [him]." So she offered him the $150,000 he had asked for but in exchange for 65 percent equity rather than the 15 percent originally requested. Hopper countered with a request that she limit her equity to 49 percent so he would remain in control. But with no competing offers from the other

3

Sharks, Greiner stood firm, claiming she would make Hopper a millionaire and forcing him to make a decision. "I'm a little gun-shy in giving up total controlling interest," Hopper remarked.

Several Sharks were struck that, having presented himself as a simple, down-home guy, Hooper now showed some business acumen. "All of the sudden," O'Leary insisted, "when money comes to the table you get crystal clear." "Wow! This is brutal," Hopper said as the show's producers used music and editing to heighten the drama. Sharks jumped in to remind him of the stakes involved, and Hopper responded with, "This is my big chance. I love this." "What a moment. Take it. Grab it," Greiner insisted. She told Hopper he would no longer have to stay in his garage and glue pieces together; instead, he would just "sit back and watch the money roll in." Grimacing and then smiling, Hopper accepted Greiner's offer. "That's America for you," she commented. That is "how you go from zero to a millionaire in the Shark Tank," O'Leary insisted.

"When Lori looked right into my eyes," Hopper remarked after leaving the set, "and said 'I'm going to make you a millionaire,' I believed her!" His website later claimed that he could now "spend his time doing what he loves, building and inventing." And, indeed, he did benefit from his share of the profits that came from additional designs (including a pink Reade-REST in support of breast cancer survivors), abundant TV and online sales, and placement in stores, including 2,500 Walmart Vision Centers. By late 2016, more than four years after the episode aired, sales had totaled over $10 million—but that was far short of the $6 million annual profit promised on the show.[4]

These dramas capture many of the elements that drive the narratives on *Shark Tank*, an immensely popular and award-winning reality TV show launched in 2009. The xCraft episode demonstrates the broad range of funding sources for entrepreneurs: crowdfunding venues such as Kickstarter, venture capitalists, and on-screen angel investors. On most episodes all five Sharks bow out or only one makes a bid (as was the case with ReadeREST), but with xCraft all of them jumped in, bidding up the valuation—though not as high as the pitchers, sensing victory, hoped for. For ReadeREST, the dynamics were in the opposite direction and deprived the pitcher of a controlling interest of more than 50 percent, though not of substantial income. While xCraft was high tech and greatly successful, ReadeREST, more typical of the products pitched on *Shark Tank*, was low tech and only moderately lucrative. These two pitches reveal common elements of most *Shark Tank* episodes: the typical kinds of interactions between Sharks and contestants, the frequent invocation of the American dream, and the appearance of the Great Recession as a factor affecting pitchers.

As a structured reality TV show, *Shark Tank* has a standard format that, like other shows in its genre, stretches if not explodes the nature of the claims about the reality it supposedly represents. Within the category of structured reality TV, this show is soft or semi-scripted, as opposed to hard-scripted, where those in charge tell cast members exactly what to say. Entrepreneurs, some naive and others savvy, pitch their ideas to five wealthy investors, each of whom has a different set of skills and a distinctive interpersonal approach. Contestants use well-rehearsed dramatic strategies to create interest in their stories and describe their offerings— a barbecue sauce of unusual pungency, an app that helps students find sources for college loans, or a device to make child-rearing easier. Though the pitchers are asking for capital in exchange for equity in their business, they are also looking for strategic partnerships from one or, ideally, several Sharks. Soon, the Sharks compliment or denigrate the contestants, who respond in clarifying, probing, confusing, and/or halting ways. One by one, each Shark says "I'm out" or makes an offer. Sometimes negotiations follow—between a pitcher and one Shark, a pitcher and several Sharks, or cooperatively among a pair or more of Sharks. After deals are reached, or not, contestants walk away and talk in front of a camera about their pleasure, pain, and prospects. And another camera pans over the Sharks, who offer a postmortem, sometimes criticizing one another and always commenting on the pitcher's performance.

Shark Tank, in its current incarnation, is the brainchild of Mark Burnett. Hailed by *Adweek* as "the most powerful producer in television," the British-born Burnett presents himself as a self-made American man.[5] Both of his parents were factory workers in England. After arriving in America in 1982, he became a nanny in Beverly Hills. A second job as a nanny brought him into the orbit of a successful businessman whose mentoring helped launch his career, initially as an entrepreneur on a small scale. In 1991, Burnett worked with friends to develop the first of several adventure challenges ideally suited for television. In 2000 he had his first major hit with *Survivor*, followed in four years by *The Apprentice*, which featured Donald Trump.[6] Entertainment and corporate successes ensued, and Burnett eventually built a fortune worth about half a billion dollars.

Burnett's ascent to organizational and financial heights through reality TV built upon the kind of smaller-scale, supposedly individualistic success stories *Shark Tank* promotes. He adapted *Shark Tank* from *Tigers of Money*, a show that originated in Japan in 2001 and then spread to almost thirty nations, often with the title *Dragons' Den*. Emboldened by his success with *Survivor* and *The Apprentice*, Burnett began to contemplate an American version of *Dragons' Den* as the Great Recession intensified, and he launched *Shark Tank* in 2009. Since then, *Shark Tank* has attracted an average viewing audience as high as 8.5 million and was often the show most watched by the coveted eighteen-to-forty-nine demographic. Although the show's viewership peaked with season six in 2014–15, it still manages to attract millions of viewers.[7] It won four Emmy Awards for Outstanding Structured Reality Program and two Critics' Choice Awards for Best Reality Series. Backed by major global corporations and eventually becoming part of Burnett's own media empire, *Shark Tank* has compelled the attention of viewers, critics, and imitators. Millions watch it on ABC, CNBC, Hulu, and YouTube. Every year, tens of thousands try to secure a role in an episode. Even greater numbers react to it in podcasts and on sites such as Facebook, Instagram, Twitter, and Tumblr. Scores of journalists follow it in old media and new. Students from third graders to those in MBA programs reenact its dramatic format. On television screens and at least one theater stage, knockoffs follow its lead, sometimes satirically, other times appreciatively.

Five of the six mainstay Sharks appear on most episodes, and all of them present dramatic and carefully crafted stories of overcoming obstacles to rise to fame and fortune. Barbara Corcoran began with a side job of renting apartments and then in 1973, determined to be her own boss, used a loan of $1,000 to launch her own real estate firm. Twenty-eight years later she sold it for $66 million. Mark Cuban started his career as an entrepreneur by selling garbage bags at age twelve so he could buy an expensive pair of basketball shoes. Now worth over $3 billion, he controls a sports and media empire. Already an entrepreneur by his late teens, Daymond John became a branding expert after working out of his home in Queens in 1992 to launch FUBU ("For Us, By Us"), a line of hip-hop clothing that grew into a business with billions of dollars in sales. At age eight, Robert Herjavec migrated with his family from Croatia to Canada with only suitcases and twenty dollars in hand. Though he grew up in a family that struggled to make ends meet, he eventually flourished as a computer security entrepreneur, heading a company that has had a phenomenal growth rate. Another Canadian, Kevin O'Leary, having begun his career when he opened a lemonade stand as a kid, started a software company that he eventually turned into the Learning Company. In 1999 the toy company Mattel acquired it for over $4 billion. Lori Greiner is an inventor who also has a keen eye for what others develop, which she sells on QVC.

Burnett and the Sharks serve as aspirational models for those who apply to appear on *Shark Tank*, for the winners and losers who actually appear, and for some of the millions who track the drama on television. Aside from entertainment value, many factors help attract rapt attention from contestants and viewers. First are the Sharks' rags-to-riches stories, which often contain some but not all of the truth. Then there are the trajectories of their careers, which involve making money by investing, speaking, and writing. Also in play are their presentations of themselves as colorful, successful, engaged, sometimes sympathetic and sometimes cynically skeptical businesspeople. Finally, at work is the possibility that they might support entrepreneurs with capital and advice — or at least that the show will provide publicity for contestants' products.

Shark Tank promotes the idea that everyone can be, needs to be, and should be an entrepreneur. "Entrepreneurship," historian R. Daniel Wadhwani has remarked perceptively, "has come to be imbued with an authenticity that transcends economic and political calculus."[8] Every episode proves that entrepreneurs can be made or unmade and offers a window into a particular and currently prominent aspect of modern finance capitalism: entrepreneurship, especially in its startup or early phases, is characterized by taking on risk when much is still unknown. The entrepreneur as a heroic figure, so prevalent in *Shark Tank*, emerged beginning in the 1970s for a variety of reasons. From the 1950s on, antibureaucratic, Marxist, and countercultural rebels attacked large corporations and their organization men (who worked in the bureaucracies of large corporations) for their power and complacency.[9] On the Right, the writings of Ayn Rand and of the Chicago school of economics as popularized by Milton Friedman in his 1962 *Capitalism and Freedom* helped turn freedom, private enterprise, and deregulation into powerful guides for public policy.[10] With the elections of Margaret Thatcher in 1979 and Ronald Reagan a year later signaling the rehabilitation of the once-vilified capitalist, many conservatives heralded the reemergence of unrestrained private enterprise. In 1985, Reagan announced that the 1980s would be "the age of the entrepreneurs," though like others he conflated the term with "operators of small businesses."[11] Then the collapse of the Soviet Union opened the floodgates to the celebration of capitalism, especially in its dynamic, entrepreneurial form. Now, in the words of historian Christian Olaf Christiansen, advocates saw capitalism as not only triumphant but "also democratic, cool, revolutionary, egalitarian, liberating, anti-hierarchical, self-transcending, and, not least, capable of moral self-governance."[12]

At the same time, globalization, especially the international success of

Japanese corporations, undermined the achievements of what many saw as self-satisfied leaders of American corporations and, more generally, of those who celebrated the nation's free-enterprise system. In addition, in the 1970s corporate raiders increasingly launched attacks on once-heralded American companies. Deregulation disrupted old patterns that had governed enterprises. Women and people of color challenged the hegemony of white males. Immigration brought ambitious and innovative talent to American shores. New methods of financing, changes in laws governing corporate formation, reengineering of staid corporations, and university-sponsored labs provided key institutional bases that fostered change. New technologies and downward pressure on costs made corporations leaner as they eliminated middle managers, outsourced some positions, and made others temporary. The dramatic ascendancy of new technologies created new heroes—young, irreverent entrepreneurs who embraced disruption and creativity rather than constancy and tradition.[13] Service sector companies, including financial ones, ascended over manufacturing and extractive industries just when consumption gained in prominence over production.[14] All this, the British historian Anthony Sampson has observed, was "part of a profound change in the social atmosphere which was turning against all the assumptions of collective responsibility which lay behind company men."[15] Opportunity increased, often at the expense of security.

The entrepreneur emerged into a prominent position in American life during the last third of the twentieth century. The term itself, continually invoked on *Shark Tank*, can be capacious and vague. Participants in and observers of *Shark Tank* deploy the word in ways that range from the trite to the somewhat precise. Of course, entrepreneurship has a long history in America: in the eighteenth century, Benjamin Franklin in the civic realm; in the nineteenth century, the captains of industry such as Andrew Carnegie in the economic sphere. A key moment occurred in 1942 when the economist Joseph Schumpeter emphasized the process of what he called "creative destruction" as "the essential fact about capitalism."[16] *Innovation, initiative*, and *opportunity*—these are key words that many contemporary observers deploy as they work to capture the protean and often elusive meaning of entrepreneurship.[17] The definition that currently dominates the scholarly field emphasizes the cognitive ability of entrepreneurs to identify opportunities. This has resulted in an emphasis on micro-level developments, a perspective that *Shark Tank* usually reflects.[18]

Historical conditions have shaped the meaning of entrepreneurship. Schumpeter, writing at a time of heated debates about social and economic systems in a world marked by turmoil, emphasized both the context of capitalism and the power of disruption. In the 1970s many hailed the entrepreneur as a self-employed figure. Later on, as globalism and new technologies upended well-established corporations, innovation rose to prominence. More recently, the focus on opportunity that enterprising individuals build on echoes what viewers see on *Shark Tank*: the centrality of the heroic individual who operates in broader contexts that are out of sight.[19]

Over time, in both popular and academic discussions, as well as in the business world, the focus has shifted from the organization man to the entrepreneur. In the 1950s and well into the 1960s, those who worked at midlevel jobs in large and stable corporations were capitalism's emblematic figures. Schumpeter worried that the emphasis on bureaucratic organizations and scientific principles threatened the free-wheeling innovator. In *The Organization Man* (1956), William H. Whyte expressed concern about the complacent conformity of a world populated by white, male, college-educated employees in a secure niche at the center of the occupational world and their wives in the center of the domestic world. With *The New Industrial State* (1967), John Kenneth Galbraith seemed to honor the new corporate-based social order, which the business historian Alfred D. Chandler prominently featured in his *The Visible Hand: The Managerial Revolution in American Business* (1977).

We can chart how, over time, the entrepreneur became the nation's totemic symbol in several ways. "Connotations of the word 'entrepreneur,'" write scholars K. H. Vesper and W. B. Gartner, who did not fully acknowledge that this was truer in popular culture than among most academics, "began to shift from notions of greed, exploitation, selfishness, and disloyalty to creativity, job-creation profitability, innovativeness, and generosity."[20] "Since the 1970s," note the historians R. Daniel Wadhwani and Christina Lubinski, "entrepreneurship has provided the framing language with which businesspeople and policy makers describe what drives markets and economies."[21] Very early in the 1970s, mentions of the word *entrepreneurship* in the *Harvard Business Review* began to climb, and then they accelerated toward the end of the decade before reaching a plateau in the early 1980s.[22] Beginning in the 1970s more and more universities began to offer programs in entrepreneurship. Although there may have been courses on the subject as early as 1947, the University of Southern California claims to have offered the first program in entrepreneurship in 1971.[23] A decade later, more than 300 universities supported courses on related topics. In the United States by the beginning of the twentieth century, close to 200,000 students enrolled in more than 2,200 of these courses at more than 1,600 institutions.[24]

The era initiated by Ronald Reagan's presidency and punctuated by the end of the Cold War saw entrepreneurship gain a fuller hold in higher education, corporate life, and the American imagination. In the quarter century after 1980, Fortune 500 firms lost in excess of 5 million jobs. At the same time the nation witnessed the creation of more than 34 million jobs. Until the 1970s there had been a long-term decline in the formation of small businesses, but the number hit bottom in 1972 and then began to increase. By the mid-1990s, corporations with 500 or fewer employees were responsible for roughly 50 percent of the American workforce, sales, and private GDP. At the same time, approximately one in six companies had been in existence for a year or less. "The younger generation of the 21st century," an enthusiastic observer noted in 2005, "is becoming the most entrepreneurial generation since the Industrial Revolution," with almost 6 million people under age thirty-four trying to launch new enterprises.[25]

If one major shift is from the organization man to the entrepreneur as the totemic figure, another is from *free enterprise* to *entrepreneurship* as the preferred language to describe the virtues of the American economic order. As the historian Lawrence Glickman has shown, the celebration of free enterprise originated in the 1920s and began to wane in the mid to late 1970s.[26] As it receded, the hosannas to entrepreneurship took its place. *Entrepreneur* became a useful term for a number of reasons. *Businessman* was gender specific. *Capitalist* might suggest a certain rapaciousness. As all-encompassing and convenient alternatives, *entrepreneur* and *entrepreneurship* suggested excitement and innovation. As Glickman so wonderfully shows, *entrepreneurship* sounded beautifully democratic, open to everyone everywhere. It substituted for the defensiveness of *free enterprise* a bold assertiveness. And it was seemingly apolitical—eliminating the necessity of mentioning corporations, government, or unions.

What we learn from studying *Shark Tank* and contemporary American entrepreneurship more generally is the pervasive popularity of the cult of the entrepreneur. Together they offer a robust but highly problematic vision of America's political economy. Whereas references to the organization man and the language of free enterprise fulfilled the cultural needs of an earlier time, invocations of the entrepreneur and entrepreneurship do the same today—they provide a comprehensive and largely reassuring (albeit often distorted) vision of what American capitalism and society are and can be.[27] Ironically, *Shark Tank* invites contestants and viewers to think of themselves as venturesome individuals who through hard work and imagination can transform their lives and the world, even though the show itself is an international franchise backed by megacorporations and the Sharks are organization men and women. The show reflects the outlook of powerful corporations even as it offers a fantastical dream that those who compete on it and those who watch it might somehow achieve riches through highly individualistic activity. All this happens with the show (and other entrepreneurial celebrations) revivifying the American dream once again, despite all the evidence that America's present and future are not so rosily perfect.

All these trends and events underscore the ways in which *Shark Tank* reflects and amplifies the power of neoliberalism as a force that has transformed the world we live in. In lectures he delivered in the late 1970s, the French philosopher Michel Foucault asserted that what made "American neo-liberalism" distinctive was how universal entrepreneurship was, so much so that each person could be understood as an "entrepreneur of himself." As "a whole way of being and thinking," he wrote, entrepreneurship was not "just an economic and political choice" but a "utopian focus."[28] In the years after he spoke, neoliberalism became widely used by social scientists and cultural critics to explain major transformations, especially the erosion of social welfare systems and increasing reliance on individual initiative in the last quarter of the twentieth century and into the twenty-first. As David Harvey wrote in his pathbreaking *A Brief History of Neoliberalism* (2005), neoliberalism provides "a theory of political economic practices that proposes that human well-being can best be advanced by liberating individual entrepreneurial freedoms and skills."[29]

Self-government instead of government power stands in a central place in neoliberalism's vision. Although it embraces the individual's autonomous power, it also recognizes that capitalism's institutions, especially cultural ones like *Shark Tank*, powerfully shape people's experiences and options. Beginning in the late 1970s, with politics deadlocked and people's pessimism about the effectiveness of government power ascendant, neoliberalism held out the hope that individuals could operate successfully, often on their own, in spheres other than political ones. Neoliberalism profoundly affects how people experience the world—how they think about themselves and others. Neoliberals celebrate competition, freedom, opportunity, and of course entrepreneurship. Rather than rely on the social safety net of the welfare state or forms of collective action, ambitious citizens are to welcome the benefits of transformative technologies and globalized free trade.

On *Shark Tank*, this means that pitchers' hopes (and those of some viewers) rest on startup business ventures that in turn rely on optimistic celebrations of individualistic new beginnings and unbounded opportunities. The show, its producers, and the Sharks provide evidence of the impact of neoliberalism's vision. Celebrity power and models of successful entrepreneurship come together to inform eager and attentive audience members on how to be properly self-governing, neoliberal citizen-entrepreneurs. This happens in spite of the fact that—indeed, precisely because—the show appeared right when the Great Recession revealed how problematic were the promises of a neoliberal order. *Shark Tank*, and its related media enterprises, offered a full range of strategies that buttressed a neoliberal vision at a time when social insecurity and economic inequalities prevailed: the show emphasized individual initiative at the same time that it hid the power of structural injustice and frequently offered vague evocations of the rags-to-riches, individualistic American dream. Yet it is important to acknowledge that neoliberalism can be a problematic concept. It is more cogent as a view from on high, with distance smoothing out inconsistencies and fluctuations, than as an explanation of the often-contradictory responses experienced below; as a totalizing concept, it can barely hide the messiness of historical experiences; and it is hard to reconcile with the counternarrative of contemporary America as polarized.[30]

Shark Tank underscores key changes in investing.[31] Historically, funding for new enterprises has come from friends and families, banks, and stock and bond markets. Although there were precedents for venture capital financing such as the New England whaling and textiles industries of the nineteenth century, after World War II it emerged in the form we know today, as the domain of informal networks of a small number of wealthy families and institutions that fund the early stages of ventures. A key moment came in 1946 with the founding of American Research and Development Corporation, a firm that specialized in providing capital to startups in the hopes that one huge success would more than offset some failures and moderate successes. Over time the federal government also played critical roles in fostering transformative innovations, for example, by funding military research that led to technological transformations in the wider economy, as well as by passing legislation such as the Small Business Investment Act in 1958 and the Small Business Innovation Development Act in 1982. By the 1970s and especially the 1980s, venture capital investing had emerged as a significant factor in the American economy. By then the dominant elements were clear: the importance of Silicon Valley; the use of limited partnerships; the reliance on funding from sources such as sovereign funds and the endowments of nonprofit institutions; the focus on specific high-tech sectors; and the promise of huge rewards from a very small percentage of all investments placed. Over time, noncorporate, individual angel investors and online crowdfunding platforms also became increasingly prominent.

Sharks and most contestants occupy a relatively small and specific niche in the world of investing. Today, those launching new ventures can take advantage of a wide range of funding sources. Most rely on friends, family members, mortgages, and/or credit cards. Higher up the funding chain are angel investors such as the Sharks—individuals who lend their own money in exchange for equity. Banks are among the institutions that provide funding. An intrapreneur is someone who works in a large corporate or nonprofit organization that funds innovation internally. Those who organize venture capital and private equity funds gather money from others (including institutional sources such as pension funds, endowments of nonprofits, and sovereign wealth funds) and then, pooling this money, invest in a new or ongoing enterprise. They anticipate that some of their investments will fail, others will yield modest returns, and a few will provide spectacular profits. Also important is the stage at which an entrepreneur seeks funding or an investor places a bet—ranging from the earliest stages to those much later on.

A series of statistics clarify the nature of jobs, new business, and entrepreneurship. Around 80 percent of new businesses garner their funding from the owner, friends, and family. Almost 70 percent of new ventures are created in people's houses. Only 1 percent of new businesses obtain funding from venture capitalists. Despite popular impressions, people thirty-five years old and under create only 16 percent of new businesses, while those over fifty create three times that number. More than half of small businesses fail within their first four years. Entrepreneurially oriented firms come in many forms—startups, existing small businesses, and existing large ones as well. Small businesses, defined by the federal government as those with 500 or fewer employees, which make up over 99 percent of all businesses, have accounted for slightly over two-thirds of new jobs in recent years—with startups responsible for a greater share than existing ones. Large corporations, those with more than 500 employees, are responsible for the creation of one-third of new positions.[32]

Cold statistics paint a very different picture than popular sources do. Dramatic narratives of a small group of nerds, or of one lone one, in a garage coming up with an idea that transforms their lives and the world are compelling but hardly representative. *Shark Tank* presents more varied but nonetheless specific options. The show features more business-to-consumer products than business-to-business ones, and more products than services. The aspiring contestants are relying on one or more angel investors. Contestants are whiter, younger, and more often native-born than the general population. They pursue a narrower range of opportunities than do small businesses generally and transformative entrepreneurs specifically—few of the contestants are interested in bricks-and-mortar retail stores, health care, high tech, real estate, or the professions. Most frequently, the Sharks invest at an early stage of an enterprise. Sometimes they do so when revenues remain scant, more often when there is some track record promising future success.

In a challenging and often risky world, *Shark Tank* represents a variety of business models. Although not visible on the show, at the top are executives of established corporations like Sony, which controls the international *Shark Tank / Dragons' Den* franchise, and ABC (now a division of Disney Media Networks), which produces the show and then distributes it to CNBC (now owned by Comcast) for syndication. Mark Burnett heads the production company that bears his name and in which MGM eventually acquired a major interest. Between the exodus from a remote island in *Survivor* (2000) and from Egypt in *The Bible* (2013) came *Are You Smarter than a 5th Grader?* (2007), *The Celebrity Apprentice* (2008), and, of course, *Shark Tank* (2009). Beyond the entrepreneurial heights reached by the Sharks, and sometimes by the pitchers, are contestants who struggle to make a living, failed pitchers who are laughed off the set, and many amateur copycats, including elementary school children, who pitch their ideas in *Shark Tank*-inspired competitions.

Focusing on changes in media industries helps us understand the emergence of reality TV generally and *Shark Tank* specifically as popular entertainment. Deregulation, pressure to reduce labor costs, and technological changes from the 1980s on unleashed powerful forces that helped transform television. The proliferation of cable channels compelled old and new networks to find inexpensive formulas for filling seemingly endless hours with what media scholars Raymond Boyle and Lisa W. Kelly call "a reproducible format that has a definite *outcome* and which is full of *conflict* and *jeopardy*."[33] The 2007–8 strike by the Writers Guild of America provided an opportunity for media corporations and producers to shift from scripted to unscripted television programs. Standardized formats helped contain costs, and deployment of media outside the boundaries of the shows themselves increased revenue. Globalization made it possible to import models developed in one nation across borders and into scores of others, with imported models taking the lead in the ratings more often than American ones. As networks reduced the number of offerings they produced, show development shifted to production companies, which employed anywhere from one to more than a thousand regular employees. They also relied on contingent labor, which grew or shrank corporate payrolls as situations required. Major international corporations snapped up production companies, increasing consolidation in a sometimes chaotic field.[34]

Shark Tank as reality television is more carefully choreographed and ideologically inflected entertainment than reality.[35] As Mark Burnett remarked in 2004, reality TV deals with "contrived situations creating genuine emotions."[36] Media scholar Laurie Ouellette captured this more amply when she wrote, "While this fare was pitched as spontaneous and real, it was also tightly edited and carefully packaged with high doses of voyeurism, suspense, gossip, sensationalism, melodrama, affect, and cruelty."[37] As a structured or formatted show, *Shark Tank*, rather than relying on handheld cameras in a jungle or an urban apartment, is staged in a studio and features a small number of judges who are telegenic and skilled performers. Instead of turning supposedly ordinary twentysomethings or subjects of makeovers into celebrities, it transforms the Sharks, already-successful businesspeople in their forties and older, into people who are famous outside their previous, more limited domains. Other shows build drama over a long period of time, at the end of which one contestant emerges victoriously; in contrast, on *Shark Tank*, the Sharks can anoint multiple winners and turn down several losers in each series of episodes. Whereas when Burnett produced *Survivor*, editors compressed hundreds of hours into less than one for each episode, on *Shark Tank* the scripting is easier and the editing more contained.

The timing of *Shark Tank*'s ascendancy could hardly have been more emblematic. The Great Recession, which underscored the power of economic risk and social instability, opened up space for *Shark Tank*'s appeal. "When we started *Shark Tank* back in August 2009," remarked a Sony executive almost nine years later, "people could not get bank loans. Then this show hit the landscape and became a place where everyday Americans got a chance to have a Shark invest in their dream."[38] The first signs of the Great Recession, ones that few recognized at the time, appeared in the spring of 2007. The filming of the first episode probably occurred in February 2009—not long after the bankruptcy of Lehman Brothers, the passage of the Troubled Asset Relief Program, the inauguration of Barack Obama, and the federal government bailout of Citigroup, General Motors, and Chrysler. Between then and the show's premiere on August 9, 2009, the Dow Jones hit a low of 6,627 and the National Bureau of Economic Research declared the recession over in the United States, even though the unemployment rate remained high and housing foreclosures continued to climb to record levels.

Although not always visible in episodes of *Shark Tank*, the dramatic events of 2007–9 transformed the nation and shaped the reception of *Shark Tank*. Ratings of shows on HGTV, the home design and remodeling channel, dropped dramatically during this time because people did not want to be reminded of the housing crisis. Consequently, those in charge of *Shark Tank* may well have learned how to play the recession successfully.[39] "The Echoes of Lehman in Our Time of Distrust" was the headline of a mid-September 2018 story in the *New York Times* that commemorated the tenth anniversary of the disappearance of the century-and-a-half-old investment bank. "[It] was a moment that cleaved our country," wrote financial reporter Andrew Ross Sorkin, and it was a key factor in Trump's rise to the presidency. "Its effects still echo in the way we live today—in the attitudes that pervade our economy, our culture and our politics." Although Sorkin emphasized how the economic turmoil "broke a sense of trust … in the very idea of experts and expertise," the popularity of *Shark Tank* and of entrepreneurship more generally suggests that one exception to the revolt against expertise was the enhanced faith in businesspeople, such as the Sharks, who could help ordinary Americans overcome economic adversity.[40]

An examination of *Shark Tank* reveals how it focuses on key aspects of American entrepreneurship but hides others. Airing at a time when tens of millions of Americans face uncertainty born of changes in technology, globalization, and public policy, *Shark Tank* presents useful information on several levels, in effect offering a dramatic version of business education that many viewers may take more literally than they should. Viewers can learn how to become successful entrepreneurs by managing risk, making their case to investors and customers more effectively, increasing the scale of an enterprise, recognizing the importance of exclusive rights through patents, minimizing the impact of government regulation, determining the value of a company, and bargaining effectively. More ambitiously, *Shark Tank* also offers to contestants and viewers alike often-vague versions of the American dream and a chance for ordinary people to catch the entrepreneurial brass ring. Work hard, take risks, rely on your individual talents, dream big, embrace the advantages of market forces, and you, too, like the Sharks, can rise from rags to riches—even in a world where so many forces seem arrayed against you.[41]

Entertaining Entrepreneurs provides a window into how mass media tells us about the opportunities, traps, and dynamics of entrepreneurial capitalism at a time when tens of millions of Americans are facing challenges that threaten their economic and psychological well-being. Stepping aside, we can see how the show, as well as many related texts, pretends to teach viewers how to navigate the shoals of uncertain times when a hyperemphasis on the power of markets propels them to rely on their own self-directed resources. It promotes and is steeped in the marketization of everything, promising that the market can support viewers' dreams. Yet at times, *Shark Tank* hides or fudges as much as it reveals. The Sharks' emphasis on selling and investing makes invention and production minor sideshows. The invocation of a Darwinian struggle in which only the fittest survive offers a limited vision of what successfully achieving the American dream involves. The show's treatment of the dynamics of race, ethnicity, class, and, to a lesser extent, gender is often muted and opaque. Aside from occasional discussions of patents and even less frequent discussions of regulations, the role of federal, state, and local public policy—so powerful in shaping enterprises—is absent from the show. This is a very significant omission because, despite the vision of entrepreneurial individualism, the federal government has played critical roles in fostering innovation. It has done so through fiscal and monetary policy, programs fostering small businesses, and the support of research in the military, government labs, and universities.[42] As a populist version of more high-powered and momentous competitions in the entrepreneurial arena, *Shark Tank* celebrates small-scale, often family-based enterprises but frequently gives too little attention to the larger forces that might shape and even limit the fulfillment of an aspiring entrepreneur's dreams. In other words, in line with Burnett's intentions and the audience's interest, this is usually Main Street, petit bourgeois capitalism rather than the version dominant on Wall Street, in Silicon Valley, or among the powerful 1 percent.

In exploring the ways *Shark Tank* uses entertainment to try to teach citizens about how the economy functions, I consider issues that historians and cultural critics often do not treat simultaneously. The recently emboldened field of the history of capitalism and the even newer one of the history of entrepreneurship focus on the nation's intensified embrace of market fundamentalism and on the powerful, both aspects of the American economy that *Shark Tank* vividly conveys. The show also demonstrates the centrality of celebrity culture in American life, exemplified by the wealthy Sharks and aspired to by many of the show's contestants and viewers. Hovering over the program is the profound appeal and importance of the rags-to-riches and self-help traditions, even as *Shark Tank* emphasizes how aspiring entrepreneurs can benefit from funding from and strategic partnerships with the wealthy and successful. The show highlights key aspects of globalization at a time when this force, along with neoliberalism, is transforming the lives and aspirations of many members of its audience, often in adverse ways. The biographies of Burnett and the Sharks, as well as the lives of those they promise to transform, dramatize the dynamics of social mobility, a subject that, along with issues of economic inequality and insecurity, commands the attention of those who live in and observe American society. To explore broader connections, I have placed *Shark Tank* at the center and then linked it with popular books, TED Talks, movies, other TV shows, social media, firsthand observations, and interviews. Additionally, this book juxtaposes such media treatments with current discussions among journalists and social scientists about capitalism, public policy, celebrity culture, inequality, insecurity, class relationships, technology, and globalization.[43]

When researching this book, at crucial moments I came up against the fact that those involved in the show were more inclined to protect the brand than to reveal very much about what lies behind it. In an attempt to go beyond the oft-repeated stories Sharks tell, in early January 2019 I emailed the six regular Sharks to ask whether they would answer my inquiries. Cuban quickly responded and invited me to ask him questions over email. I did so, seeking information on where he lived in Pittsburgh; what kinds of jobs his parents had; his experiences and identity as a Jew; how he reconciled the influence Ayn Rand had on him with his support for Hillary Clinton in 2016; the organizational structure and personnel involved in his *Shark Tank*-related enterprises; and how he defined the American dream. He again replied quickly, this time saying, "Pass. This is supposed to be about shark tank. Not my biography."[44] The other Sharks never responded to my emails; I suspect Cuban alerted them to the scope of my inquiries. I understood how Sharks want to control what others know of them and, more important, how a historian and a reality TV personage differentially approach the relevance of certain issues.

When I tried to get information from others involved in the show, it became clear that I was up against an understandable effort to avoid providing information. For example, friends of friends made it possible for me to contact Dan Fuchs, the show's director. When I asked him about editing, gauging audience responses, and data collection, he wrote back, "I think I may refer you to one of our producers who may be able to help you better." Whether or not he did refer me, I never heard back from a producer. I also wrote to Sony's publicist for the show, and she responded by saying, "We have to run your request by our executive producers, Legal and Business Affairs before proceeding." I am still waiting for a response.[45] In addition, though I corresponded with several contestants, their signing of lengthy nondisclosure agreements prevented them from providing much useful information.

Later on, when I talked to someone who had worked in reality television for decades, though not on *Shark Tank*, she told me my inquiries would inevitably run up against several roadblocks. Anyone willing to talk would worry about the risk of making a mistake and whether they had permission to speak openly about a wide range of issues. Above all, people involved in reality TV hesitate to talk to an outsider about the fine (and sometimes not-so-fine) line between the real and genuine, on the one hand, and the constructed, on the other.[46] After all, though many understand the show as entertainment, to a considerable extent its status and power rest on its ability to convince those who watch that it is genuinely real. A television executive explored with me a range of reasons for industrial secrecy: there are significant legal obstacles that block revelations; the Sharks themselves have ample reason to protect business secrets; people are cautious in an intimate, relationship-driven world; and memories of the quiz show scandals of the 1950s persist and discourage openness about what happens behind the scenes. It's also important, he said, to sustain mystery and help audience members suspend disbelief, because to reveal more publicly might undermine belief in a show's authenticity.[47] "Reality shows," TV critic James Poniewozik has noted, "both appealed to the thirst for authenticity—though their setups were contrived and their stories edited—and promised a peep into realities more exciting than your own."[48]

It turns out that what we see on *Shark Tank* with pitches like those for xCraft and ReadeREST is the tip of the iceberg of entrepreneurial visions in America. The story of how Elizabeth Holmes, the founder of the blood-testing startup Theranos, captured the imaginations of supposedly savvy investors underscores some of the moral and economic pitfalls that result from the unbridled celebration of entrepreneurship so common in the early twenty-first century, including on *Shark Tank*. A dropout from Stanford and someone obsessed with modeling herself after Steve Jobs, Holmes founded the company in 2003, when she was nineteen, and at one point she was worth $4.5 billion on paper. In March 2014, when Theranos was flying high, Holmes gave a TED Talk that helped feed the media frenzy about her invention, which promised to transform American health care and the lives of hundreds of millions. Poised and convincing, she stood on

In 2003, Elizabeth Holmes, a nineteen-year-old college dropout, founded Theranos, a company that she promised would transform health care. Theranos hit a peak valuation of $10 billion in 2013, but three years later, after *Wall Street Journal* articles revealed problems with the company's blood-testing technology, stock in the company was worthless. Holmes, seen here at a 2015 conference, copied Steve Jobs's signature look, black turtleneck included. Mike Blake / Reuters / Newscom.

stage dressed in a black outfit similar to what Steve Jobs wore when he un-veiled a new Apple product. She wove the story of the death of her beloved uncle with narratives of hardships that ordinary people faced because they could neither afford proper health care nor have their illnesses diagnosed before it was too late. In the process she promoted Theranos's diagnostic tests, which would dramatically lower costs and overcome people's fear of needles, and celebrated individualism, transformative technology, human rights, and democracy. Yet she both violated the key precepts of Silicon Valley venture capitalism and echoed its hype, aspirations, and reliance on brilliant and innovative technological solutions.

The fascination Holmes and others had with Jobs was powerful and emblematic, something that John Carreyrou highlights in *Bad Blood: Se-crets and Lies in a Silicon Valley Startup* (2018). People who tracked the way entrepreneurs in Silicon Valley were transforming the world saw in Holmes the hoped-for female equivalent of Jobs. In a chapter titled "Apple Envy," Carreyrou remarks that "for a young entrepreneur building a busi-ness in the heart of Silicon Valley, it was hard to escape the shadow of Steve Jobs." Walter Isaacson's biography *Steve Jobs* appeared in late October 2011, less than three weeks after the subject's death. Soon after, colleagues of Holmes started to realize that she "was borrowing behaviors and manage-ment techniques" Isaacson had described, and they "could pinpoint which chapter she was on based on which period of Jobs's career she was imper-sonating."[49]

In 2015 Carreyrou published articles in the *Wall Street Journal* that re-ported on the frauds Holmes had allegedly perpetrated. His book later dra-matically and fully focused on the blazing haze of falsified revenue and scientific tests, hyped public relations, nondisclosure agreements, threats by high-powered lawyers, and military-style secrecy that had until then prevented fired and skeptical employees from talking. The crash of Theranos, as well as some of the more problematic aspects of *Shark Tank*, raises issues about the downside of upscale dreams—in this case, like others on a smaller scale, involving dashed hopes, lost jobs, and drained capital.

The Apprentice

MARK BURNETT AND THE AMERICAN DREAM

In *I Love Capitalism! An American Story* (2018), Ken Langone told of his life as the grandson of Italian immigrants and the son of working-class parents, of digging ditches before he went to college and eventually becoming a billionaire by building businesses, especially Home Depot. "The thing I can't and never say is that I'm self-made," he remarked. "I'm not. To say that would be an injustice to all those people who brought me to the party."[1] His list of those who helped him was extensive and included his father, who provided a bad example of what it meant to be a businessman; his mother, who had grand aspirations for her son; an economics professor and dean at Bucknell, whose support made it possible for him to graduate; his father-in-law, who helped him get started on Wall Street; colleagues at the firm there, whose laziness served as negative models; the 400,000 employees at Home Depot; and God and his Roman Catholic faith.

Whoever wrote the copy for the dust jacket for *I Love Capitalism!* unabashedly played the Horatio Alger card, however. Langone's story, the copywriter rhapsodized, "doubles as a passionate defense of the American Dream," portraying as it does "a country in which any young striver can reach the maximum potential of his or her talents." And when Langone insisted that "capitalism is brutal" and only the fittest survive, he failed to note that, as he'd said elsewhere, success goes to the most well-connected and even the luckiest.[2] Nor did he mention the ways government support helps businesses flourish. After all, public roads bring to Home Depot goods to sell and customers to buy them, and publicly supported schools taught the company's workers the numeracy and literacy they need to function effectively. More generally, immigration policy, fiscal policy, tax and monetary policy, a stable legal system, public support of education and research, and specific legislation, such as the Small Business Innovation Development Act of 1982, have all helped foster enterprises.[3]

Langone's book is hardly unique in its blind spots. *I Love Capitalism!* is similar to scores of best-selling books on entrepreneurship that follow the familiar traditions of inspirational biographies and how-to books. As one perceptive observer reminded me, "No one authors a book that says 'Work hard, lose your family, tolerate defeat, and if you are very lucky, you might get rich!'"[4] Instead, books in the genre confidently offer romantic and carefully crafted stories to inspire Americans through difficult times, encourage them to follow where the authors suggest they go, and of course anchor positive narratives about their own brands. Given the rarely acknowledged but frequent use of ghostwriters for such books, one should not be too surprised by their commonalities. But no matter who is behind the words or whether the books are self-published or produced by major commercial houses, these books immerse readers in a universe where public relations, curated lives, carefully constructed images, and cliché-ridden bromides thrive.

The books bearing the Sharks' names are no different. Together Mark Burnett, the Sharks, and those writing on their behalf offer an inspirational and secular version of how to achieve the American dream. They emphasize celebrity status, new technologies, serial entrepreneurship, and overcoming obstacles as the roads to and results of success. And coming on the heels of the Great Recession, these books were among many cultural productions that promoted a vision of entrepreneurship that promised guidance in a world where incomes were stagnant, communities were fragmented, and a tiny slice of the American population captured greater and greater shares of wealth and income.

Mark Burnett's biography and vision dovetail to underscore the themes *Shark Tank* highlights. His quintessential and carefully constructed story of a startup entrepreneur whose sharp intelligence, salesmanship, ambition, and hard work built a fortune serves as a model for the show. Central to his narrative are the marketing of the self and the risk-taking, individualistic entrepreneur who through struggle, passion, and determination achieves the American dream. Under Burnett's direction, *Shark Tank* claims that successful businesspeople rely on everyday smarts and assertive entrepreneurship. For Burnett and his Sharks, as well as for most contestants and some viewers, climbing to the top involves mastering the art of selling, battling to become the fittest and thereby survive, and promoting values that weave together egalitarian and elitist strands. Along with *Survivor* and *The Apprentice*, *Shark Tank* provides dramatic and problematic versions of life stories in which ambitious individuals can succeed in a Darwinian world.[5]

"Ever since I was a child," Burnett remarks in the opening sentence of *Dare to Succeed: How to Survive and Thrive in the Game of Life* (2001), with perhaps more than a hint of retrospective and strategic exaggeration, "I've cherished the American Dream." Born in 1960 to parents of genuinely humble backgrounds, Burnett grew up in what he calls "London's gray and grimy East End." Later his family moved ten miles east to Dagenham, where his parents worked different shifts in a Ford factory.[6] As a child, he recalls, he avidly watched American television shows, and he claims they later lured him to a California characterized by fortune hunting and street smarts. Among his favorite shows were *Bonanza*, a Western set in the 1860s that took its title from the prospect of getting rich in mining, and *Starsky and Hutch*, the story of two Southern California police detectives. Burnett also asserts that he learned an important lesson from his parents. Determined not to live a life filled with regrets, as he felt his parents had, Burnett was driven, in Daymond John's words, by a "fear of missing out, or leaving opportunity on the table."[7]

Burnett traveled from working-class England to the pinnacle of the entertainment world by a circuitous route. At age seventeen he went directly from secondary school into the military and then a year later joined the British Army's prestigious Parachute Regiment. He served in Northern Ireland from 1978 to 1982, years of violence between the Irish Republican Army and British troops, and in the Falkland Islands during the war there in 1982. After finishing his four-year tour of duty, in October 1982 he flew from London to Los Angeles "with just $600 cash in my pocket and a deep fear of failure," as he tells us, using typical rags-to-riches tropes. Yet he was convinced, he says, that "I could do anything I wanted in America. All I had to do was work my ass off."[8] He claimed that at the L.A. airport he heard the voice of his mother, who had always encouraged him to achieve his dreams but told him to be careful in doing so. Though he'd intended to head for Central America, where he could earn money training paramilitary forces, he decided to stay over in Los Angeles instead. A friend from back home met him at LAX and told him he had arranged for Burnett to interview that evening for a job as a nanny in Beverly Hills. The parents offered him the position because Burnett convinced them that they were getting a nanny and a security guard in one.

That soon led to a similar position with another wealthy family, this one in Malibu in a household headed by Burt Borman, "a savvy business-man willing to mentor his twenty-three-year-old babysitter about how to achieve success."[9] It was here that Burnett claims he honed his skills as an apprentice. When he met houseguests, he "learned the ways of the business world by continually asking them question after question about how they got to where they were, what mistakes they made along the way, and how they conducted their businesses."[10] This provided contacts and information that would prove extremely useful in Burnett's future. Surely recognizing that Burnett had ample aspirations and talents, Borman hired him to work in his insurance office, a job whose steadiness Burnett appreciated, though he realized it would neither make him rich nor sate his adventuresome restlessness. So, two years later, following his mentor's advice to start small, Burnett rented a section of a fence on Venice Beach. After seeing a "flurry of green" change hands when vendors on the beach plied their wares, he'd "decided to become an entrepreneur." On weekends he sold T-shirts he'd bought for two dollars and had silk-screened. They sold for nine times what he'd paid for them.[11] Burnett was skilled at selling and quit his job in the insurance office to launch a series of successful startups, initially building his T-shirt enterprise, then quickly going on to, as he insists, make a killing in real estate, and then develop a credit card marketing business.

Eager for something more creative that appealed to his competitive urges and drew on his experiences as a paratrooper, in 1991 Burnett focused on *Raid Gauloises*, a French TV adventure competition that involved strenuously racing through rough and dangerous terrain for days on end and sleeping little at night. The following year he organized and led a five-person team that competed in the *Raid* in Oman, raising the funding for it and securing television coverage in the Los Angeles market. Still in his early thirties, he was a young man who, he later wrote boastfully, had "no MBA or other traditional academic training to guide" him as he "began hobnobbing with the money men" in the entertainment industry, guided by a belief that he was embarking on a path that meant he "had the potential to be incredibly successful."[12] Although his team failed miserably, Burnett remained determined, hoping to "learn from my failure to keep my epic dream alive."[13] Hell-bent on winning a contest that combined adventure and entertainment in a challenging physical environment, he put together a team for the 1993 competition in Madagascar and this time finished respectably. More important, he secured a national broadcast on ESPN, for which he sold sponsorship.

His experience with *Raid Gauloises* convinced him that such competitions would have immense appeal on television because they combined drama, adventure, and environmental engagement. He could work on them not just as an on-the-ground adventurer but as a producer of commercially successful shows. So in the early 1990s Burnett began to develop a television series, *Eco-Challenge*, for which he purchased the American rights and which aired from 1995 to 2002.

Many observers credit this show as the urtext of late-twentieth-century reality TV. Seen by a billion people in 140 nations around the world, it launched Burnett's career as a major producer. He had a compelling ability, media producer Noah Pollack noted, to passionately pitch a story by painting a dramatic picture and putting investors and executives in the scene. And he was able to identify and successfully pursue key members of a cast.[14] Developing this series, as well as later ones, also required the ability to assemble a team, raise money from sponsors, secure television coverage, obtain permission to shoot on location from governments and interest groups such as environmental organizations, and organize an enterprise located in both Los Angeles and remote places. Burnett wrote at length about how the road was not always smooth because along the way he had to keep pitching networks until he found the show a home; fight with executives for creative control; invent new business models; balance the claims of competing stakeholders and permission granters; and gather funding in order to avoid risking bankruptcy. He and his team members also arranged transport for people and equipment; secured product placement agreements and advertising, which sometimes seemed elusive; protected participants from disease, poisonous snakes, and technological challenges; ensured utmost secrecy when it mattered; and wove together visions of a show that included adventure, entertainment, and some version of reality.

Burnett eventually moved from *Eco-Challenge* to *Survivor*, for which he had secured the North American rights in 1998 and which launched in the summer of 2000. In the process, he came to realize that he "didn't belong in a purely documentary world" but "in the dramatic" one.[15] *Survivor*, built on a Swedish predecessor, *Expedition Robinson*—which puts an asterisk next to any claim about Burnett's originality—was a tremendous success. In its first season it attracted as many as 51 million viewers, and the season's finale had an audience of 125 million. For more than a score of years it ranked among the most widely watched television shows. *Survivor* mixed entertainment and life lessons by providing dramatic, metaphorical enactments of dog-eat-dog competitions that would later be echoed in at least two of the shows Burnett produced: *The Apprentice* and *Shark Tank*. "Success isn't handed to any of us," even those who attended the right schools, he remarked about the show, using both meritocratic and Darwinian language. Rather, it is something "we have to battle for . . . because each person atop the success pile means there's less room for someone else."[16]

On *Survivor*, sixteen people are transported to a remote location where they struggle to survive, cooperate, and compete. In each episode they vote to eject one of their peers from their tension-filled community, until only one contestant remains and takes home the million-dollar prize. It was, Burnett noted, "something akin to 'Gilligan's Island' meets *Lord of the Flies*, meets *Ten Little Indians*."[17] With the feel of spontaneity but driven by the calculated orchestrations and interventions of more than 130 members of the production team on site and back in California studios, it combined Machiavellian politics, group dynamics, self-discovery, and a struggle to survive. As cultural studies scholar Keat Murray has astutely observed, *Survivor* deploys social Darwinism within an imperialistic framework, links the consumption of goods to upward mobility, and in the process underscores how it is possible "for capitalism to rationalize its own practices and naturalize the increasingly polarized social structures produced by cutthroat competition."[18]

When Burnett discussed working on the episodes of *Survivor* that took place in the Amazon basin, he talked of how threatening the environment was. He watched ants "swarm over other live insects or the carcass of a dead animal, picking it clean within a matter of hours." This reminded him, he said, "of the swarms of people living in the urban jungle—everyone crammed into cities and fighting for a place. Just like ants, people on the whole are industrious but will also pick your bones clean, given half the chance." After having what he called a "spiritual awakening" in the Amazon, he turned to thinking about "the setting of an urban jungle for a new show," which eventually emerged as *The Apprentice*.

The new show, he recounted, would examine "social psychology through reality TV" by exploring "a way to deal with the competitive brutalities of our daily lives in cities, which can be every bit as harsh as living in a jungle." In life and on his shows, people "who Jump In make it—the others get eaten," he remarked, using "Jump In," the title of his book, to evoke the importance of seizing opportunities. Thus, *The Apprentice* would be about "people wanting the American dream, wanting to get rich, wanting recognition." Writing in 2005, when almost no one anticipated the crash of the housing and financial markets that began not long after, Burnett described the show as focusing on "aspiring moguls looking to be hired and mentored by a true leader of industry." That leader turned out to be Donald J. Trump.[19]

The Apprentice, which premiered in 2004 and starred Trump until 2015, when he intensified his bid for the presidency, featured a familiar mix of competition and ruthlessness. It moved these qualities from distant, exotic locations to a stage set of a corporate boardroom in Trump Tower. More than a dozen aspiring entrepreneurs in each season competed in tasks meant to reveal their business acumen. One contestant triumphed at the end of each season, capturing the opportunity to earn an annual salary of $250,000 running one of Trump's companies. The others memorably listened to Trump say "You're fired," apparently leaving the losers without any safety net to cushion the fall.[20] *The Apprentice* prefigured some of the key aspects of Trump's campaign in the 2016 Republican primaries and the presidential election, as well as of his presidency. Among these features were politics as theater, the power of humiliation, the appeal of plain speaking and directness, the ascendancy of individualism in face of supposedly failed government social programs, and the often-brutal and always-dramatic triumph of winners over losers.

Shark Tank premiered in the late summer of 2009. Its formula was different from that of *Survivor* or *The Apprentice*. It was not a winner-take-all competition that took place over a long series of episodes, with one contestant eventually triumphing at the end of the season. Instead, each hour-long episode featured a series of self-contained mini episodes in which contestants competed not against one another but rather for funding from a school of wealthy and famous Sharks. What intensified the interest in and the poignancy of *Shark Tank* was its timing, as it launched at a critical moment of the Great Recession. For an apprehensive and eager audience, the show could underscore the challenges and opportunities uncertain times presented.

Propelled by the success of these reality shows, by the end of the second decade of the twenty-first century Burnett had achieved fame and fortune far beyond what he could have imagined when he got off a plane at LAX a quarter of a century earlier. Now he was president of MGM Digital and Television Group and had served as executive producer for network and cable series, miniseries, and feature films, including *The Celebrity Apprentice, Fargo, The Bible,* and *Are You Smarter than a 5th Grader?*—shows

Donald Trump and Mark Burnett joined forces for the reality TV show
The Apprentice, which played a major role in Trump's political ascendancy. Burnett's
next major venture was *Shark Tank*. John Barrett / ZUMAPRESS / Newscom.

that aired in more than seventy nations and were seen by tens of millions. His productions have won many awards: ten Emmys, five Producers Guild Awards, and seven Critics' Choice Awards. Burnett was reportedly worth just under $500 million in 2019.[21]

A critical element in Burnett's own narrative of his life was the role Trump played in motivating him. He told his readers that reading Trump's *The Art of the Deal* (1987) when he was selling his T-shirts on Venice Beach inspired him "to Jump In, take risks, and pursue a career as an entrepreneur."[22] In the words of a reviewer for the *New York Times*, as quoted on the cover of *The Art of the Deal,* Trump "makes one believe for a moment in the American dream again." From Trump Burnett learned that the very "strategies that applied to selling T-shirts [applied] to selling TV shows."[23] Trump, in turn, agreed to star in *The Apprentice* and also wrote an introduction to Burnett's *Jump In! Even If You Don't Know How to Swim* (2005) in which he described the book as "the inspirational rags-to-riches story of an American immigrant." Burnett, he wrote, was someone who "transformed hard work and an inspired vision into the realization of the American dream."[24] Burnett drank deeply from the well of classic American self-help practices when he took seminars from Tony Robbins, a guru of multilevel marketing and author of *Unlimited Power: The Way to Peak Personal Achievement* (1984) and *Awaken the Giant Within: How to Take Immediate Control of Your Mental, Emotional, Physical and Financial Destiny!* (1991).[25]

From his own life story, Burnett developed equally inspirational lessons, which the Sharks also articulated in their books. "The path to success twists and turns," he remarked, "and bumps and grooves can make the journey frustrating, but these difficulties also make the destination even more rewarding." Because unexpected events and threatening setbacks are inevitable, he advised people to rely on "flexible action," always having the courage "to take new and different" paths as necessary. As he wrote in the dedication to *Jump In!,* "Always remember in order to succeed you must be willing to fail." Risk-taking entrepreneurs are more admirable than unimaginative MBAs or managers of mature corporations who stifle creativity, he said, an opinion that later reverberated when the Sharks made clear their opposition to many kinds of expertise. Embrace the competitive urge because it builds character and yields success. Dream bold dreams, but realize that to fulfill them you need to take "little victories." Trust your gut feelings, believe in yourself, take risks, and be passionate and courageous about what you do. Develop your natural talents, especially for salesmanship. Perseverance builds strong character because if people stop moving "forward, always forward, disregarding risk and seeing only results," they "will wither." In the words of his favorite quote from the Bible, "Suffering produces perseverance; perseverance, character; and character, hope." Or in Burnett's own words, which reflect clichéd advice literature, "If you have hope, in anything you do, you can make it."[26]

Don't give in to fears, Burnett advised, because competition focuses the mind and sows the seeds of success. What matters ultimately, he claimed in ways that invite skepticism about whether for most people there is such a clear distinction between the pursuit of money and higher aspirations, is not success marked by money earned and wealth gained but success proven by goals pursued and achieved. If at times Burnett relied on inner-directed notions of character building, he also evoked an other-directed vision of achievement, best realized, he said, when "overhearing people honestly rave about something I've produced."[27] What had worked for him would also, he hoped, work for those who watched his shows and read his books. "So if you have an idea, a passion, a belief," he told his readers at the very end of *Jump In!*, "go ahead, Jump In. What are you waiting for?"[28] Though he advised those who followed him to balance self-reliance with reliance on carefully chosen team members, he more prominently and frequently emphasized individualistic self-determination.

Burnett understood that the Great Recession and long-term economic changes provided the contexts that intensified interest in *Shark Tank*. Writing in 2013, he argued that "Americans face unprecedented hardships" because job security was disappearing. In response, he said, "people of all ages and backgrounds are reclaiming their future by creating their own opportunities." Into the breach came the Sharks and *Shark Tank*, he observed, as he undercut the emphasis on self-made individualism but nonetheless evoked ideas about self-determination. The Sharks served "this new crop of entrepreneurs" by offering them access to successful, self-made "moguls who [were] looking to invest their own money in the right people with the right ideas." The show, he emphasized, gave "real people a platform to catapult their dreams and ideas into successful businesses," in the process proving that "with a little ingenuity and a lot of hard work, they can all transform their lives and their communities."[29] Burnett claimed that the American dream drove him to come to the United States and shaped his ambitions once there, even though he also said that he was only passing though Los Angeles when he decided to stay. He usually deployed language that was vague, simple, nationalistic, and trite.[30] "I discovered who I was in America," Burnett announced. "I was entranced by the American Dream.... By 1990 I was living that Horatio Alger vision."[31]

As Langone might have suggested, such invocations overlook key aspects of the story of Burnett's career. While Burnett had a keen eye for what new ventures would work in America, the shows key to his career—including *Raid Gauloises, Survivor*, and *Shark Tank*—were ones others had originated and for which Burnett relied on the franchise. In addition, especially important to his career were the three women he married. Roma Downey inspired his turn to religious-themed shows, such as *The Bible*, but by the time he met her in 2004, Burnett was well on his way to fame and fortune. His first, brief marriage in the late 1980s, to Kym Gold, was strategically useful. The stepdaughter of a prominent Hollywood publicist (at whose company, Faces, Burnett was a vice president), Gold had the skills of an entrepreneur, as she proved early on when she helped him develop his business selling T-shirts and later when she founded True Religion, an immensely successful clothing line.[32]

Even more influential was his second wife, Dianne Minerva, whom he met in 1989, married in 1992, and divorced in 2006. Her memoir portrays Burnett not as an individualistic entrepreneur but as a businessman crucially assisted by others: she tells of the many people who helped Burnett develop his enterprises in vitally critical ways. And though one must view such claims skeptically, she also describes her own contributions to their common enterprises as a connector, executive, and innovator: "We worked hand-in-hand to launch *Eco-Challenge*" and then "we gave birth to a show that would change television history, *Survivor*. . . . With all due respect to Mark, I was often the Horatio to his Alger in our rags-to-riches story . . . the behind-the-scenes kingmaker, and the muse who delivered his 'signs,' as well as his personal cheerleader."[33] Over time, tensions in the marriage developed. They attended a Tony Robbins seminar titled "Unleash the Power Within," during which Robbins advised audience members to write on an index card what they most wanted in life. She wrote "Family," she later reported, while he jotted down "more money." What this meant became clear to her with the success of *Survivor*. Now that they had "hit the jackpot at the lottery machine of TV network programming," she wrote, things changed dramatically for the worse. "Where he'd once said 'we' and 'our,' he now substituted 'I' and 'my.'"[34]

"The thing I can't and never say is that I'm self-made," Ken Langone remarked. Unlike Burnett's, Langone's tale telling is more accurate and complete, albeit less familiar and less culturally resonant. To be successful, supposedly self-made individuals rely on others and on cultural and social capital in order to transform themselves from self-directed entrepreneurs into leaders of large, complex organizations. After all, his background in England, his good looks, and his experience as a paratrooper had shaped

Burnett profoundly. Moreover, from the moment he stepped off the plane in Los Angeles, many people provided important lessons, contacts, and boosts that helped him become successful. This contrasted with the stories he told of how he rose from rags to riches as a hardworking, ingenious individual. "Like Trump," journalist Patrick Radden Keefe observed, "Burnett seemed to have both a jaundiced impression of the gullible essence of the American people and a brazen enthusiasm for how to exploit it." A producer on *The Apprentice* commented, "We have to subscribe to our own myths, [and] Burnett is a great mythmaker," someone who both hyped dreams and seemed to believe in them.[35] And among what he promoted was the promise of making it big in America at a time when tens of millions struggled to do so. The ways he promoted himself—through the story of his life, the advice he offered, and the television shows he helped create—offered readers and viewers hope in troubled times. To some, all this was entrepreneurial wisdom; to others, lifelines that promised more than they actually delivered.

School of Sharks

Each Shark has a distinctive story, skill, and role on the program. However, they share much in common, especially how they view entrepreneurship, what they look for in contestants, and what they believe in. They serve as role models for aspiring entrepreneurs but also as investors who must be persuaded if a contestant is going to win. What they look for is usually not what Joseph Schumpeter described as "creative destruction," represented by a venture "that incessantly revolutionizes the economic structure from within, incessantly destroying the old one."[1] Rather, intentionally or not and in line with currently prominent academic approaches to entrepreneurship, they look for "the nexus of two phenomena: the presence of lucrative opportunities and the presence of enterprising individuals."[2] Their preference for compelling stories, fascinating and ambitious risk takers, and the possibility of getting a substantial return on their investments means they usually emphasize micro-level developments rather than pay attention to the broader forces at work in the world.

Although experimentation with the cast has continued, when the show debuted the producers in fairly short order settled on a group of six—Barbara Corcoran, Mark Cuban, Lori Greiner, Robert Herjavec, Daymond John, and Kevin O'Leary—of whom five normally appear in any given episode.[3] Yet in order to sustain interest and prevent ratings from falling, many guest

Sharks (mostly celebrities or successful entrepreneurs) have appeared—sometimes multiple times, but more often only once or twice.[4] All of the six principals were present by season three, and all served as regulars beginning in season four. For the Sharks, according to David Eilenberg, a producer involved early on, being in the tank involved "personal brand building," making money, and "philosophical buy-in" in terms of a commitment to "promoting entrepreneurship" on a "really feel-good show."[5]

Though all of the regular stars came to *Shark Tank* with successful résumés and some degree of public visibility, since the show's launch all have continued to present carefully crafted life stories and advice to promote themselves and what they believe it means to achieve entrepreneurial success in a shark-infested and dangerous world. In the Sharks' speeches on the lecture circuit, their work as consultants, and the words of wisdom they offer in popular books and on websites, they deploy celebratory narratives of their lives to drive home their recommendations for developing successful businesses. Notwithstanding the fact that two of the six are Canadian, they ask readers, viewers, and contestants to follow them in fulfilling their particular but usually insufficiently explained version of the American dream.

Early in the show's history, episodes began with five Sharks marching forward confidently and then standing outdoors in front of a huge American flag and between two expensive sports cars. The narrator introduced them one by one over footage of them shaking hands to close deals. Surrounded by symbols of their achievements, they entered, exited, or piloted a speedboat or sports car; or sat in or got out of a private jet. For *Dragons' Den*, the show on which *Shark Tank* drew, the producers, sensitive to the implications of the Great Recession, eliminated such objects of envy from the opening—and the American producers eventually did so as well. The first episode also featured headlines announcing "Store Closing" and "Bankruptcy," images that later disappeared.[6]

The presentations of the Sharks, shaped by producers, literary agents, public relations experts, and ghostwriters, provide windows into what *Shark Tank* promotes about American entrepreneurship. They exemplify key aspects of celebrity culture: the celebration of democratic heroes who contribute to the community's well-being; the role of mass media in creating and broadcasting fame; and the ways in which notoriety relies on the assumption of a difference between a public person and a more "real" private one.[7] On the one hand, the entrepreneur-as-judge can appear mean, arrogant, and demanding; on the other hand, the judge's authenticity as a successful operator in the dog-eat-dog business world reassures contestants and audiences. As skilled entrepreneurs, the Sharks remain both accessible and formidable. By getting to know the personal stories of the Sharks, even in carefully shaped narratives, audience members feel they have pierced the often clandestine and mysterious business world.[8] Above all, the stories told of them and the roles they play on-screen fit familiar albeit incomplete versions of how to achieve success in a world where self-governance has replaced the promise of support from public sources.

Barbara Corcoran

The stories told by Barbara Corcoran (b. 1949), an empathetic but usually tough-minded investor, rely on the clever trope that the lessons she learned from her mother enabled her to overcome adversity and build a real estate empire in New York City.[9] And there was plenty to support her claim that growing up in a hardscrabble household profoundly shaped her rise from rags to riches. She was the second-oldest of ten children who lived in Edgewater, New Jersey, a long, thin strip of a town on the western shore of the Hudson River, opposite uptown Manhattan. She grew up on the ground floor, where she shared a bedroom with five sisters; her four brothers inhabited another bedroom. Her father, a foreman in a factory, and her homemaker mother slept on a convertible couch in the living room. Adversely affected by dyslexia, young Barbara performed poorly at school. When she was eight, she related retrospectively, Sister Stella Marie, a nun who taught at her school, "pulled me right up out of my chair. She was inches from my face, and she said, 'If you don't learn to pay attention, you will *always* be stupid.'"[10] Corcoran wasn't able to do well academically in parochial school and had to attend a public high school.

After Corcoran earned a degree from Saint Thomas of Aquinas College in 1971, she taught school for a year but then found herself approaching her midtwenties, living in her parents' home, and working at a series of dead-end jobs. She was restless and ambitious, and her moment came when she met a man who called himself Ramòne Simòne while she was wait-ressing at a Fort Lee, New Jersey, diner. He claimed that he was from "the upper echelon of French-Spanish society" and had a career as a major real estate developer, and when he offered Corcoran a ride home in his Lincoln Continental, she accepted.[11] Several months later, she said yes to another of his offers: to help her start her life in Manhattan by paying for a week in the women-only Barbizon Hotel. Once she was there, he gave her a hundred dollars to go to Bloomingdale's and buy an outfit appropriate for a young career woman with expansive aspirations in New York. The following morning she landed a job as a receptionist at a real estate firm on the Upper East Side, and a few days later she moved out of the hotel and into an apartment on East 86th Street, which she shared with two young women. A few months after that, she convinced Simòne of the viability of her plan to launch a rental agency. He loaned her $1,000, and together they formed Corcoran-Simone, splitting the equity as 51 percent for him and 49 percent for her. Working out of her apartment, Corcoran made a simple but clever modification to an ad for a rental apartment that hyped its value, and the apartment was leased soon after. She had increasing success renting apartments over the next two years, and in 1975 she turned to the buying and selling of Manhattan real estate.

But before long, she found out that Ramòne Simòne was really Ray Simon, someone with not only a fabricated name but also a not very prestigious background and a faltering career. His business went bust, and he and Corcoran moved into a series of apartments in New Jersey. One night he came home and announced he was going to marry their secretary. Though she was humiliated, she soldiered on and continued to work at their real estate business. Under her leadership the company grew large enough to have more than a dozen salespeople. Corcoran dissolved the partnership with Simon in 1978 and, still in her twenties, formed the Corcoran Group with a modest amount of funding from the settlement with Simon. Success came quickly when she developed innovations that helped transform her fledgling real estate office into one of the premier firms in the city. In 1981, she captured attention in a media- and data-hungry real estate world with *The Corcoran Report,* a publication that reported trends in local real estate, with the *New York Times* featuring it in a story.[12] "I must be in the middle of some kind of Catholic miracle!" she later recalled thinking, for the newspaper article "put me square in the middle of the Manhattan real estate game."[13] In 1984, she married Bill Higgins, a former FBI agent from a privileged background.[14]

From 1978 to 1992, the Corcoran Group grew to employ hundreds of salespeople and generate tens of millions of dollars in commissions, although the path upward was not always smooth, especially given the boom-and-bust cycles of Manhattan real estate. One of Corcoran's most important successes came in the mid-1990s when she won a legal battle with Donald Trump over a $2 million commission. Corcoran later claimed she was drawing not on her lawyers' advice but on her mother's lesson that "you've got to bully a bully," and the judge announced that the only damages in the suit were to Trump's "bruised ego."[15] By the late 1990s, with over $2 billion in sales for the Corcoran Group, she had fulfilled her dream of becoming "the queen of New York real estate." With a young son at home and a successful business at work, she was ready for a change.[16] In September 2001 she sold the firm, now with $5 billion in sales and 2,150 employees.

Corcoran chronicled this journey in a book coauthored with Bruce Littlefield. She cast her story as a tribute to her mother, at one point saying to her directly, "All my life, you never told me I couldn't. You only told me I could."[17] The book is organized cleverly around a series of "Mom's Tales." Her mom's genius, Corcoran remarked, was that she insisted that each of her children had a unique gift. In Barbara's case it was her imagination, which helped her figure out how to fill in the blanks when she did not have an answer at hand.[18] "You're going to have to learn to use what you've got," Barbara's mother told her, pointing to her "great personality." "Since you don't have big breasts," she supposedly said, "why don't you tie some ribbons on your pigtails and just be as sweet as you are."[19] The other lessons were less anatomically revealing but nonetheless clever. Growing up with nine siblings taught Corcoran how to compete for attention. "Perception creates reality," another of her mother's lessons, meant that it was important, in dress and in business, to develop "the image of success." Her mother taught her that "moms can't quit," and so when there was a dramatic downturn in New York's real estate market, she knew that she too had to give 110 percent. Looking back on how she had deployed what her mother taught her, she remarked that she had "already achieved what most people would have called the American Dream." Using the $1,000 Simon had loaned her and turning it into a "billion-dollar business" confirmed what she, with some justification, called an "amazing rags-to-riches story."[20]

After she sold the Corcoran Group, sad about losing the pleasures of the world she had created, Corcoran set out on a path of reinvention—initially writing a real estate column for the New York Daily News, briefly serving as a political commentator on television, and then appearing as a weekly real estate commentator on The Today Show. That brought her to the attention of the producer Mark Burnett, someone exceptionally skilled at casting, and in the summer of 2009 she appeared as a regular during the first season of Shark Tank.[21]

Robert Herjavec

A sympathetic but tough Shark with expertise in new technologies and an on-screen preference for dramatic flair, Robert Herjavec (b. 1962) is one of two Sharks hailing from Canada and one of three who took advantage of being in the right place at the right time when the computer industry took off. Like Burnett, Corcoran, and Daymond John, he rose from humble origins to great heights.[22] Born into a Roman Catholic family in Croatia (then part of Yugoslavia), Herjavec grew up on a farm in a community whose pervasive poverty, he later claimed, created a we're-all-in-this-together ethos. His father was jailed twenty-two times for speaking out against Marshal Tito's Communist regime and then threatened with permanent incarceration at Bjelo Otok, the Yugoslavian equivalent of Robben Island in South Africa, where Nelson Mandela was imprisoned. In 1970, after his family was barred from entry into the United States because of inadequate papers, the eight-year-old Herjavec migrated with his parents to Halifax, Nova Scotia, with two suitcases and little cash. He and his family briefly lived in a friend's basement apartment there before moving to Toronto, where they again lived in a friend's basement apartment. Herjavec's father took a factory job earning $76 a week sweeping floors because better jobs went to those who spoke English like a native.[23] As a child Robert delivered newspapers and, aspiring to a career in entertainment, had bit parts acting in television commercials.

Life in Canada was tough. Having left a world of egalitarian poverty in Croatia and knowing no more than a dozen English words, Herjavec was now living in a socially stratified, often hostile environment. Schoolmates teased him for speaking with an accent and dressing like a greenhorn. His parents struggled to make a go of it. His father walked two miles to work in order to save bus fare, something that his son later insisted taught him the value of perseverance and the importance of not complaining. A greedy door-to-door salesperson cajoled his mother into buying an expensive vacuum cleaner that the family could ill afford. From this and other experiences young Herjavec learned resilience, and though he later said they also left him with "an emotional scar," they compelled him to pursue success. If it took money "to be treated well," he said in one of three how-to memoirs written with the help of John Lawrence Reynolds, "I would find a way to become so wealthy that no one would take advantage of me or my family again." In time, he said retrospectively, "my life unfolded like the classic 'immigrant makes good' tale: teased at school for my poor English and different customs, supported by a father who walked miles each way to a menial job, loved by a mother who believed in her son and encouraged him to pursue his dreams, and determined to justify the sacrifices my parents made for me."[24]

Herjavec went to the University of Toronto, where he majored in English and minored in political science. After college, he held a series of jobs—waiting tables, selling men's clothing, making phone calls for a debt collection agency, serving as a gofer for movie productions, and using his knowledge of Croatian to be a television network field producer in Sarajevo for the 1984 Winter Olympics. After seeking to rise as a producer in the Canadian film industry, he was fired, leading him to set aside his interests in entertainment for work in the growing computer industry. This ended his hopes—temporarily, it turned out—of achieving his vision of cruising "through Beverly Hills wearing sunglasses and a million-dollar smile."[25]

Herjavec entered the computer business with no technical knowledge and persuaded his boss to hire him by promising to work without pay for six months. He sold IBM equipment for the database company LogiQuest while waiting tables at night to make ends meet. As he often recounts, fired again, this time from his position as general manager at LogiQuest and threatened with a $5 million lawsuit, he struck out on his own. Initially working from the basement of his home and financing the venture with credit cards and a mortgage, in 1990 he launched BRAK Systems, an internet security software firm. Ten years later he sold the company to AT&T Canada for figures variously estimated at between $30 million and $100 million. He then went to Silicon Valley to restructure a struggling company for sale to Nokia for $225 million.[26] In 2003 he founded the Herjavec Group, a computer security firm that quickly experienced dramatic growth. Starting out with 3 employees and $400,000 in revenue, ten years later it had 165 employees and $125 million in revenue. Before long it was the leading Canadian IT security company and one of that nation's fastest-growing technology corporations.

Most of the Sharks are circumspect about their private lives, but not Herjavec, who has written extensively and emotionally about details others might want to protect. He brags about having a home on a private island in Miami where other wealthy celebrities live, including Oprah, Julia Roberts, and Jim Carrey. His principal residence is a 50,000-square-foot mansion outside Toronto. "Rich beyond his dreams," wrote a reporter for Toronto's *Globe and Mail*, who used a gender-confusing analogy, "he wanted a house that would symbolize his Cinderella-like transformation from struggling immigrant to mogul." And that is what he got. "The ceilings are about as high as the Sistine Chapel's," the reporter announced.[27]

Fame is central to Herjavec: being on national television, he remarked, "catapulted me into celebrity status." Despite saying that this had "little impact on my life," he engaged in celebrity name-dropping, telling us that he has connected with the likes of Bono, Celine Dion, Sylvester Stallone, and Mick Jagger. He relished the chance to "meet people I admire for their achievements both in and out of the limelight—people who, like me, are driven by their need to take their talents and abilities to the maximum level."[28]

Yet wealth and celebrity status had its downside. After a painful separation and then divorce from his first wife, he worked to repair his sense of failure and the damage to his family life caused by his near-total absorption in his business. Determined to heal himself by helping others, he accepted a priest's recommendation that he work in Seattle preparing food and serving it to the homeless. In his mere two weeks there, his "sense of worthlessness began to fade" as he experienced "feelings of accomplishment" when he helped people vastly less privileged than he. His experiences caused him to reconsider his long-held belief that people could pull themselves out of whatever situation they found themselves in, and led him to honor every individual's worth.[29] Herjavec's story is hardly unique. A common message on reality TV is that engaging with others' problems can be powerfully satisfying.[30]

"We all need someone to enrich our lives," Herjavec wrote about the period when his marriage was ending. Putting aside a lingering sense of depression, he soon found "light flashing from a source" he'd never known before. He accepted an invitation to appear on *Dancing with the Stars*, where in early 2015 he met the television performer Kym Johnson, whom he married a little over a year later.[31] Nor has Herjavec limited himself to expressive performances on television. Whether he's scuba diving, playing golf in celebrity tournaments, running marathons, or racing Ducati motorcycles and Ferrari automobiles, he celebrates aggression, competitiveness, and winning.[32]

In 2006, the producer of the Canadian version of *Dragons' Den* invited Herjavec to appear on the program. His success there prompted Burnett to invite him to perform in a similar capacity on *Shark Tank*, which he did beginning with the first season. "The prospect was terrific, especially the ego-boosting thought" that *Shark Tank* would generate an audience ten times the size of the Canadian versions. "The kid from Croatia had made it—a major U.S. network television show!"[33]

Daymond John

Daymond John (b. 1969) is an African American entrepreneur who, having used branding in the fashion industry to build his fortune, deploys the same talent on *Shark Tank*, on which he is often reserved and coolly confident. On the program, he said in one of several books written with the help of Daniel Paisner, he serves as the "fashion guru with a good gut for trends in popular culture and lifestyle." If some of the Sharks are "ruthless deal makers" and others are "easily won over by flash and publicity," he is, he insists—hiding the fact that he values shrewdness and successful investing more than populism—"the People's Shark" and the "champion of the underdogs."[34]

John grew up an only child in Hollis, Queens—ten miles east of Manhattan and literally across the tracks and three miles south of the home in Jamaica Estates where Trump spent his early years. While Trump started out in a five-bedroom, four-and-a-half-bath faux Tudor house, the John residence was more modest, albeit freestanding and owner occupied. His mother, once a contestant in the first Miss Black America competition, was a disciplined, ambitious woman who worked up to three jobs at once and still found time to pursue her dream of being a successful entrepreneur, albeit without success. His father, a computer programmer, was Trinidadian. When John was nine or ten, his mother sued for divorce and his father moved out of the house. By the time he was twelve, having realized that his father habitually lied to him and his mother, John cut off all contact with him. In a neighborhood where most children grew up with only one birth parent, John later noted, he "went from aberration to statistic."[35] His mother's boyfriend soon became like a father to him.

Life was tough, and John and his mother sometimes had to rely on food stamps and didn't have enough money to pay for utilities. Even as young as six years old, John claimed, he "ran every kind of hustle," and as he grew older, he bent the rules even more. For young John, making money was about getting power, as he said later. Extra money was "the measure of the man you might become." From age ten on, he always had at least one job, some legit, others barely so, and some not so at all. "Get rich or die tryin'" was the credo he and his friends lived by, knowing full well that by the time they reached the age of twenty, they might be dead or in jail.[36]

John watched as rap music, gangs, and drugs brought money into his neighborhood. He later remarked that he and his friends looked at drug dealers as entrepreneurs.[37] As early as middle school, he learned how to behave from hip-hop, break dancing, and rap music, and he grew up aware of the presence in Hollis of major figures such as the hip-hop musician LL Cool J and the record producer Irv Gotti. As he later recalled, his youthful aspiration to match Trump's achievements, especially as a branding expert, impelled him to succeed.[38] He was determined to become rich, and at some level, he realized that it was possible to do so by combining ambition, hustle, style, and business acumen. With his mother's warning to avoid dangerous choices and aspirations fixed in his mind, he carefully navigated among competing temptations, aspirations, and cautions.

A turning point came around when he was twenty. He realized that going to college was out of reach, partly because he was dyslexic. But for John, as for two of the other Sharks, dyslexia had a silver lining: it taught him how to compensate for what he could not easily do.[39] On weekends when he went out of town with friends to concerts that featured hip-hop artists, white kids came up to him and offered to buy, right off his back, clothes that in the 'hood seemed run-of-the-mill but in the suburbs were cool and desirable. Quickly realizing there was money to be made, John traveled to concerts, festivals, and trade shows with suitcases filled with knockoff goods he could obtain cheaply and sell for handsome profits. Then he hit on a transformative idea: because his mother had taught him how to use a sewing machine, he could make tie-top hats at home and eventually persuade rap artists to promote them. Aware that African American celebrities like Michael Jordan, Danny Glover, and Whoopi Goldberg were setting trends nationally and that African Americans were repurposing brands not initially intended for them, like Tommy Hilfiger, John was beginning to realize there were markets for him to capture.

Then came a second and more transformative tipping point. In 1991, when John was just twenty-two, the outdoor clothing company Timberland distanced itself from the inner-city African Americans its brand appealed to.[40] An executive "used the phrase *urban market* to describe his undesirable customers," John noted retrospectively, "but we knew . . . he meant . . . us inner city kids—low-income blacks, whites and Hispanics who lived in what less-enlightened types might have called the ghetto." Until then someone who had supposedly been "color-blind when it came to clothes," now John was inspired to build a line of clothing specifically for the "urban market" Timberland had rejected. "Cater to us, and we'll follow you anywhere," he wrote years later. "Reject us and we'll drive you into the ground."[41] One night, sitting around with friends, he realized that his tie-top hats needed a label, and he hit upon "For Us, By Us"—FUBU—a name that was a retort to Timberland. The name, he claimed, was designed to "reinforce for our customers that we were just like them." He and his partners believed "it was the kind of name that could start a movement—away from the big department-store brands that seemed to cater to rich white kids and toward a self-styled clothing line that was inclusive, affordable, and shot through with street cred."[42]

Working out of a van with friends, he stood outside the New York Coliseum and sold $800 worth of his hats in one night, and then he deployed a number of tactics to attract attention and boost sales. With three partners from his neighborhood, John developed a fuller line of stylistic clothing that reflected his pride in his community. "A legitimate hustle," he wrote later, "but a hustle just the same."[43] John and his partners quickly and innovatively developed a series of bold marketing strategies. They offered hip-hop and rap musicians free FUBU items, a move that helped transform the brand from a regional into a national one. Using what he later called "guerilla marketing," he persuaded LL Cool J to pose for pictures wearing FUBU clothing and then distributed promotional pictures. In 1994 he traveled to Las Vegas to pitch his brand at a trade show. This helped John and his partners make FUBU successful, and they left Vegas with $400,000 in orders. Back in New York, he figured out how to build "a *business* out of a hustle."[44] After being turned down by banks and lending agencies, he persuaded his mother to take out a mortgage to fund the company. Mothers, he said later, are "the ultimate angel start-ups, our true angel investors."[45]

John, his partners, and his girlfriend turned his mother's house into a factory where a West Indian sewer cut patterns and Latinxs worked on ten industrial-grade sewing machines. John and his associates continued to promote the FUBU line at clubs and on music videos. As he has recounted, they also found time to fend off neighbors and city officials who could not help but notice the range of disruptive and illegal activities involved in running a factory out of a residence. His mother, seeking to secure outside sources of financing, took out an ad in the *New York Times*. This led to an alliance with brothers Bruce and Norman Weisfeld, sons of Holocaust survivors, who were connected with Samsung's textile division and experienced in the financing and distribution of clothing. John struck a deal with the Weisfeld brothers that enabled him to quit waiting tables at Red Lobster and his African American partners to quit their day jobs. They rented an office on the forty-eighth floor of the Empire State Building, moved manufacturing out of the family home, and kept FUBU a company wholly owned by African Americans.[46]

Eventually the FUBU brand had sales of $6 billion and John himself was worth several hundred million dollars. FUBU and John earned multiple awards, wealth, and recognition far beyond what he could have imagined. Flush with cash and giddy with success, he gave away bundles of money to petitioners, bought fast cars and costly jewelry, purchased expensive real estate, and threw lavish parties. "I was like a lot of guys from my neighborhood when they first make it big," John remarked later, "wearing my money and not buying in to the conventions of the corporate workplace."[47] The path to success had been rocky, with plenty of growing pains—ones that involved dealing with counterfeiters, staying ahead of the fashion curve, and building a team that drew on talent in New York's diverse population.[48] Although he kept his private life as private as possible, he nonetheless had to acknowledge that his divorce and absence from his children's lives meant that he "lost [his] family during FUBU's climb."[49]

One day John got a phone message from Mark Burnett's office and learned that Burnett was thinking of asking him to join the Sharks as someone who "might bring a kind of street sensibility to the panel." This "would play like a show about the American dream." John knew he was ready to move beyond his triumphs at FUBU and admired Burnett's brand, which "symbolized hard work, dedication, quality, and the same entrepreneurial spirit that moved me and my boys at FUBU," but he had reservations: he "didn't want to be part of a show that was aimed primarily at the African-American market," preferring instead "to swim in the mainstream, not in some fringe puddle off to the side." But after his initial hesitation, John signed on, reassured that Burnett had in mind a capacious role for him. "When you're out there trying to reinvent yourself," he wrote later, "and grow your reputation as a motivational consultant and empowerment entrepreneur, the exposure that could come my way from this one show was like winning some brass ring."[50]

Lori Greiner

With a real estate developer father and a psychologist mother, Lori Greiner (b. 1969) grew up in an upper-middle-class household. Though she once said, "I wanted to make sure I was self-sufficient" as an adult, that remark hid the privileges from which she benefited and which remain invisible to most of those who watch her on television and read what she wrote.[51] She attended Loyola University, close to where she had grown up on Chicago's Near North Side, and majored in communications with a focus on journalism, television, and film. During her collegiate years she worked for the *Chicago Tribune* and sold jewelry on the side, demonstrating an entrepreneurial drive that before long led to her breakthrough moment.

In 1996, Greiner took out a $300,000 loan and developed her first commercially successful product, a specially designed cabinet for organizing and displaying earrings. She got the idea one summer while she was on a massage table and she supposedly "raced home with [her] mind on fire," determined to get it into JCPenney stores for the Christmas shopping season. She called the store's corporate headquarters in Texas and arranged to meet an executive there. He was interested in her earring organizer and said that if she could convince a dozen stores in the Chicago area to carry it and sales were successful, he would make sure it got into stores throughout the nation. On following weekends, she went to two stores and pitched her product directly to customers there, aided by her husband, who acted as a shill. Then she traveled to nineteen cities in twenty-one days. Successful sales of the organizer set her on the road to success as an inventor, entrepreneur, and eventually a Shark. To amplify her impact, in 1996, still in her twenties, she founded For Your Ease Only, Inc., a firm that focused on product development and marketing. In the following years she took out more than 120 patents and invented more than 500 products, many of them organizers designed for women that have together grossed more than $500 million in sales.[52]

In her only book, *Invent It, Sell It, Bank It! Make Your Million-Dollar Idea into a Reality* (2014), written with the help of Stephanie Land, whom she called her "writing partner," Greiner followed the entrepreneur's inspirational-memoir-plus-how-to-advice formula but did so in some distinctive ways. The book was markedly less personal than those by other Sharks; it spoke minimally of her life before college and paid scant attention to the importance of her parents, who, she remarked without elaboration, gave her "the mindset that I can achieve anything I want to." Without providing much detail, she nonetheless much more fully acknowledged the importance of her husband to her career, dedicating the book to him as someone who "stood by me, loved me, and made me believe in myself." As she tells it, her success story explicitly undergirds her advice, which—unlike that of other Sharks—is usually more practical than rhetorical. Yet when she is rhetorical, she is relatively circumspect. Thus she claims that her "fair share of hard knocks" made her "stronger and better," but whereas others dwell on how specific setbacks impelled them forward, Greiner never lets the reader in on precisely what her "hard knocks" were.[53]

Yet despite these not-very-original invocations of self-sufficiency, there are hints of a counternarrative.[54] Greiner writes of the importance of social media, which involves reliance on the inventiveness of those who help develop and handle her media presentation. She insists that individualism is more important than family wealth but discusses at length how to acquire funding from government agencies, venture capitalists, banks, and crowdfunding sites. She emphasizes the importance of self-reliance but talks of surrounding yourself with people who can help you. She minimizes the importance of a formal education and does not seem to acknowledge the connections between her college major, her early ambitions to become a journalist, movie director, or playwright, and her often-dramatic creativity in public arenas. Thus, her claim of self-reliance seems to conflict with the unexplored power of the cultural, social, and economic capital that surely stemmed from her early experiences, including her upper-middle-class upbringing and her college education.

The success of Greiner's QVC show, *Clever and Unique Creations by Lori Greiner*, launched around the year 2000, may well have persuaded Mark Burnett to anoint her as a Shark. "When I accepted the opportunity to appear on *Shark Tank*," she later remarked, "I saw it as a mere extension of the kind of mentoring, partnering, and investing I had done throughout my career." Although she unconvincingly insisted she "didn't set out to become a public personality," that indeed happened.[55]

Kevin O'Leary

On *Shark Tank* Kevin O'Leary (b. 1954) plays the role of the tough-minded, unsentimental, disciplined investor whose only concern, he says emphatically and repeatedly, is MONEY. "Here's how I think of my money: as soldiers," he said in one episode. "I send them out to war every day. I want them to take prisoners and come home, so there's more of them."[56] During the program's first season, after he made an especially bold offer to a contestant, Corcoran sarcastically remarked, "Well, aren't you Mr. Wonderful." O'Leary readily adopted the nickname, turning an intended insult into a mark of pride.[57]

O'Leary told his life story and offered advice in two books, one of them written with his "literary collaborators," the ghostwriters Lisa Gabriele and Bree Barton, and the other with the assistance of his stepfather and Gabriele.[58] Immigration was central to his background. His maternal grandfather migrated from Lebanon to Canada in 1904 and eventually became a successful businessman. After he died, O'Leary's mother inherited the business and then married Terry O'Leary, "a charismatic Irish extrovert," but also a drinker, carouser, and gambler, whom she had hired as her lead salesman.[59] O'Leary's parents split and his mother remarried, this time to George Kanawaty, an Egyptian who was working on his Ph.D. at the University of Illinois. So the family relocated to Champaign-Urbana. In 1963, when O'Leary was nine years old, his mother followed his stepfather to postings in developing countries where he worked for the United Nations. Initially young O'Leary went along with them, but at age thirteen he enrolled in a Canadian boarding school. In 1970, his family was together once more, this time in Ottawa, where O'Leary attended a public school.

In many ways young O'Leary had experiences not unlike those that other Sharks reported in stereotypically mythological tales undergirded by some reality: at a young age he opened a lemonade stand where he "was crippling the competition," and he had his first television appearance as a child.[60] Although he didn't rise from poverty to wealth, he had his own version of a life transformed and lessons learned. From often-traumatic family experiences, especially his mother's struggles to protect the family from her first husband's recklessness, O'Leary claimed he learned early on how vitally important it was to gain financial independence. His early experiences, he remarked retrospectively, were "harrowing, heartbreaking, but always thrilling and invigorating," making him "ready to face new challenges."[61]

O'Leary went off to college and then to business school at the University of Western Ontario. There, he compensated for his difficulty reading due to dyslexia by producing a promotional film for the MBA program. Echoing other Sharks' antipathy to expertise, he later insisted that the principal gain from earning an MBA, which he did in 1980, was graduating with a Rolodex filled with the names of "brainiacs with the books, but utter zeroes when it came to making money and building a business." Moreover, a four-month stint as a brand manager for cat food at Nabisco in the summer between his two years in the MBA program confirmed that he would not follow his peers into large corporations. No, he was a risk-taker who wanted to make lots of money and do so on his own terms.[62]

Fresh out of the MBA program, O'Leary founded Special Events Television (SET), a firm that produced short films, mostly on hockey. He was bought out by one of his business partners and in the fall of 1983 he focused on television graphics developed on personal computers, at the time clunky machines with more promise than power. At a key moment he realized the lucrative potential of new technologies. Working out of the basement of his home, O'Leary and a colleague formed SoftKey Software. Learning from what Microsoft was doing, he realized there was money to be made by having manufacturers, such as Hewlett-Packard and Epson, license the software and bundle it with the hardware they sold—in this case the millions of personal printers just beginning to come on the market. Before long, he met a university student named Linda Greer. Using what he later called the "O'Leary Onslaught," in 1990 he persuaded her to marry him.[63]

When funding from an investment company fell through at the last minute, he relied on money from his mother and from the proceeds from the sale of SET to tide the firm over until it was possible to launch an initial public offering. Around 1985, SoftKey moved out of its improvised headquarters in O'Leary's basement and into an office suite of 10,000 square feet. On paper, O'Leary was now wealthy, but he realized that he was also responsible to shareholders, whom he could also make rich.[64]

With sales of personal computers exploding, the enterprise grew dramatically as SoftKey added to its quiver a whole range of educational and business programs such as spreadsheets and dictionaries, acquisitions built on aggressive expansion, and innovative marketing and distribution strategies. SoftKey was emerging as a formidable software firm worldwide: it was hiring associates, driving down costs, seeking to understand what consumers and stores wanted, making licensing deals with existing software companies, controlling the distribution chain, realizing that it was important to commit to software that consumers purchased more than once, and acquiring competitors. Flush with acquisitions and bolstered by funding from two private equity firms, in 1995 O'Leary set his sights on the Learning Company (TLC), a prominent player in the educational software field.[65] SoftKey bought TLC, adopted its name, moved its headquarters from Toronto to Cambridge, Massachusetts, and shifted its listing to the New York Stock Exchange. O'Leary had gone from a basement apartment to Wall Street in ten years and now led a company that could offer consumers materials from the likes of *Sesame Street* and *Sports Illustrated*. Four years later Mattel acquired TLC for several billion dollars. In the following decades, O'Leary pursued a number of business ventures, including in 2008 O'Leary Funds, which within four years managed over $1.2 billion.

In 1996, O'Leary's career took a different turn when he began appearing regularly on Canadian television. In 2006, compelled by his business acumen and the colorful personality he'd already revealed on-screen, the Canadian producer of *Dragons' Den* invited O'Leary, along with Herjavec, to serve as on the inaugural program. Three years later Mark Burnett brought both of them in for the premiere of *Shark Tank*.

Mark Cuban

Mark Cuban (b. 1958) is by far the wealthiest of the Sharks, and on *Shark Tank* he conveys a reserved shrewdness.[66] His Jewish grandparents came to the United States from Russia and Romania, and his paternal grandfather changed his name from Chabenisky to Cuban at Ellis Island. His father and his uncle owned Regency Products, a modest auto upholstery enterprise founded in 1953. His mother was active in the Jewish community and held a series of jobs outside the home.[67] In his early years, the family lived in modest middle-class apartments in the Squirrel Hill section of Pittsburgh, a vibrant Jewish neighborhood filled with synagogues as well as restaurants and stores offering kosher food. Around 1968, the family moved to Mount Lebanon, one of Pittsburgh's mostly Jewish suburbs. Initially, they occupied a three-bedroom, one-and-a-half-bath house 1,079 square feet in size, before moving in 1975 to much larger home in Mount Lebanon. Over time, his parents ascended the class ladder, going from lower-middle-class residences, where their parents had lived in the mid-1950s, to middle-class homes by the time Mark graduated high school.[68]

Like other Sharks, Cuban—and those who wrote of him—repeated foundational stories that, although surely having much more than a grain of truth, nonetheless cleverly drove home certain lessons through didactic dramas. Unlike other Sharks, Cuban has published relatively little in the way of biography or advice in a focused manner, though it is nonetheless possible to piece together the story of his life.[69] "He displayed a penchant for business from a very young age," reported the author of *Mark Cuban: The Life and Success Stories of a Shark Billionaire*.[70] One of his foundational tales focused on when, at age twelve, he sold garbage bags door to door in order to afford a pair of expensive sneakers. Soon after, when workers at the *Pittsburgh Post-Gazette* went on strike, he delivered Cleveland papers in his hometown. During his high school years, he earned money from several jobs, including buying and selling stamps and coins. "*If* I ever grow up," he reportedly told himself, he hoped to run his own business with "as much doubt as confidence."[71] He spent his first year of college at the University of Pittsburgh before transferring to Indiana University, from which he graduated in 1981 with a B.S. in business administration. During college, he earned money bartending, giving disco dance lessons, developing a chain mail business, and operating a successful bar. For nine months after graduating, Cuban worked in Pittsburgh at Mellon Bank. Employed to more fully incorporate computers into the bank's operations, he learned he had a knack for computer work. His next job, also in Pittsburgh and lasting about the same length of time, involved working for a company that was trying—unsuccessfully, as it turned out—to bring franchising to the television repair business.

In 1982, at age twenty-three, with no money and no job prospects, Cuban moved to Dallas, driving there in his beat-up 1977 Fiat and crashing in an apartment he shared with guys from his college years. His first job in his adopted city was as a salesman at a local software store. At that point, the only PC experience he had was on a primitive home computer on which he'd attempted to teach himself BASIC. As he would do throughout his career, Cuban studied the latest scientific and technological findings and figured out how to monetize them. He pored over software manuals, built a client base, and earned extra money as a consultant. Then, nine months into his job, his boss fired him because he had closed a personal deal with a customer rather than follow his boss's instruction to open the store for the day. Having learned, as other Sharks had, that he was not cut out to be a traditional organization man, Cuban set out to start his own company. He could not say, he later remarked, that he prepared for his "journey into entrepreneurial territory" by writing up a business plan while on vacation with his friends who "got drunk, did stupid tourist tricks and ate at greasy spoons."[72] Yet once back in Dallas, he began to act decisively.

Like Herjavec and O'Leary, Cuban initially knew little about computers but set out to build his fortune by taking advantage of opportunities in the early days of the technological revolution driven by the proliferation of personal computers. In 1983, relying on a loan of $500 from a customer at the store where he'd worked, he founded MicroSolutions, a computer and software distribution and installation company. By building on the trust he had established with customers at the store, making contacts with sales-people at other computer stores, and cold-calling major computer companies, he secured contracts with a series of small-business owners. In his first year, he earned $15,000; seven years later he sold MicroSolutions to CompuServe for $6 million.

Living in Dallas, Cuban missed listening to Hoosier basketball games, so in 1995 he joined friends from his college days in developing AudioNet (soon renamed Broadcast.com), which transmitted sports events not easily accessible on radio or television. In 1999, near the height of the dot-com boom, Yahoo! purchased the company for $5.7 billion in a deal *Fortune* magazine later called one of the "worst internet acquisitions of all times."[73]

Cuban believed that you had to strike it rich only once and then protect yourself from downside risks. After the sales of MicroSolutions and Broadcast.com, Cuban used financial strategies to protect his gains.[74] Then, like other Sharks, having achieved more than most Americans, he hardly sat still. He continued to develop companies in the sports, computer, and entertainment fields. In 2000 he made a major investment in the NBA team the Dallas Mavericks and became the majority owner. Cuban turned around the struggling team by inspiring confidence in players and reaching out to fans through messages on his blog. Under his leadership the team thrived, making it to the playoffs in 2001 and the NBA finals in 2006, and then winning an NBA championship in 2011. Unlike owners who watched on high from skyboxes, Cuban placed himself courtside and was intensely involved in the team's performance. As was widely reported in the media, his passionate executives embroiled Cuban in conflicts with NBA leadership, referees, and players, which led to a long strings of fines and eventually an investigation into whether the Mavericks had a corporate culture hostile to women.

Already a powerful and often controversial figure, in September 2004 Cuban moved more formally into television. Nine months after Trump debuted on *The Apprentice*, Cuban starred in a new ABC show, *The Benefactor*, on which contestants competed to win $1 million from Cuban by showing what they could achieve in life. The show lasted for only nine months, but it was probably among the reasons that Cuban came to the attention of Mark Burnett. Cuban first appeared as a guest judge on *Shark Tank* in 2011 and became a regular Shark the following year. The addition of Cuban to the tank was transformative. According to producers of early shows, he "changed the rules of the game." He "lit the other Sharks up" and "play[ed] games with them." Others, they said, were playing checkers while he was playing chess.[75]

Sharks on Stage

Burnett selected the Sharks carefully, gathering people with varied expertise and backgrounds. The Sharks have strong, distinctive styles that shape how they respond to a pitch. Reality TV judges, note scholars Raymond Boyle and Lisa W. Kelly, "perform a certain 'nasty' role that has become appealing to audiences schooled in reality television. . . . However this does not necessarily make them appear inauthentic, as their ruthlessness is again legitimized by their off-screen achievements within the demanding world of business."[76]

The male Sharks often characterize the two female Sharks as not sufficiently tough. For example, John wrote—incorrectly—that Corcoran is "a real softie" who "buys into almost every idea that gets pitched," someone who is "almost too sweet" and "seems to want to trust everybody and find the hope and possibility in every prospect."[77] Corcoran has revealed empathy at key moments (as do most of the men, some less frequently than others), but she can also display a quicker wit and sharper tongue than many of her male peers. While Lori Greiner admitted that she had "become known as 'the warm-blooded shark,'" she did not think "being kind or compassionate" made her "any less competitive in the business world." Indeed, like all of the Sharks except Kevin O'Leary (and even him on very rare occasions), when she looks at contestants, she often identifies with them because she sees in them reflections of her own history and aspirations.[78] Greiner carefully threads the needle when giving advice to women:

on the one hand, she warns female contestants not to "let any men put you down or be chauvinistic to you," yet on the other hand she tells women not to "think of yourself as a female.... If in your mind you say, 'I'm a woman, how are they going to react to me?' you're already making yourself nervous and inferior, so don't. You're on a level playing field and you're just as good as them—if not better."[79]

Of the four men, Mark Cuban and Daymond John are often the most kindly and empathetic of the Sharks. Usually they remain quiet at first and only reveal their reactions to a pitch after the others have jumped in. Cuban frequently sits there, Buddha-like, with a sardonic smile. Even with losers, at the end he almost always sends pitchers off with best wishes. Although John has remarked that his own background makes him "root like crazy for the little guy," more often than not he acts with restrained interest backed by calculated business judgments. He observed somewhat inaccurately that on-screen, Robert Herjavec comes "across as mean and menacing," although he also acknowledged that off-camera he is kind and friendly. As a "very shrewd businessman" Herjavec incorrectly claims that he "cuts through all of that and gets to the core of a deal" by taking "all the emotion out of it." While O'Leary, John observed, is a "sweetheart" off the air, especially if the Sharks are not talking about money, on air O'Leary plays the bad cop to the good cops his peers often appear to be. John characterized O'Leary as someone who, as a "venture capitalist by trade," is "all about the cash," who "tells the truth," and who "doesn't stop to think about hurt feelings."[80] Or as Greiner put it, "Kevin is ruthless and has an acid-tipped tongue."[81]

Each of the Sharks not only has a vivid, often unique style but also occupies a specific niche undergirded by distinctive skills and experiences. Queen of the online television shopping channel QVC and an inveterate inventor of niche items, Greiner justifiably claims an ability to launch a product quickly and widely as she moves it from concept to sales. Corcoran almost never has the opportunity to help a pitcher in real estate, the field where she was initially so successful; rather, her skills seem as generalizable as those of any Shark. Like the others, she makes it clear that there are business sectors into which she cannot and will not venture. John claims he occupies what he calls "the pop culture slot on the panel," an expert when it comes to "fashion, music, lifestyle goods and services," although he also has considerable experience in branding, manufacturing, and distribution.[82] Herjavec relies not only on his knowledge of new technologies but also on his love of sports and music. Cuban's range is even wider, encompassing as it does the many sectors where he has investments, including sports, entertainment, and new technologies. O'Leary plays the role of the shrewdest investor, focusing on valuation and return seemingly regardless of sector.

All of this helps make the Sharks' interactions keen and contested. Although in private they may get along well, on *Shark Tank* they are skilled actors who interrupt, cooperate, and clash. They hurl insults at each other more often than compliments. Alliances form among them and then shift on a dime in unexpected ways. Part of what makes the show exciting are the compelling, often rapidly changing processes of negotiation.

The Sharks appear on *Shark Tank* for varied reasons, including the opportunity to invest their own money in promising enterprises. Another incentive is the fees they receive for their appearances. The 2014 North Korean hack of Sony's emails made public a testy exchange between Cuban and a corporate executive that revealed Cuban's compensation for season five was around $900,000. From the start, the pitchers had to cut the production company in on deals. For the first four seasons, the producers had required that the contestants hand over 2 percent of operating profits and 5 percent equity of companies the Sharks invested in. In 2013, Cuban, by then a popular and essential regular, told the producers that unless they eliminated this requirement he would no longer participate. This clause, he insisted successfully, not only would discourage skillful and knowledgeable investors from agreeing to appear but also smelled of predatory influence.[83] "Economically it's an amazing show," remarked a producer involved in early seasons. Aside from what the Sharks are paid, there are no expensive "talent fees" in addition to production costs, which themselves are low compared with those for shows filmed off-site, such as *Survivor*, or even those filmed in a studio with an audience. In addition, the Sharks, rather than the production company, "produce the prize money themselves."[84]

What was also clear from the hacked emails was that there were complicated, momentous, and often arcane contractual issues about the Sharks' obligations to promote the show and the rights of the Sharks or Sony to copyrighted materials, including phrases and gestures.[85] When the show's producers first approached John, he was surprised that he had to invest his own money, that the contract had an exclusivity clause that barred him from regularly appearing on other television shows, and that the producers expected him to, in his words, "put my expertise and my reputation on the line, too, pledging to do whatever I could to help each venture I supported achieve some kind of success."[86] He was also reluctant to join the show because having aspiring entrepreneurs approach him with a request for funding was already a common experience, as it surely was for his peers. In the end, it was Burnett's brand that convinced him.

For John and presumably the others, the most compelling reason for becoming a Shark was that it gave them opportunities to amplify their brands by moving in new directions through potentially profitable investments, media exposure, and celebrity status. All of them were at a turning point in their lives when they joined the show, though some more than others. They had achieved wealth and fulfilled the American dream, but they'd often done so in somewhat circumscribed realms. Now they were ready for something more adventuresome and expansive. John put it best when he said, "When you're out there trying to reinvent yourself and grow your reputation" in new ways, "the exposure that could come my way from this one show was like winning some brass ring—or, the lottery." When John at first hesitated to sign on, a Hollywood agent called to say he would be crazy to turn down the chance to appear on *Shark Tank*. "I've got superstar movie actor clients," the agent told him, "who would give their right arms to be on a prime-time reality show."[87]

The Sharks' Entrepreneurial Vision

In books, interviews, and on-screen appearances, and on websites, the six principal Sharks articulate their visions of what entrepreneurship involves and what they expect from supplicants. There are some distinctive elements even though by and large they all evoke remarkably homogenous visions of American life. In contrast to Herjavec, who has a macho and Darwinian vision, Corcoran expresses feminist commitments, something that also pops up in her *Shark Tank* appearances. She is keenly aware that she entered the New York real estate world when it "was a business worked by women and *owned* by men," a pattern she successfully challenged.[88] All things being equal, she wrote, it's best to hire women because they will work harder since they have more to prove, and because they have more collaborative styles and are more pragmatic, truthful, and fun to work with. Besides, she remarked, driving her point home, "choosing a woman puts you on the cutting edge, since women are taking over anyway."[89]

What makes John's vision distinctive (markedly more so in his books than in his on-screen appearances) is his emphasis on the African American experience. In *Display of Power* he focused on race, mostly on pages shaded in a darker color than the rest of the book. He explored how, growing up, he and his peers had struggled to be color-blind in a world where authority figures taught them "to shoulder all this disregard and disrespect just because of the color of our skin." He talked of how slowly most people, especially bankers, came to realize the considerable purchasing power of the African American community—something that impelled him to keep as much money as possible in that world. In a nod to the historically situated and culturally resonant alliance between blacks and Jews, he acknowledged how his Jewish business partners had opened up job opportunities for African American youth and incorporated him into their family celebrations, including bar mitzvahs. "Black and white equals green," he said, and noted that GTFM ("Get the F***ing Money!") was the name of the holding company his neighborhood partners had formed with the Weisfelds.[90] In his most recent book, *Rise and Grind* (2018), John doubled down on his use of African American inflections and language, speaking of the importance of the hustle, dropping in the word *man*, and talking about "street or slang definitions" of the word *grind*, some of which, he noted, "aren't exactly appropriate for a family audience."[91]

Despite these distinctive elements, to a remarkable extent the Sharks' advice to aspiring entrepreneurs, their judgment about what to invest in, and their outlooks on the world have much in common. Rely on gut instincts, not elaborate business plans, they advise, even though they know that business acumen and concrete plans make for a successful pitch. Following the tradition deeply imbedded in American advice literature, they see failures as inspiration for doubling down and moving on. They look for pitchers who work hard, show ambition and drive, take daring risks, and recognize the importance of selling and, especially, of establishing reciprocal relationships with customers. Particularly in the early stages of a career, 24-7 devotion to work, even at the cost of family life, is essential. What matters, Cuban wrote, is "getting so jazzed about what you do, you just spend 24 hours straight working on a project."[92] Whittle "lives down to the bare essentials," Greiner insisted. This might seem like "all work and no play, but it isn't, because when you're doing what you love, work is play."[93] Several of the Sharks pay particular attention to elements they consider essential: John, the importance of branding; O'Leary, customer acquisition costs; and Cuban, core competencies. New technologies, they assert, change the dynamics of success—quickening the pace of change, upsetting established patterns and hierarchies, and making it possible for from-the-bottom-up entrepreneurs to move more nimbly than mired-in-the-mud corporate executives. With the possible exception of O'Leary, they aver that passion drives successful entrepreneurs more than the pursuit of money.

Theirs is an anti-institutional vision. Despite evidence to the contrary in their own careers, they counsel others to rely not on banks but on family, partners, sweat equity, and self-financing. They are antibureaucratic, appreciating nimble corporations and skeptical of the complacency of large, well-established ones. Though some of them have formal educations relevant to their careers, they collectively believe that earning an MBA is hardly a key to success because theory learned in the classroom is unimportant. For example, having achieved enormous success as an entrepreneur by relying on what he characterized as his own intelligence and character strengths, Herjavec remarked that he would "pit one entrepreneur with vision and determination against twenty MBA grads and expect the entrepreneur to win." He contrasted someone "who prefers a calm, mature and stable work environment," where the workday ends at 5 P.M., with a person "seeking to benefit from unforeseeable opportunities and adrenaline-raising crises."[94]

Central to the success of *Shark Tank*, Mark Burnett, and the Sharks themselves are the often-compelling, carefully constructed stories of how their lives and the show they participate in prove the viability of the American dream, however vaguely participants and the program define its meaning and scope. Herjavec is among the most rhapsodic. He sees little that can in the long run deter an ambitious entrepreneur. Commitments to competitiveness, passion, and growth undergird his vision of the American dream, which he sees as more possible south of the Canadian border, even though he often uses the word *American* to include all of North America. "There's a side to the magic element" of *Shark Tank*, he asserted, "that says something about the greatness of America." Putting aside all the show's glitz, he continued, what the show is truly about is "you and me and every American who harbors a dream."[95] He appreciates how America gives people second chances. Because the widely shared "entrepreneurial spirit" is "the essential core of success in a free-enterprise society," he insisted, in the United States "it's assumed that anyone who has made a lot of money has found a secret to wealth that any other American, with enough luck, energy and determination, can duplicate."[96]

When the Sharks articulate what the American dream means, what is especially striking are the ways in which they are outsiders—as women, an African American, a Jew, Roman Catholics, an immigrant, and someone (O'Leary) with multiple ethnic identities, and dyslexics.[97] Some of their narratives, however intentionally dramatic, are more compelling than others, such as Herjavec's realization that his experience as an immigrant meant he would always be an outsider and would "never lose [his] need to prove [himself] over and over"; John's "hip-hop version of the classic rags-to-riches story"; Corcoran's narrative of moving from a hardscrabble New Jersey household to the top of the heap in the Manhattan real estate world; and Burnett's journey from working-class Brit to nanny to media mogul.[98] It's not hard to believe that Burnett knew what he was doing when he picked the six key Sharks and then helped curate their stories.

Social Visions and Political Engagements

A key element in the Sharks' stories is the intricate relationship between politics, entertainment, and celebrity. As the media scholars Susan J. Douglas and Andrea McDonnell have shown, cable TV, the internet, and reality TV have played critical roles in the dramatic explosion of celebrity culture in the early twenty-first century. Promoted by "the celebrity production industry" and "connected in often deeply meaningful ways to audiences," famous people such as the Sharks become "the conduits for our dreams—if they can do it, I can do it," their status suggests. Their stories include the promise of "upward mobility, especially in an era of increased inequality between the rich and everyone else," and "work to justify economic and social hierarchies."[99] Sociologist Joshua Gamson has shown how a highly elaborate celebrity-producing industry mixes authenticity and artifice, just as the Sharks do. It continually offers audiences "tidbits of the 'private' selves of public figures" that rest on the illusions of reciprocity and intimacy. Picturing celebrities as ordinary people adds credibility to the myth of the self-made person because "the ordinariness of celebrities keeps the door to success, measured as fame, always somewhat ajar; interested and determined individuals can always kick it open."[100] By identifying with famous people, individuals can imagine roads to success and power. So it should come as no surprise that the Sharks carefully weave together their roles as celebrities, investors, and entrepreneurs. Thus, O'Leary watches fans oohing and aahing Daymond John but appreciates even more how John directs attention away from himself and toward the products up for sale. While Herjavec's take on the role of celebrity in his life involves bragging about his own fame, O'Leary's approach, characteristically, is more explicitly strategic, all about treating fame as a currency to deploy wisely.[101]

The Sharks inevitably used their celebrity status to enter the political fray, especially after Donald Trump became a presidential candidate. Each Shark's relationship with Trump has ricocheted over time, throughout his candidacy and then presidency, and serves as a litmus test for their political engagement. A few weeks before the 2016 presidential election, soon after the release of the tape in which Trump bragged about grabbing women's genitals, Corcoran went on MSNBC to describe her experiences with Trump and advised young women to stand up to bullies.[102] Two days later, on CNN, she insisted that it was "preposterous" for the presidential candidate to claim that he had never sexually harassed or assaulted a woman. To back up her statement, she told a story about the only time she was in a room alone with him, when she and Trump's second wife, Marla, were both pregnant. Corcoran said, "He compared my breast size" to that of his wife "by putting his hands in the air" as if to offer comparative measurements. Corcoran had trouble going to sleep, she said, when she thought of Trump as president.[103]

Cuban also used his access to media to criticize Trump.[104] An early supporter of Trump, he eventually, the media reported, changed his mind about whom he would back in 2016. Before the election he offered to donate $10 million to Trump's favorite charity if the candidate would appear with him on television and discuss policy at length. Trump never responded, but Hillary Clinton did, inviting Cuban to sit in the front row as her guest during a presidential debate. Soon after, Clinton lauded Cuban for hiring rather than firing apprentices and sharing his profits with his employees. After the election, Cuban criticized Trump for a backward-looking economic plan, for threatening to start a trade war with Mexico, and for false claims of voter fraud.[105]

As a young man, John was inspired by the figure of Donald Trump in Trump Tower, by Trump's ability to create the Trump brand, and by Trump's book *The Art of the Deal*, though he claimed the book only confirmed his own mother's wisdom. Trump served as John's lodestar, someone who "represented everything money and power could buy in a city like New York" and who was doing "Branding 101." During his junior year in high school John worked as a messenger for the investment bank First Boston and was charged at one point with delivering a packet to Trump. He went to Trump Tower, determined to meet "The Man," but one of those "beefy, 300-pound, brick-eating security guys" shoved him "out of there like [he] was at a bowling alley." As John "slid across the floor on the way to the door," he said to himself, "Okay, there's always a next time."[106] However, as media sources often revealed, he publicly supported Hillary Clinton in the presidential election, and once Trump was elected, John reminded Americans that their success depended on their skills and initiative, not on help from a president.

Though at times Herjavec found Trump to be an alluring figure, he opposed Trump's immigration policies. For a while O'Leary campaigned for the top leadership position in Canada's Conservative Party, a party Herjavec also supported. O'Leary's candidacy prompted extensive comparisons of O'Leary and Trump—two brash, wealthy reality TV stars who entered politics as advocates of lower taxes and deregulation. However, they differed on many policy issues, including support of NATO, same-sex marriage, and, most notably, immigration. "I'm of Lebanese-Irish descent," O'Leary said in mid-January 2016. "There's no walls in my world. I wouldn't exist if Canada had walls."[107]

While Greiner was silent on both Trump and politics, O'Leary and Cuban, both libertarians, were the most explicit about not just Trump but also their political outlooks more generally. O'Leary had read Ayn Rand's *Atlas Shrugged* (1957) early in life and had realized that "either you believe in the intrinsic concept about the pursuit of wealth and why it's good for you, or you don't.... To me there is darkness and light," socialism and capitalism.[108] In 2011, as North America was recovering from the Great Recession, O'Leary remarked that "the true capitalist, the entrepreneur ... sees adversity as opportunity and carves a confident path through the financial rubble. More than governments," he continued, using neoliberal language, "these trailblazers are the true paramedics of the ailing global economy."[109]

Cuban spelled out his political commitments when he wrote the foreword to Gary Shapiro's *The Comeback: How Innovation Will Restore the American Dream* (2011), in which Shapiro argued that the American dream could only be made possible by opposing unions and supporting fiscal responsibility, free trade, and immigration of highly skilled workers. In his foreword, Cuban, who had named his yacht after Ayn Rand's *The Fountainhead*, made his commitments clear. Entrepreneurial innovation, not more government aid, would bring true progress. Restarting "America's innovation engine" would "get America back on track and reassert our preeminence in the world."[110] His one book, *How to Win at the Sport of Business* (2011), has a subtitle that pithily captures his social vision: *If I Can Do It, You Can Do It.*

Though they make for good stories, the Sharks' insufficient and incomplete personal histories, as told in their books and other media, contribute—often inadvertently—to a neoliberal outlook on the world. The Sharks devote virtually no attention to the ravages caused by the growing inequality that their own triumphs represent. Faced with the powerful and tragic forces unleashed by the Great Recession, they double down on optimism and the promise of the American dream. In their view, self-governance dominates while the power of family, government, corporations, and cultural institutions remains largely offstage. In their life stories, the advice they offer, and how they judge pitchers on *Shark Tank*, two narratives exist in unresolved and unacknowledged tension with one another. One relies on the trope of the self-made individual and deploys folk wisdom that emphasizes ambitious risk-taking, gut instincts, learning from setbacks, and antipathy to powerful institutions. The other narrative, mostly a subtext that they ignore but that can be seen in their lives, emphasizes that much of what they accomplished depended on timing, family, friends, and associates, as well as on the cultural traditions that shaped them.

Corcoran, Herjavec, and John did rise from rags to riches. Yet all the Sharks, not just these three, constructed narratives of their lives with dramatic stories that purported to show how, almost by themselves, they overcame obstacles to their success. To varying degrees but to considerable extents, they all overlooked or minimized qualifying or contradictory evidence. Most of the Sharks told of how, early in their lives, they demonstrated ambitious entrepreneurial talents, but later on they were usually in the right place at the right time. Timing was elusive but crucial — the advent of new technologies helped Cuban, Herjavec, O'Leary, and Corcoran advance their careers. For John, emerging cultural and stylistic relationships between African Americans and white youths opened up entrepreneurial opportunities. To be sure, not everyone so situated achieved what they did, but they owe their achievements to many uncontrollable factors in addition to their own drive and talents.

With their carefully crafted and dramatic formulations, the Sharks offer advice that can hide as much as it reveals, especially when it comes to receiving help from friends and family. Even Greiner insists that failure and adversity, rather than privilege, were what shaped her. Family members played crucial roles, some more acknowledged than others — Corcoran's mother was influential but not her father; for Herjavec, it was the opposite; and John's mother had a powerful positive role in direct opposition to the negative influence of his father. And what role, one has to wonder, did religion and ethnicity play? O'Leary gives some sense of what his parents and their cultural traditions brought to the table, and John richly renders how African American communities and traditions played crucial roles in his ascendancy. But how Corcoran's and Herjavec's Roman Catholicism, as well Corcoran's Irish heritage and Herjavec's Croatian background, shaped their lives goes unexplored. As for husbands and wives, the Sharks reveal little. Corcoran mentions the initial help from Simon and the tech advice from Higgins, about whom she says little more. With Herjavec, there's a disappearing first wife and a very present second one, though in his telling, neither of them played any role in shaping his career. John tells us even less about his spouse. Beyond family members, to a considerable extent the impact of friends and, even more so, business associates generally remains opaque. To be sure, John emphasizes the role of the Weisfeld brothers, but he rarely if ever mentions his African American partners by name, let alone highlights their contributions. Overall, for most of the Sharks, it seems that entrepreneurs are geniuses who act alone, without the aid of mentors and business partners. But the specifics of their own lives and the acknowledgments sections of their books, which list the names of those who helped them, contradict this idea.

Support from institutions also matters. Although Cuban, Greiner, and O'Leary all had extensive university educations, their narratives don't share what they usefully gained from those educations. Their insistence that they learned the most out in the world, not in the classroom, is the tip of the iceberg in their individualistic anti-institutionalism. While John does highlight the importance of the Weisfeld brothers, Greiner's vagueness about her source of financing at an early and crucial point in her ascendancy is more typical of how the Sharks elide, hide, minimize, or contradict the fact that friends, families, and institutions helped launch and sustain their careers. All of the Sharks often (although not always, and some more than others) portray themselves as more independent and less organizationally embedded than they actually are. From reading what they wrote and what is written about them, you would think they were solo entrepreneurs rather than the organization men and women they became. The federal government also played a role behind the scenes in their success by developing key technological innovations, yet they failed to acknowledge that contribution. Above all, the tension between the Sharks' socially embedded lives and their individualistic advice finds its counterpart in the similarly unresolved tension between the Sharks' telling contestants they can make it on their own and their making it clear that in order to do so, contestants need the financing and strategic partnerships the Sharks themselves offer.

Then there are other caveats of note. Perhaps no more so than any sample of greatly successful figures, Burnett and some of the Sharks have found themselves embroiled in personal and professional problems, among them divorces, lawsuits, deals gone bad, and business reversals.[111] Although the television show uses the word *billion* frequently, only Cuban is a billionaire; for several of the others, the word refers not to their personal wealth but to the cumulative revenues of enterprises with which they are associated. As a headline in Toronto's *Globe and Mail* noted in 2012, "Kevin O'Leary's Not a Billionaire: He Just Plays One on TV."[112] Despite their emphasis on going it alone, most if not all of the Sharks have emerged as philanthropists, often marked by self-interest and noblesse oblige.[113] Moreover, skepticism is in order when life stories seem too triumphalist and inevitable: we understand our lives in retrospect (and in these cases with the help of ghostwriters) even though they are messier day to day and even year to year.

In *I Love Capitalism! An American Story*, Ken Langone correctly insisted he was not a self-made man because so many people, institutions, and traditions helped him on his journey from rags to riches. In the lives of Burnett and the Sharks, ambition, hard work, intelligence, and a willingness to take risks have been important, to be sure. But so too have factors we can see in the stories of their lives but that often play bit parts in the individualistic advice they offer: timing, for example, along with cultural, social, and economic capital. Were we to keep Langone's perspective in mind as we brought the stories the six Sharks and Burnett into harmony with the wisdom they proffer, we would encounter worlds very different from the presentations they offer and that are made on their behalf by ghostwriters, public relations experts, and copywriters.

Shark Tank, it turns out, is but a small part of the world of cultural productions that promote American entrepreneurship. Some of the writings on the topic of risk-taking businesses are scholarly and others are in the vein of enthusiastic or practical, even humdrum advice. *Shark Tank* exists alongside books, TED Talks, and websites that offer to transform the world—their promoters promise that the skills and ideas put forth in these productions will bring about a utopian world that enriches not just entrepreneurs but billions of others, even as Americans recover from the Great Recession. In contemporary America, enterprises such as Walmart, Chick-fil-A, Hobby Lobby, and Amway connect enterprise and Christianity.[114] In contrast, Burnett and the Sharks offer a secular, albeit inspirational, vision that melds personal striving, worldly success, and entrepreneurship with the promise that this powerful and familiar combination will help Americans successfully navigate a dangerous world.

The Artifice of
Perfectly Pitched Dramas

On June 11, 2019, I drove with a friend to Babson College in suburban Boston to attend a meeting of Walnut Ventures, where experienced angel investors listened to pitches and then decided whether to consider investing their own money in what their website describes as "seed and early stage companies." This enabled me to understand the artifice on which *Shark Tank* relies and how atypical and problematic its episodes are as examples of entrepreneurial investing.

Walnut Ventures is one of about three dozen such investing organizations in New England, which vary in their heft and formality. The thirty or so of us in the room (mostly white men ranging in age from their mid-thirties to their late seventies) listened to four pitchers. Each spoke for fifteen minutes and then fielded questions for about the same amount of time. Then they left the room so the potential investors could discuss their proposal in confidence. The moderator asked who was interested in taking the next step of carrying out due diligence, and usually a handful of people raised their hands, and one among them agreed to lead that effort. They promised to report their findings on a listserv for others who might be interested once more information was available.

What struck me was how different this venue for

angel investors was from what I had seen on *Shark Tank*. To be sure, there were some similarities. Some of the valuations were problematic, others reasonable; the pitches varied from the stumbling to the professionally perfect; and the responses to questions ranged from evasive to commanding. Yet the differences were more striking. There were more than five potential investors watching, and they were informally seated. The pitchers sought funding for technologically sophisticated products with both high risks and huge potential, not household niche products that were more modest in their promise. The potential investors were inquisitive and polite; they tried neither to humiliate the contestants nor compete with one another. The investors were thinking of betting relatively modest amounts of money compared with the amounts seen on *Shark Tank*. At this stage, there were no bids, only polite inquiries and quiet discussions. Whereas *Shark Tank* involves carefully crafted pitch productions, Walnut Ventures, like many of its peers, expected applicants to present their proposal using a formulaic pitch deck. Overall, what I was witnessing were low-key moments that had relatively little artifice (especially on the part of potential investors) and even less drama. It turns out that reality is very different from reality TV.

Shark Tank has its own depiction of early-stage investing, one that does not rely on the pitch decks that are so widely employed elsewhere and are explained in detail in Evan Baehr and Evan Loomis's influential 2015 *Get Backed: The Handbook for Creating Your Pitch Deck, Raising Money, and Launching the Venture of Your Dreams*. In advising readers on how to shape a pitch deck, which is composed of a series of PowerPoint illustrations, Baehr and Loomis stressed the importance of building a problem-solving team that can take advantage of opportunities by identifying the market and competitors and then laying out the financing. "Entrepreneurs," they emphasized, "hold the keys to innovation, new jobs creation, and deep, personal fulfillment. That is, if they are courageous (or should that be crazy?) enough to give it a try."[1] Barbara Corcoran supplied a blurb for the book's cover: "Successfully raising money requires sharing a big vision in a clear way," she wrote. "Anyone who comes to pitch on *Shark Tank* should read this book first." But despite Corcoran's endorsement, *Shark Tank*'s formula does not allow contestants to use a pitch deck.

Yet in their own ways, the show's episodes involve carefully orchestrated dramas that use elaborate artifice to convey authenticity. At the center are carefully edited negotiations showing how the contestants persuade Sharks to act as investors and mentors. The contestants and Sharks project their sincerity, aided by pre-filming planning by contestants and members of the production staff, on-screen performances that at their best resemble those of professional actors, and elaborate postproduction editing. The show offers dramatic stories of eager entrepreneurs pitching their ideas to wealthy and experienced angel investors who respond with a mixture of funding, support, and humiliation. If product placement plays some role in many television shows, it is absolutely central to *Shark Tank*, in part because Mark Burnett is especially adept at it. Moreover, the show enables the pitchers, the Sharks, and the production company to develop other financially enriching platforms that hype the pitched products and tout the Sharks as skillful entrepreneurial investors.[2]

As media scholar Mark Andrejevic perceptively noted, in a society marked by inequality, insecurity, and uncertainty, "the work of self-promotion" is increasingly important, and reality television promises "what might be described as 'attention capital,' or 'public image capital,'" which "can eventually be exchanged for other forms of capital."[3] Branding—of Mark Burnett, the show, the Sharks, the pitchers, and their projects—is one of the principal ways aspiring contestants gain traction in precarious times. Sharks like to think of themselves as investors, entrepreneurs, and educators, but it is also accurate to see them as entertainers and actors.

Shark Tank is backed, produced, and broadcast by powerful corporations that rely on surveys of what viewers prefer, and over time episodes have become more dramatic, polished, and staged.[4] Sony owns the format, which means that the American version relies on a proven structure whose basics cannot be modified.[5] On the first episode, broadcast on August 9, 2009, viewers saw the Sharks sitting in private jets and expensive sports cars and lounging in front of piles of cash; images of newspaper headlines provided evidence of economic troubles in the nation. These were "the worst economic times since the Great Depression," the announcer declared, and "the Sharks are the last chance for the entrepreneurs to get financial backing they desperately need." On early episodes, the pitchers passed between two tanks where images of sharks appeared and then walked through a door and entered the set. The Sharks sat behind a long table, and as the episode developed, an off-camera narrator with a not-very-resonant voice provided the information that connected the narrative.

In later episodes, the show's basic format remained intact, but some details changed. Over time, the Sharks came to sit separately rather than together at a long table—something that encouraged competition rather than cooperation among them. Eventually, either a narrator with an impressive voice or, more typically, a Shark who was not bidding at key moments told viewers where things stood, heightening expectations, competitiveness, and a sense of drama. As time went on, the set became more well crafted: to the pitcher's right there appeared a sizable, elaborate, and colorful display of the product, heightening its attractiveness. The producers accepted fewer outlandish products, and pitches became more polished.[6] Music came to play a major role in heightening tension and emotion. Pitches increasingly ended with clever turns of phrase. By season ten, the show, hailing a "decade of dreams," insisted that it had contributed to the recovery from the Great Recession, though of course the Federal Reserve Board, the Treasury, President Barack Obama, and Congress played much more significant roles. "It's been ten years since *Shark Tank* ignited America's entrepreneurial spirit," ran the announcement at the beginning of a series of episodes, "and we're still blazing a trail for those who take their fate into their own hands by working hard, by working smart, by thinking big and chasing their dreams."

Contestants are painstakingly selected and coached, and the on-screen dramas, far from being spontaneous, are carefully staged and edited. Conceiving, producing, and then broadcasting a show involves what a knowledgeable insider likened to "a military operation" deploying hundreds of people organized and titled in ways familiar to insiders but arcane to an outsider like me.[7] There is an unbreakable rule of the franchise that successful contestants must get an investment at least equal in dollars to their original ask, which affects the outcome of winning pitches.[8] Burnett and his team know how to play on the emotions of the audience to convince them that what they see is authentic.[9] Producers heighten tension by making sure that each hour-long episode contains a variety of contestants—from innocent to shrewd and bland to compelling, aspiring entrepreneurs who fail miserably or succeed wonderfully. A pitcher's appearance may be preceded by a moving background story, and the pitches themselves, supported by appropriate props (for which contestants have to pay), have a rehearsed, animated cleverness. The fun begins after the pitch, with the start of negotiations, and ends somewhere along the spectrum from humiliation to triumph for the contestant. In between, the Sharks compete or cooperate, in the process revealing their distinctive styles and niches.[10]

The pitchers arrive on the show through a more competitive process than do the Sharks. The production company holds open casting calls in cities around the nation. In addition, in search of interesting companies run by dynamic and fascinating leaders, people associated with the program make appearances at trade shows and keep their eyes on crowdfunding sites such as Kickstarter; in fact, it was on Kickstarter that they discovered founders of xCraft.[11] However, the most common road to the show is through an application on the show's website. In a given year, 30,000 to

50,000 aspiring contestants apply this way, using a catchy phrase for the application subject line and likely including attention-getting visual and written materials. If this application is sufficiently compelling, someone from the casting staff calls the applicant and then sends an email packet, to be returned by the applicant within a few days. This packet contains a contract, forty to fifty pages long, that restricts future actions and contains instructions on how to make a video in which the person operating the camera asks a set series of questions. Then, after submitting the video and signed contract, the applicant waits.[12] "The odds of an entrepreneur making it through the grueling audition process is roughly one in 4,000," according to one *Forbes* article. "Only 104 contenders made it on air from a sea of 40,000 rejects in the 2015/2016 season. You are more likely to get into Harvard with a 5.6% acceptance rate or be born with an extra finger or toe."[13]

As the public has grown more familiar with the show, aspiring contestants have carefully watched and studied previous episodes before applying, especially once they know they might appear. In some cases, representatives from the production company talk several times a week with a potential pitcher who has cleared initial hurdles, helping the pitcher improve the presentation. Even if they are invited to come to Los Angeles for several days of rehearsals, contestants are continually warned that they might never appear on the show.[14] And other perils await. For example, Greiner remarked that Aaron Krause, who offered the eventually successful Scrub Daddy, "practiced, and practiced and practiced, preparing an answer for every question he thought the sharks could possibly ask," but she asked one question, about the smell of the product, that he had not anticipated. It was vitally important, she advised, for pitchers to "have rehearsed every gesture, every phrase, and every joke a million times; by the time they are presenting to us on the show, they could pitch their product walking backward."[15]

When pitchers finally appear on the show, they start their presentation with a compelling opening, sometimes involving an attention- and sympathy-grabbing story. Then, drawing on a display of props, they usually walk over to the Sharks and offer each a sample of their product, often individually crafted to match the personalities, features, or interests of each Shark. After carefully calculating—or in some cases carelessly miscalculating—what their company is worth and what the Sharks might promise to invest, contestants offer the Sharks an equity percentage in exchange for a set dollar figure. They have some knowledge of the often-contested metrics that the Sharks use to determine a product's worth. They end their formal pitch, usually with a catchy phrase that highlights why they are seeking financial and strategic support.

Most contestants are well prepared by the time they present on the show. They know full well that they need a combination of passion, personality, and knowledge of data relevant to their business. They have to be ready to offer a plan for how they will spend the money a Shark invests and how the Sharks will earn money on their investments, preferably quickly. Contestants assess in advance which Shark or Sharks they would prefer to work with and how negotiations might proceed. Greiner counseled contestants to modify their pitch on the fly depending on what the Sharks conveyed through their language, gestures, and questions. Above all, she urged them to "be authoritative, clear, and excited!"[16] In the Sony-sanctioned *Shark Tank: Jump Start Your Business: How to Launch and Grow a Business from Concept to Cash* (2013), the marketing expert Michael Du-Dell advised pitchers to "craft an opener that's compelling enough to grab [the Sharks'] attention from the start" and then follow up with a simple pitch that tells a story about their own experiences, avoids exaggeration, stays focused, and anticipates questions that might well arise.[17] To this, two executive producers added that pitchers should acknowledge weaknesses and strengths and exude confidence while remaining appreciative and gracious.

Not surprisingly, as *Shark Tank*'s audience grew, the Sharks realized that some of pitchers were what they called "gold diggers," aspiring entrepreneurs who came on the show only for the publicity. For example, season six contestants Erik Berkowitz and John Devecka, the founders of a karaoke machine called Singtrix, later indirectly confessed that this was why they appeared. Indeed, they asked for $1.5 million in exchange for 5 percent equity, which valued their company at $30 million and involved such a small piece of the action that it would normally have led to a rejection, but in this case four Sharks made bids — and they grew frustrated and angry when they realized Berkowitz and Devecka were there not to close a deal but to garner free publicity.[18] "You are the classic, 'You're dead to me.' You gotta go," O'Leary announced with his usual flair and bluntness.[19]

Filming on *Shark Tank* takes place over a compressed period of time. With so many other obligations, including familial but especially corporate and promotional ones, Sharks can come to Los Angeles for only relatively brief but obviously intense stretches of time, normally twice a year. Estimates are that it takes ten to seventeen days to shoot a series of episodes at the Sony Pictures Studio in Culver City, California.[20] The Sharks remain on the set or nearby for twelve hours straight and watch around eight pitches, each of which can last anywhere from less than half an hour to two hours or more.[21]

If contestants feel discomfort and pressure during taping, so do the Sharks, even though they have less at stake. According to some sources, the producers intervene at key moments, sometimes communicating over concealed earpieces that the Sharks wear but the audience cannot see. Although they would do so carefully because the Sharks cherish their independence, they might prod the Sharks to clarify what they are doing, compete more with each other, or ask pitchers about an especially moving back story. Though in the end each Shark decides independently how to bid and whether to accept an offer, on occasion a producer will, as one article observed, "nudge the investors to compel entrepreneurs to clarify an aspect of their story for the benefit of the audience."[22]

The Sharks prepare carefully for their on-screen appearances. The night before she appears on a show, Greiner wrote, she discusses with her husband what is likely to happen, and then the next morning her "whole team gather[s] for last-minute preparations." Hair and makeup can take up to ninety minutes before taping begins. On the set, the Sharks listen to recorded music designed to amp up their energy and enthusiasm. The Sharks have no idea of what is coming before a pitch begins, though when stagehands place props in from of them, they might get an inkling. Then the doors opposite them open, and contestants enter the set. The pitchers follow instructions by silently coming to stand on an X marked on the floor, which the camera operators have used to preset the focus of their cameras — but the silence in which the contestant approaches also creates a pause that heightens tension.[23] In what has been labeled a "staredown," the contestants hesitate in painful silence for up to a minute before starting their pitch. The Sharks, as Greiner noted, "furiously scribble down the financials, the retail history, and the valuations," while off-screen (but nearby on the set) at least one associate of each Shark is taking notes. However, "nothing matters except the people standing there," Greiner remarked, "pitching their hearts out in the hope that one of us will believe their idea is worth our investment of time, effort and money." Then "a crackle of energy ... surges through the room when" a deal is struck, or, alternatively, "the entrepreneurs' disappointment is crushing."[24]

The Sharks feel pressured to make quick decisions, figuring out on the spot whether a pitch captures their interest and merits their investment, judging how to best structure a deal, and deciding whether and with whom to cooperate or compete. "We're hungry, and we're miserable," Herjavec said when he described what it felt like onstage. With multiple cameras rolling, bright lights raising the temperature on the set, and millions of viewers watching their every gesture and facial expression, the Sharks are under intense pressure physically and psychologically. Once a Shark settles into his or her seat, Corcoran said, "it's like you're in a war zone" and "you can't come up for air."[25] Over time, the producers developed techniques that intensified drama and the human interest dynamics. Especially important are clips several minutes long that capture the lives of pitchers before they appeared on the show. For example, in one instance the producers arranged to film a contestant taking a shower because he said that was where he got his best ideas.[26]

We might suspect that the on-screen tension is staged. Indeed, someone with years of experience as an investor correctly reminded me that "with staff and producers feeding [the Sharks] information, in addition to the extensive rehearsing of the contestants," the pitches are "more Shakespeare than VC."[27] Journalist Richard Feloni, who often writes about the show, commented that the Sharks themselves "insist it's not staged. Rather, they say, it's the natural byproduct of on-edge people dealing with substantial amount of money." Although their relationships have been described as familial, John, a usually mild-mannered Shark, expressed the Sharks' dynamics in vivid and violent terms: "Listen, I don't care if you're my brother—if we go play football I'm gonna try to crack your head open."[28] Of course, pitchers as well as Sharks experience the stress of appearing on a television show that millions will view and that might determine the contestants' futures. Raymond Boyle and Lisa W. Kelly, scholars of reality television, remarked that many of these shows rely on "a reproducible format that ... is full of *conflict* and *jeopardy*."[29] Indeed, the producers keep a therapist on duty to talk to contestants after their pitch and make sure they are holding up. The experience, Corcoran reported, "was so overwhelming for one entrepreneur" that he fainted while standing before the potential investors. "He just, like, hit the floor!" she said. "You won't see that, though. And too bad, because it would make for great TV."[30]

Before an episode airs, producers and staff complete an impressive process of shaping it into narratives. "The real alchemy of reality television is the editing," wrote journalist Patrick Radden Keefe. It involves "sifting through a compost heap of clips and piecing together an absorbing story." An editor who had worked on earlier shows Burnett produced said, "You don't make anything up. But you accentuate things you see as themes."[31] For each hour-long show, which is actually forty-three minutes long without ads, editors create a series of eight-to-ten-minute dramatic segments. Varied techniques enhance the suspense. Herjavec has emphasized the "importance of listening quietly to build drama" during filming; when a pitcher is losing focus or has nothing more to say, the Sharks remain silent, "an effective, almost theatrical technique."[32]

Central to the editing process are highly skilled professionals who are part of the writing staff but whose titles do not include "writer"—since reality TV largely does not employ members of Hollywood unions and guilds, calling these staff members "writers" would breach the uneasy compromise that now exists between reality TV production companies and labor unions. Their role begins during filming, when a member of the creative staff takes notes and thinks about how to draw on key moments to create a compelling story by using these notes to create the first version of the episode. This material is then handed over to an associate or junior editor, a more technically oriented person who revises it for a more senior colleague to view. Footage shot on the set is interwoven with material shot outside the studio that provides context for the story. Although they are constrained by the actual outcome of an episode, editors and producers engage in protracted, technical, and circular negotiations as they use compelling highlights and reverse engineering to develop a powerful story line.

The editing process is tightly focused on the goal of keeping viewers tied to the show. Drawing on a music library, possibly one developed in house over time by people at Mark Burnett Productions or in a commercial library, to intensify the drama editors select brief music sequences to insert under the dialogue and behind the action, perhaps one labeled "intense but nostalgic" or "total defeat." They work hard to increase the likelihood that viewers will not change channels when an advertisement appears, using what those in the trade call a "blow" or "button"—a tense series of glances, gestures, more glances, and dramatic music—to end the segment on a cliff-hanger before a commercial break. The editing process also eliminates the stumbles we all make when we speak. Editors cut repetitions and what those involved in producing the show consider "unsexy" moments, especially when the pitchers and the Sharks delve into financial details that are of little interest to audience members or, presumably, difficult for them to understand. They also eliminate moments when Sharks use swear words or fight more contentiously than seems desirable. All this enables the producers to control the episode's pace and build its emotional content, whether that emotion is manufactured or arises spontaneously.[33]

The drama does not end once editing is complete. Verbal assents, handshakes, and hugs are not the same as legally binding contracts. Each Shark has a team of experts—perhaps an accountant, a marketing expert, a lawyer, and an organizational expert—who together carry out due diligence in order to verify the pitcher's claims, financials, acumen, organizational skills, and reputation. And even at that stage, some contestants walk away. For example, the founders of evREwares, a novelty sticker company, decided not to accept what both parties had agreed to on-screen—that Cuban would purchase the entire company. Yet those deals that last often enhance the investing Sharks' income and command their attention. To varying extents, the Sharks and those who help them manage their investments remain in contact with those they have invested in. For example, John claimed that he spends around a dozen hours a week on projects related to his *Shark Tank* investments.[34]

Moreover, every hour-long show includes a short update on a past pitcher and how successful (but rarely, if ever, how unsuccessful) they have been since appearing on the program, which further publicizes the pitcher's product and enhances the value of the investments backing them. Corcoran is especially adept at taking advantage of such opportunities. "I'm the queen of updates!" she said. "I know how to pitch an update better than anybody! And get it bought, boom, booked."[35] One of the most dramatic examples is Cousins Maine Lobster, a food truck operation founded by two cousins in which Corcoran invested $50,000 in exchange for 15 per-

The January 21, 2016, episode of *Beyond the Tank* featured Barbara Corcoran going Down East to celebrate the success of Cousins Maine Lobster cousins and cofounders Jim Tselikis and Sabin Lomac. She visited them in Maine, where they grew up, though they'd launched their food truck company in Los Angeles. Here are iconic images associated with their business: an informal place setting for the lobsters, a bib featuring a picture of a lobster, and people eating outdoors outside a New England–style home.

cent equity. Her financing, her recommendation that they sell franchises, and her ability to secure the cousins spots on national television shows helped the company to expand rapidly to $20 million dollars in sales and at least twenty trucks. On a breathless update segment lasting almost two minutes, Corcoran joined the two cousins and their franchisees in Maine, going out to sea to harvest lobsters from the traps and then returning to land, where she toasted all her new cousins.

The producers deploy a variety of techniques as they assemble a show. They have some contestants bring along celebrities to hype their product, typically a famous athlete or entertainer who pitches an item or demonstrates how to use it. Then there are special themed shows, such as those featuring young entrepreneurs, businesses launched by college students or military veterans, or products made in the United States.[36]

Pitches can fail because of a range of issues: a poor presentation, the lack of a business plan or demonstrated record of sales, an absurdly high valuation, a market that is too limited because of seasonality or lack of scalability, legal problems with patents or regulatory approval, or a clash of strategies between aspiring and proven entrepreneurs, especially over whether it is better to license or self-produce a product.[37]

Treatments of gender, race, and social class often don't play out as powerfully on the show as they do in public discussions. The producers of *Shark Tank* tread cautiously when it comes to identity politics. As the National Women's Business Council reported in 2015, the percentage of contestants who are white, male, and middle class is higher than in American society outside the tank. Race hasn't been the focus of much attention, as we can see by how carefully Daymond John approaches the topic. The coincidence of the show and the Great Recession prompted the producers to pay some attention on the show to how some Americans struggled during the downturn, even as the contrast between wealthy investors and those markedly less fortunate remained largely unexplored.[38]

Perhaps because networks consider women to be an important target audience for reality TV shows, gender has received the most extensive and to some extent politically charged focus. At key moments gender has provided dramatic resonance on *Shark Tank*.[39] Nothing better illustrates the gender dynamics of the show than an episode that appeared in season five on April 10, 2014. Erin Bickley and Jenny Greer, each the mother of three children, offered their own line of shapewear called Hold Your Haunches. In the one-minute prequel filmed in their hometown of Macon, Georgia, the two pitchers clinked wineglasses and remarked that they were "two sassy southern moms." "Don't let our southern accents deceive you," they declared. "When it comes to business, we're as tough as the peach pit." Noticing that when they looked into mirrors, their "reflections ain't what they used to be," they had searched for ways to improve their appearance and found no acceptable line of shapewear products on the market. So they decided to create one themselves, and the camera captured scenes of them designing items and walking through their factory. They knew how capital intensive their business was, so onto *Shark Tank* they came.

As they walked into the tank and gave their spiel, the camera focused on the smiling faces of Corcoran and Greiner but also showed the faces of more skeptical, unsmiling men. The two female entrepreneurs, speaking in heavy southern accents, introduced themselves as the "Head Haunchos" in a play on the name of their shapewear line. They asked for $75,000 for a 20 percent equity stake in their product line, which offered "smoothing and slimming support" women could wear "from carpool to cocktails." They concluded their initial pitch by asking, "Who's ready to get into our pants?" Their trademarked motto was, "A girl has a right to look tight!"

The three men quickly declared they were out. O'Leary took on the role of the chauvinist. What would happen, he asked, if a woman wearing one of their products met a single man? At this point Greiner interrupted and told him not to pursue this line of questioning. O'Leary nonetheless persisted, asking what would happen on the third date when the secret was revealed. Brushing past Greiner's continued objection, he raised his voice and emphatically insisted, "This is a kind of false advertising." Bickley responded that makeup and bras were similarly deceptive. Cuban, remarking that he understood that "every tush needs a push," declared himself out because this was not a product that drew on his "core competency." Then Herjavec also declared himself out, acknowledging that this was also outside his ken.

Together Corcoran and Greiner challenged the men on their responses. Corcoran led the way, asking, "Why is it that every time there's a female product on this show, you guys go out right away?" Cuban looked surprised, and when Corcoran insisted that she and Greiner had invested in many products for men, Cuban asked them to name one. Before they could answer, O'Leary interrupted to insist that he did not want to be part of "this fraud" and "false advertising" and then declared himself out. Making it clear that the three men had exited before even hearing the practical details of the business, Greiner and Corcoran asked about sales, production costs, and profit margins. When the pitchers responded, Cuban and Herjavec quickly acknowledged that their data was impressive. Greiner, glancing over to Corcoran for assent, announced that they wanted to make an offer so that later on they could "show our *male* Sharks how they missed out" on a terrific opportunity. Greiner knew her customers and the power of QVC, and, relying on her and Corcoran's ability to get this product line into major retailers, she was ready to make an offer. Corcoran, though desiring to join in, thought it best that Greer and Bickley left the tank temporarily so the two female Sharks could agree on their strategy.

Once they could talk confidentially, Greiner said to Corcoran that she wanted to prove something to their male counterparts by acknowledging that as women they better understood the pitchers and the product. However, she was aware that, as in many other instances, 20 percent equity was too little to merit the time and energy commitments she would need to make as an investor. When the contestants returned, Greiner announced that their joint offer was $75,000 for 40 percent equity. One of the pitchers winced, and O'Leary asked, "What kind of greed is this?" Corcoran jumped in and told Greiner to mention a "sweetener," a credit line of $100,000. The contestants briefly paused and then accepted. As she got up to hug Greer and Bickley, Corcoran turned to each male Shark and said, "You're a loser." She then pointed toward Greer and Bickley and said, "She's hot"; pointed toward herself and Greiner and said, "We're hot"; and finally pointed to the male Sharks and said, "You're not." The camera then captured the two contestants high-fiving as they walked away, one of them saying, "It feels so great to be validated by these women ... two expert, genius women."

In the short and intermediate term, the impact of the *Shark Tank* appearance was tremendous for Hold Your Haunches. Echoing the 1973 tennis competition between Billie Jean King and Bobby Riggs, the episode soon came to be known as "the battle of the sexes." The company quickly sold more shapewear than in the previous two years, which was only possible because they had increased their inventory when they learned when their episode would air. Because of what had become known as the *Shark Tank* effect—just by appearing on the show, pitchers raised their product's visibility and drove increases in sales—overnight their number of email subscribers leaped from 800 to more than 10,000, with 4,000 eager customers placing their names on a list so they could be informed when Hold Your Haunches had restocked.[40]

Nine months later, *Shark Tank* broadcast a two-minute update. The two successful pitchers had appeared on other national platforms, and the company had expanded its product line and improved its website. With only $165,000 in sales in the year before they appeared, Bickley and Greer now reported that in six months they had reached $1.5 million in sales, which had enabled them to move out of a playroom in Bickley's house and into a larger commercial location. The show featured Corcoran and

Greiner arriving on large tractors at the Georgia National Fair, where the Head Haunchos received an award from the state. Corcoran announced how proud she was of the successful contestants because they were "walking, talking examples of what women can do in America. The guys," she continued, "did not believe in them but," she said as she pointed to herself and Greiner, "these two smart women bought in, and now look at them." Then one of the Haunchos remarked how pleased they were that Corcoran and Greiner had got "behind" their company, and now the four women "were making behinds look amazing everywhere." At that point, the camera showed the women walking away from behind.[41]

This battle of the sexes highlights the importance of gender even as it underscores the fact that *Shark Tank* is more part of the problem than the solution. The late-summer 2015 report by the National Women's Business Council examined the role of women on *Shark Tank*. Although they were relatively well represented as contestants, there was room for improvement. They tended to make pitches in areas one might think of as women focused: food and beverages; fashion, clothing, and accessories; education, child development, and products for children. They were less present in areas such as technology; fitness, health, and sports; and games and entertainment. Men were significantly more likely to negotiate on the show, although when they did negotiate, women did so as successfully as their male counterparts. Corcoran was the Shark who invested most frequently in companies led by women; Greiner, though more receptive and sympathetic in terms of questions and comments, was nonetheless not especially inclined to invest in what female pitchers offered. The study found Herjavec to be the "most egregious offender," the least likely to invest in women. "Overall," the report concluded, "*Shark Tank* is doing a good job of having women on the show, an okay job of presenting women as serious entrepreneurs, and a not great job of treating its female sharks the same as it does its male sharks."[42]

In passing, the report of the National Women's Business Council mentioned another concern. Daymond John, its authors noted, was "the only person of color on *Shark Tank*" and made a higher percentage of offers to "contestants of color," however few they were, than any of his peers. Overall, the vast majority of the pitchers were white, with 3 percent Asian American, 6 percent African American, and just over 2 percent Latinx.

The interaction between John and Billy Blanks Jr. on May 11, 2012, in season three effectively captures key dimensions of how race sometimes plays out on *Shark Tank*.[43] Blanks offered an exercise video called "Billy Blanks Jr.'s Dance with Me" for $100,000 in exchange for 20 percent eq-

Billy Blanks Jr. appeared on *Shark Tank* on May 11, 2011, to offer the Sharks the opportunity to invest in his dance-based exercise program. The episode was filled with drama, especially the heart-wrenching story of Blanks's broken relationship with his father and Daymond John's theatrical backstage pursuit of Blanks. Here, near the opening of the episode, Blanks and one of his dancers demonstrate the vigorousness of the exercise routine.

uity. Right off, Blanks announced that his father was Billy Blanks Sr., who in the 1980s had developed the enormously successful Tae Bo (tae kwon do boxing) fitness program, which sold 1.5 million copies in its first year. Now up for sale was Blanks Jr.'s workout program, which incorporated a wide variety of dancing styles. At the beginning of Blanks's pitch, the camera panned over the Sharks without paying special attention to John, and when it did capture John, he didn't show a particularly high level of interest. Indeed, if the editing captured the Sharks' reactions accurately, Corcoran and Herjavec expressed the greatest degree of engagement. However, when Blanks and his associates started to perform, the camera captured John responding positively, smiling and bobbing his head, and at one point Blanks called out, "C'mon, Daymond." He then invited Cuban, who, he noted, had once taught disco, to come up and dance, which he did, rhythmically and enthusiastically.

Four minutes in, the drama intensified when Blanks revealed that his father was unwilling to invest in his son's enterprise and that Blanks and his wife had recently been homeless. Three Sharks—Corcoran, Herjavec, and O'Leary—announced that they were out, even as they expressed admiration for Blanks's independence and drive. Now it was John's turn, and he announced his close business relationship with Zumba, a wildly successful dance fitness program: more than 10 million people have taken Zumba classes, which are offered in more than 200,000 fitness clubs in 180 countries. He made an offer of $100,000 for 50 percent equity, contingent on Cuban's joining him (which he quickly did); on the use of Blanks Jr.'s name; and on Zumba's commitment to act as distributor for "Dance with Me." Now things got sticky. Blanks worried that Zumba would swallow up what he had lovingly and distinctively developed. All the Sharks understood that John and Cuban envisioned Zumba as a delivery system that could quickly extend the reach of "Dance with Me." Just as John was about to withdraw the offer, John and Cuban realized it was best if Blanks went backstage to talk with his most important partner, his wife. When Blanks returned and hesitated, Corcoran, Cuban, and especially John expressed regret, and Blanks, having turned down the offer, left the tank.

Now John appeared particularly concerned. He said, "Look, if I don't do this, I am going to regret it," and dramatically exited the tank to go backstage and talk with Blanks and his wife. "I'm going to do the deal," he said as he left, the cameras following him. With the three of them sitting down backstage, John said, "I've never done this before.... You make me want to help you." John persuaded Blanks to accept the original offer as he remarked, "Don't make me cry." Both Blanks and his wife made clear how much John's exceptional intervention meant to them. Then the show ended with handshakes and hugs.

It turned out that Zumba rejected the deal, but Blanks struck a new one with Lionsgate Entertainment, a major distribution corporation, to launch the video, now renamed "Billy Blanks Dance It Out." In this case as in others, the *Shark Tank* effect worked its magic: after the video came books, an international trainer certification program, television and Broadway appearances, and music videos. This helped Blanks and his wife earn the title "America's First Family of Fitness" and his product become the "fastest-growing fitness-based dance program in America."[44] "From homeless to millionaires, a true rags to riches story," remarked a reporter.[45]

There are interesting aspects of how race played out in this *Shark Tank* episode. Common elements in the life stories of Blanks and John—their troubled relationships with their fathers; their identity as African American men; and their aspirations as entrepreneurs who wanted to build lifestyle brands—seem to have had an outsize effect on the outcome of the pitch. John made the largely unprecedented move of going backstage after negotiations ended badly, and both Blanks and John were emotionally moved about getting and giving help. Yet until John broke with tradition, there was nothing about his reaction to the pitch or the pitcher that distinguished him from the other Sharks. Indeed, a journalist noted that when Blanks demonstrated his program and showed a number of dance moves, "Barbara seem[ed] to be enjoying it the most."[46] Given how extensively John in his books referenced his African American identity, what is striking—in this instance and in most others that involved an African American pitcher—is the absence of any reference to African American traditions and common experiences. This is especially notable in comparison with what usually happened when female entrepreneurs were pitching: in those cases, gender was front and center, especially in interactions between the entrepreneurs and the female Sharks.

A 1999 *New York Times* story titled "Trying to Stay True to the Street" amply captures the racial landscape John had to navigate. To begin with, as he became more successful he had to become more respectable. The *New York Times* article noted that early on, he worked "any get-rich scheme he could think of," including selling crack cocaine, making his story "a Horatio Alger tale updated" for the contemporary world. "Although being known as a former drug dealer may enhance a rap star's 'street cred,'" the reporter said, "it is no asset for a businessman whose clothes are manufactured and distributed by Samsung, the South Korean electronics giant." And then there was the fact that success could, ironically, cost him his original market. The article quoted a FUBU competitor as saying that John's company was "going to lose its street essence as little Johnny in suburbia starts picking up its stuff."[47]

In his books and on *Shark Tank*, John navigates the politics of race and class in complicated and often contradictory ways. In *The Brand Within: The Power of Branding from Birth to the Boardroom* (2010), he insisted on the importance of class and race even as he backed off such an emphasis. On the one hand, when discussing the origins of FUBU, he said he "wasn't thinking along any *culture, movement, lifestyle* lines in those days, at least not in any kind of full-on, fully realized way." But he went on to talk of how his anger over a Timberland executive seeing inner-city residents as "undesirable customers" spurred him to develop FUBU.[48] A joking moment on *Shark Tank* also turned out to be revealing: in the fall of 2016, a contestant pitched a device that determined whether sunscreen was still effective, and when John tried the product and his skin appeared light, he remarked, "I'm a white man now."

The reason Daymond John and the *Shark Tank* producers typically shy away from overtly acknowledging race, especially compared with how Barbara Corcoran and Lori Greiner handle gender, probably has to do with branding of both the Sharks and the show itself. John and those in charge of programming undoubtedly want to extend the reach of *Shark Tank* and likely believe that tailoring their branding for African Americans would limit their audience too much. In contrast, with two women among the Sharks and a huge audience of women, an appeal to gender has few downsides and much in the way of potential gains.

The treatment of social class and region on *Shark Tank* is usually more implicit than explicit, although judging by their language, stories, demeanor, and dress, most pitchers are middle class or above. However, working-class, small-town, and rural entrepreneurs have been featured on several episodes in ways that highlight distinctive identities. For example, in the season three episode that aired on January 27, 2012, Donny McCall's presentation of an easily installable and removable cargo rack for truck beds, called Invis-A-Rack, set off an emotionally charged debate over the plight of manual laborers in a globalizing economy. Speaking in a soft southern drawl and making an almost-unheard-of-on-the-show reference to God, McCall asserted that "the Lord handed" him the idea, inspiring him to develop the product so that he could provide jobs for workers in his struggling North Carolina town. His voiced cracked as he acknowledged that a "truck rack was not going to save the U.S. economy," but he wanted to "do something that can bring some jobs, and some hope to [his] small town" in the northwestern corner of the state. Some of the ensuing discussion focused on technical aspects of the product, the nature of the business plan, the low sales, the capital-intensive nature of the business, and the challenges of distribution.

However, the most interesting and moving discussion began when O'Leary pressed McCall on why he would not consider having the racks manufactured in Asia, something O'Leary often suggested as a way to bring down costs and increase profits. John and O'Leary tried to persuade McCall that the only way to provide local jobs in sales and marketing was to manufacture abroad; O'Leary used Apple as an example, noting that although the company manufactured abroad, it employed tens of thousands of employees at home. The tensest exchanges began when, toward the end of the segment, McCall turned to Herjavec as "the factory worker's son." "Oh no, I hear you," Herjavec responded. "You're hitting a chord with me." Holding back tears, his voice breaking, the immigrant from Croatia agreed with McCall that America was the land of opportunity that welcomed all—a note that was not terribly relevant to a pitcher from a town whose families had probably lived in the region for generations. Herjavec both insisted that Americans could survive in a global economy and that his father's experience as a factory worker was relevant to how he was responding to the pitch. This made him proud, he remarked as the camera panned over the faces of the other Sharks, who were visibly moved by Herjavec's words. Nonetheless, he declared himself out because he believed McCall was not truly focused on developing his business.

The exchange between McCall and Herjavec revealed competing visions of the American dream. McCall's perspective was underscored by his southern accent, redolent of the native-born white working class, whose lives have been disrupted by globalization, rather than the presumably more middle-class people he might employ in management and sales. Herjavec recollected the pain caused by his father's halting English and how his life had been disrupted by an earlier and different aspect of globalization. Herjavec's accent reminded attentive listeners that he was Canadian. He celebrated globalization, which, among other things, helped build his fortune and brought him across the border between Canada and the United States, where he met his Australian-born wife on *Dancing with the Stars* and then achieved additional celebrity status on *Shark Tank*, a show that traced its ancestry to Japan.

"Our heads are with the sharks, our hearts with Donny," an observer remarked at the time on the website TV Worth Watching. "This moving and informative set piece on global capitalism," he continued, "could not have been scripted any better. It's a compelling piece of television." Then he asked readers to "dive in" in the comments. And dive in they did: "Stephanie" said that the Sharks turned down an investment in American-made Invis-A-Racks "so they could make bigger profits on the backs of under-paid, under-aged, repressed workers." Herjavec's dad, she noted, had worked in an "AMERICAN" factory; because "the sharks got rich in AMERICA - they should invest in AMERICA. I won't invest another minute watching these bloodthirsty sharks." Many others agreed, with Debra Bergstrom remarking that "You Sharks are why America is Struggling!!!! They sell the USA out on a daily basis all in the name of business and the bottom line (money). . . . Every day thousands of Americans have to go home and tell their families that they lost their jobs and livelihood to a foreign country."[49]

Invis-A-Rack's post–*Shark Tank* life revealed the twists and turn of entrepreneurship in a global economy. McCall sold his idea to another company, which manufactured the racks in Iowa, not North Carolina. McCall then developed another corporation, Perrycraft, which sold various add-ons for American vehicles. A spring 2016 article revealed that "Perrycraft as a company is still located in Sparta, North Carolina; however, the products are being manufactured in Sweden."[50]

The Invis-A-Rack episode is an exception to the generally applicable rule that *Shark Tank*, its audience, and its pitchers are far from the small-town, working-class experiences rarely represented on the show. In response to the Great Recession, the show more commonly featured stories of middle-class and upper-middle-class people who had been hard-hit by a reversal of fortunes and now sought recovery by pitching their enterprises on the show. Whatever the Sharks say about the American dream, their version, which usually promises success for people in the middle class and above, reflects their commitment to cosmopolitanism and globalization rather than to aspects of diversity and inclusion in the worlds of entrepreneurship so rarely visible on *Shark Tank*.

A World Full of Pitches

How pitchers and Sharks are chosen to appear on *Shark Tank*, how the production company edits episodes, and some of what happens after an episode airs, as well as the roles that race, gender, and class play—all this hardly encompasses everything that is interesting about what pitchers and Sharks do on air. Distinctive types of pitches, including those that promise to improve society, also command attention for the dramas they set off and the entrepreneurial lessons they drive home. Pitches and products that are weird, silly, or ingenious can make for professionally crafted theatrical productions. As clever actors, the Sharks mix contempt, humility, aggression, admiration, cooperation, and competition in their responses to pitches. Careful planning and editing heighten the drama and convey authenticity even though they rely on artifice. In the end, the juxtaposition of *Shark Tank* with amateur and professional pitches by entrepreneurs in other venues underscores the television program's popularity, distinctiveness, and limitations. The range of pitches serves as a lens through which to understand what new ventures entrepreneurs consider worthy of the risk.

One type of episode features social entrepreneurship, businesses whose goals are not just being economically successful but also, more important, solving a social or economic problem, whether in a developing country abroad or in a struggling community at home.

The pitch for Hungry Harvest on January 8, 2016, underscored the nature of social entrepreneurship—doing well by doing good. The display was one of the most elaborate, featuring chalkboard signs seemingly straight from a farmers market and an abundance of fruits and vegetables, which would be sold to affluent subscribers in ways that helped reduce food waste and feed the hungry.

Part of a widespread movement in the business world and designed to capture sales among millennials, this approach does its best to minimize reliance on government programs and instead links profits to altruism. On *Shark Tank*, the two most common types of social entrepreneurship involve environmentally friendly products and links between a purchase and aid for disadvantaged people.[1]

A compelling example that combined doing well with doing good was Hungry Harvest, which appeared during season seven on January 8, 2016. Clever and intriguing, this enterprise rescued produce considered unsellable because of its appearance and delivered it to subscribers; it also donated a portion of the produce collected to hungry people and hunger-fighting organizations. Growing up in Baltimore, Evan Lutz worried about the poverty he witnessed on the streets of his hometown. As a business major at the University of Maryland, he aspired to become a successful entrepreneur, but one committed to social justice. With a friend, he hatched the idea of selling what he called "ugly" produce—items that did not conform to the perfection usually expected in supermarkets—to students, faculty, and staff. In May 2014, he launched the delivery service beyond the university.

On *Shark Tank*, Lutz, only two years out of college, asked for $50,000 in exchange for 5 percent equity in order to expand operations beyond Baltimore. His company, he told the Sharks, provided multiple benefits: subscribers would save time and money and eat healthily; local farmers would sell excess produce; food would end up on tables instead of in dumps; and hungry people and hunger-fighting organizations would receive more donations. The Sharks initially seemed impressed by the combination of entrepreneurship, potential profits, and charitable intentions. However, they hesitated when they learned that, despite growing sales, Hungry Harvest had not turned a profit and Lutz had yet to pay himself a salary. In the end, Lutz accepted Robert Herjavec's offer, which involved less-favorable terms than he had initially proposed.

But Lutz's appearance produced the *Shark Tank* effect, enhanced by his use of social media and his appearances on national radio and television. An abundance of new subscribers enabled Hungry Harvest to expand. Eventually the company launched Produce in a SNAP, a partnership with public schools and community centers that brought produce stands to places inadequately served by grocery stores; the stands offered produce at low prices and accepted Supplemental Nutrition Assistance Program benefits. By the end of 2017, Hungry Harvest was operating successfully not only in Baltimore but also in Washington, D.C., northern Virginia, Pennsylvania, New Jersey, and Florida. The company had delivered more than 3 million pounds of produce and donated more than 500,000 pounds to its partner organizations. Then in June 2018, the company announced that over the next four years it would expand to thirty more locations.[2]

Not all proposals are so worthy. Wake 'n Bacon, the Sullivan Generator, and the Cougar Energy Drink for Women provide ample evidence of the unbridled and problematic entrepreneurial vision circulating in America and obvious on *Shark Tank*. These proposals are instructive only in their hollow, exaggerated, and even outrageous premises. They also show how *Shark Tank*'s pursuit of ratings can lead to the triumph of entertainment value over a commitment to a worthy cause.

Wake 'n Bacon, which aired during season two on March 25, 2011, is an apparently innocent but nonetheless silly example of American inventiveness. Sitting in an electrical engineering class at college, Matty Sallin wondered if people could be awakened in the morning not by the buzz of an alarm clock but by the smell of bacon cooking. So he created a device that automatically cooked bacon at a designated time. On top of a tray for cooking bacon sat an alarm clock designed to evoke the look of a pig— a small wooden snout and two cut-out eyes on the front, next to the face of a digital clock, and two pig ears above. Ten minutes before the set time,

The pitch for Wake 'n Bacon on the March 25, 2011, episode was visually rich. Here, Matty Sallin introduces a prototype of his clever, humorous invention. However, the ingenuity of an alarm clock that would wake users with the smell of bacon and the charm of the clock's pig face were not enough to overcome the product's problems.

the device would begin cooking slices of bacon, awakening users with the presumably pleasant odor. Sallin came to the show with a simple prototype and made a modest ask of $40,000 for 20 percent of his company. Although Mark Cuban seemed tempted to make an offer, in the end the pitch failed because of worries about fire danger, a limited market, and the lack of a business plan. Although afterward it had a cult following, Sallin's invention never made it out of the sty.[3]

The award for unhinged entrepreneurial ambition would have to go to Mark Sullivan, inventor of the Sullivan Generator, who appeared in season three on April 13, 2012. His pitch implicitly built on the image of the inventor as a lone genius who brings into the world a product that both transforms the world and generates untold profits. Sullivan boasted he had developed more than 1,000 inventions, which had earned (for whom it was not clear) more than $1 billion annually; he also claimed he made money writing music and designing and sewing clothing. He was seeking $1 million for 10 percent equity, which would enable him to develop a generator that, by harnessing the spin of the earth, would create synthetic hurricanes and trap their energy in his machine. This would also yield, as precipitates, magnesium and $96 billion worth of gold. All this, he promised, "would leave a lasting legacy of goodness."

To say the least, the Sharks' response was to humiliate rather than encourage. Kevin O'Leary opened the discussion by asking Sullivan how long he had been "visiting Earth." Not knowing "what the hell [Sullivan was] talking about," Daymond John declared himself out. He also noted that there was a fine line between being a genius and being crazy and asked Sullivan if anyone had ever suggested he was the latter. Cuban remarked that his "BS meter was going through the roof" and declared himself out. Herjavec, tongue in cheek, asked what would happen if he gave Sullivan $50,000 and O'Leary invested $950,000. Barbara Corcoran interrupted to say she too was out. Declaring that most of what Sullivan proposed was "nut bar factor 6," O'Leary also opted out. Leaving the tank, Sullivan said his fate on the show resembled what genius inventors usually faced. On *Shark Tank Blog* Rob Merlino speculated that the producers had aired the episode "for comic relief."[4] An observer on Reddit wondered whether Sullivan was "a nut case" and dozens of people responded affirmatively. After his appearance, Sullivan continued to pursue his quest for gold, not from the Sharks but from his invention.[5]

An especially insidious pitch, for Cougar Energy Drink for Women, aired on May 18, 2012, in season three. If Barbara Corcoran and Lori Greiner represented the show's interest in celebrating women as entrepreneurs, this product moved in a different direction. The idea came to Ryan Custer when, dating a woman eleven years his senior, he realized there might be a market for products for "cougars," middle-aged women who wanted to date younger men. His drink, which the product's website called the "first gender-specific functional beverage" and which was the first in a line of products he planned for this market, promised to give women more vitality and beauty with nutrients derived from thirteen superfruits. Seeking $150,000 for 30 percent of his business, Custer claimed that what had "started as a cute phrase had become a true social movement."

Custer immediately ran into trouble. Pressed by John about sales, he revealed that in three years they had amounted to a meager $60,000, which prompted John to drop out. After tasting a sample and finding it chalky, Corcoran was next to do so. When O'Leary opted out, he noted that there was a limited market for such a niche product and said that powerful beverage producers and distributors would crush Custer like the cockroach he was, a phrase O'Leary often deployed. The remaining Sharks soon dismissed Custer as well. After the show, Custer persisted in developing his brand with a line of products, but with limited success, although Amazon continued to carry his offerings. Four and a half years after the episode aired, an article following up on what happened to Cougar Energy Drink for Women said, "Looks like the Sharks were right on this one. Not all pop culture terms are meant to be turned into business endeavors."[6]

In contrast to these examples of entrepreneurial imagination run wild are more common pitches that rely on a hard-to-achieve approach: a simple invention, a low-cost investment, a moving story, and dramatic success. Tiffany Krumins hailed from a tiny town in Georgia where she took care of children with special needs and cancer. She developed a device she called Ava the Elephant, which dispensed liquid medicine from the trunk of a small toy elephant, to make it easier for children to take liquid medicines orally. On the August 9, 2009, episode, the announcer remarked at the outset of her pitch that he was "sure she had an idea that would make millions." In reaction to a presentation that revealed her insecurity and naivete, the four male Sharks exited quickly, principally because of a frequently expressed reservation: that what she offered was an idea but not a business. That meant Corcoran was the last Shark left circling in the tank. She made clear that she loved the product and the woman who presented it. However, the initial ask, $50,000 for a 15 percent investment in order to secure a patent and develop a working prototype, made it hard for Corcoran to imagine how she could make money. So she made an offer—the same dollar amount in exchange for 55 percent equity. In response, Krumins grimaced and hesitated, but in the end said yes.

"We're going to make money on this together," Corcoran remarked. "You're going to like me a lot more than the guys." After Krumins left the set, Corcoran said that what she loved about her was "that she had great passion and more than anything else she *reminded* me of myself," an oft-heard refrain from the Sharks. And, she continued, there was "no way she's not going to make it." And with Corcoran's help, make it she did. An update broadcast a few weeks later showed the two women meeting with executives at a major pharmaceutical company that provided flavoring for medicines sold at tens of thousands of stores. Then the camera focused on the two of them boarding a yacht in a harbor of a city as they jet-setted around the world making deals. To drive home a point commonly made, Corcoran insisted that "it just goes to show you, if you have the right product with the right *person*, anyone can succeed." A second update in the next season, revealed that Avas were being manufactured in China and showed workers packing 75,000 units to ship to CVS, which had agreed to put Ava's picture on every bag of prescriptions for children. In the first year after the episode featuring the pitch aired, sales reached $2.5 million. Other triumphs followed: Krumins was a keynote speaker at a Disney Social Media Moms conference; she was featured on major websites, including Forbes.com and TVGuide.com; and she appeared on *The Dr. Oz Show*, where millions of parents heard her story and learned of her product.

Aspiring entrepreneurs can fail on *Shark Tank* because either their products or their personalities fall flat. In contrast, the perfect pitch relies on a compelling combination of exciting product and winning personality. The best example of this was Q-Flex, whose pitch illustrates several common *Shark Tank* themes: the importance of family and of immigrants, the value of persistence, and the significance of selling both product and pitcher with a compelling story. In the season six, on December 12, 2014, Hong Cao and her thirteen-year-old daughter, Andrea, pitched a simple question mark–shaped device that allowed people to massage their own backs and shoulders. Andrea had invented it in order to enable her mom, a registered nurse, to relieve the back pain that came from standing on her feet all day. They had sent off an application to *Shark Tank*, but after several weeks without a response, they heard there was an open audition in San Diego. They drove over 300 miles from San Luis Obispo and camped overnight; two weeks later, they learned they had cleared the first hurdle. In the episode, they sought $20,000 for 20 percent of their company.

The force of their stories and personalities was hard to resist: the mother was a software engineer who became a registered nurse so she could minister to people after her husband died, and the daughter, who was only thirteen, had preternatural poise. Two additional things became quickly apparent: While Andrea had wowed all of the Sharks, even hard-hearted O'Leary, three of them felt this was not an investable opportunity. Right away, Herjavec jokingly accused Andrea of lying, something that visibly disturbed the poised, passionate, and articulate teen until she learned he meant that as a compliment: she was too young to make what he called a "fantastic presentation." And when Cuban learned that Andrea had already sold hundreds of devices by going door to door, that there was already great word of mouth, and that there was an impressive gap between the cost of production and retail price, he said of Andrea, "A capitalist is born." Yet for Greiner, Herjavec, and O'Leary, the problems were hard to overcome: there was no patent, a similar product had flopped, and neither the young teen nor her mother had the business experience necessary to transform a product into a business, something several Sharks felt would require too much of their involvement on a daily basis when Andrea had school and her mother couldn't quit her full-time job.

A little over seven minutes into an almost-nine-minute segment, the camera panned to reveal Corcoran leaning over to talk to Cuban. With exactly a minute to go in the segment, though surely more in the original filming, they made an offer of $25,000 for 20 percent, promising they would get a website up right away and then run all the operations needed to grow the business—with one contingency. Corcoran insisted that Andrea be available to make sales calls. "You," she said emphatically, "are going to sell like crazy." "Deal," Andrea, always in charge, responded. What was left unsaid, perhaps ending up on the cutting-room floor, was that Corcoran and Cuban saw in Andrea something of their younger selves—a spunky, young entrepreneur with more than ample ambition.[7]

Despite competition from somewhat similar products, Q-Flex was a considerable success. Between the filming and airing, Cuban set up a website. Within a few days after the episode aired, the company had sold 17,000 items. Hong and Andrea were still working out of the proverbial startup garage, and this rapid transformation challenged their ability to keep up with demand. Hong hired several helpers (including Andrea's grandparents), and the two Sharks helped the company scale up—Cuban with marketing, technical, and legal aspects; Corcoran with more hands-on tasks. In a *Shark Tank* update in April 2014, Corcoran visited the mother and daughter in California to cheer them on. She recommended that, in order to move production out of their house, improve quality control, and make their operations more efficient, they establish a fulfillment center. Corcoran now admitted that she saw something of herself in Andrea. The camera zoomed out as Hong and Andrea walked down a street in San Luis Obispo, Andrea wearing a T-shirt with "WORK, DREAM, LOVE" emblazoned on it as she touted all she had learned and all the people Q-Flex had helped. At the end, the camera showed mother and daughter placing two Q-Flexes together, so that the two question mark–shaped items formed a heart.

Andrea continued to act as an ambitious entrepreneur, apparently using her lunch breaks at school to attend to corporate matters. A 2018 "where are they now" article on Q-Flex noted that Andrea aspired to attend Stanford and earn a degree in marketing (a degree not available at the undergraduate level). The journalist added, "For now it's nice to know that hard working Hong and Andrea have spent some of their hard earned profits on their long-term dream of a Horse Ranch in Atascadero, California." If you wondered how Andrea remained so poised, the journalist said, "she revealed her secret technique in a recent interview. She simply imagined the Sharks in their underwear during filming."[8]

If we turn to negotiations, we see how they can proceed any number of ways on *Shark Tank*. This variety is useful to producers intent on generating drama to attract and hold audiences even though it gives audience members looking for information on how to pitch an inaccurate view of what happens in the real world. Sometimes bidding is simple and goes smoothly, sometimes not. There are plenty of episodes where the Sharks make decisions in an orderly manner. Some proposals seem so absurd that all five Sharks bow out quickly. On occasion, as with Ava the Elephant, four Sharks exit and the remaining one quickly comes to terms with the aspiring entrepreneur. At other times, with seeming effortlessness and implicit understanding, two or more Sharks easily agree on terms.

Yet there are plenty of times when things don't go so smoothly. One example is the carefully developed drama of Billy Blanks Jr.'s "Dance with Me." At first, Blanks walked off the stage empty-handed, and then, in an unprecedented move, John left the tank and struck a deal offstage. There are also times when contestants pass on what seems like a highly attractive offer; this occurred when three sisters turned down Cuban's offer of $30 million to purchase 100 percent of the dating app Coffee Meets Bagel, or when Copa Di Vino's founder James Martin walked away not once but twice from compelling offers to invest in his proprietary product: wines in sealed glass containers.

On very rare occasions, skilled contestants astound the Sharks. This happened during season one, on September 13, 2009, when Jonathan Miller, who had formerly worked in venture capital, struck a deal for his customizable nutrition bars, Element Bars, with infomercial expert Kevin Harrington. Dazzling the Sharks with the brilliance of his negotiating power, he prompted Corcoran to remark, "You're like a micro or mini Shark." Herjavec said, "Oh my God, this guy's great! . . . You should forget this business. Come work for me!" and John insisted, "The best thing you sold here was Jonathan. You're a star."

More typically, drama builds gradually as two and sometimes more Sharks negotiate with each other and with the pitcher. At times, the situation can get messy and even angry. Alliances vary, but the other Sharks often prefer not to join forces with O'Leary. Perhaps spurred on by producers and the show's intense conditions, tempers flare and accusations of bad faith fly across the line of Sharks. A prime and in many ways unprecedented case came in season six on February 20, 2016, when Christopher Gray, an African American college student from Philadelphia, pitched Scholly, an app that enabled students to find college scholarships by connecting them to websites through a vast database he developed. When he explained his app, he illustrated the possible outcomes by listing a few fake scholarships referring to the show: "Lori's Zero to Hero Scholarship," "Mr. Wonderful's Stingy Scholarship," and one offered by "Bank of the Tank."

The Sharks asked how he came up with the idea, and Gray said that as one of three children raised in Birmingham, Alabama, by an unemployed single mom, he could not apply to some colleges because of the application fees—but now, as a junior at Drexel University, he had proven his skill by winning scholarships worth $1.3 million. In one year, Scholly's ninety-nine-cent app had been downloaded 90,000 times.

Less than four minutes into a ten-and-a-half-minute segment, Greiner broke into a conversation in which other Sharks were asking who Gray's partners were and how they kept their app up to date. Remarking that she had never done this before, and to the visible chagrin of Cuban and Herjavec, Greiner offered Gray exactly what he had asked for—in exchange for an immediate commitment. Gray hesitated, and then John made an identical offer, saying that, as someone raised by a single mom who had himself begun to work at age ten, this was "a personal matter." Now things got heated: Cuban and Herjavec wanted more information; O'Leary asked whether Gray wanted charity or investors; and Greiner and John made a joint offer and demanded an answer. Seven minutes into the segment, Gray accepted their deal.

Less than thirty seconds later, after Gray had exited, the Sharks threatened to devour each other. Herjavec, Cuban, and O'Leary argued that the two winners had felt sorry for Gray and had made a charitable offer without having sufficient information about how the business worked. "Sometimes it's about helping America and making the world a better place," Greiner insisted, and said that their argument was "all sour grapes." Claiming he did not want to say something rude, Herjavec got up and walked off the stage, a highly unusual but not unprecedented and perhaps orchestrated move. Cuban tried to make clear that he might have made an even higher bid—and brought more tech savvy to the enterprise—and then he and O'Leary also exited, leaving Greiner and John alone in the tank.

Scholly quickly became a huge success, even though many online evaluations were tepid. By mid-2019, almost 1 million users had the app. Gray won many awards for his entrepreneurship and spoke at conferences. According to the company's website, Gray was featured in "just about every major media outlet, including Good Morning America, Forbes, BET, USA Today, Fortune Magazine, Smithsonian Magazine, CNN, Fox News" and "in Cadillac's new ad campaign, Dare Greatly." Under the guidance of Greiner and John, Scholly hired "executives with decades of collective experience in education technologies, operations, marketing, and branding."[9]

Data provide insights into the reality TV program and American entrepreneurship. As the tenth season approached, those involved in *Shark Tank* proudly announced statistics from the first nine seasons in the show's official 2018 publication *Inside the Shark Tank*. The information they provided underscores the ways *Shark Tank* both exemplifies and differs from the wider world of American entrepreneurship.[10] Most of the successful pitchers were under the age of forty-five, in the middle to upper middle class—something evident to me in their occupations and their ability to self-finance their ventures—and white. There were exceptions: two or possibly three highly educated Asian Americans; one self-professed redneck from a small town in Alabama and another man from humble origins; and one African American man whose social and financial capital came from his past career as an NFL player. There were approximately twice as many men as women among the most successful pitchers.

As for the Sharks, Greiner and Cuban had the most successes to their credit, with about twice as many victories as John, Corcoran, Herjavec, and O'Leary had. In two instances, five Sharks joined together. Among the most lucrative victories was Ten Thirty One, a Halloween-themed live entertainment company developed in Los Angeles with ambitions to expand to New York. Cuban agreed to $2 million for 20 percent equity, placing its valuation at $10 million. In contrast, Greiner came away with 65 percent equity in ReadeREST, the simple device to hitch a pair of eyeglasses to a pocket, for a mere $35,000. Greiner landed one of the most successful products when she purchased 20 percent equity in Scrub Daddy, a versatile cleansing pad, for $200,000. Scrub Daddy had revenues of $30 million in a recent year.[11]

The kinds of products that received funding varied, but overall trends nonetheless reveal that *Shark Tank*'s successes hardly represent the wider world of American innovation. Three food products were successful: Bubba Q's Boneless Ribs, offered by the former NFL player and invested in by John; Wicked Good Cupcakes, a royalty deal between O'Leary and mother-daughter entrepreneurs; and Cousins Maine Lobsters, which Corcoran invested in. Two technology devices were funded: O'Leary and Cuban joined forces to invest in Groove Book, a smartphone app that helped people create books of photographs, while five Sharks teamed up to invest in Breathometer, a smartphone attachment that measured blood alcohol level. Three clothing items earned support: Bombas, socks linked to charity (John); Grace and Lace, fashionable knitted socks for women connected to a social mission (Corcoran); and Tipsy Elves, funky holiday sweaters (Herjavec). In addition to Ten Thirty One, Cuban invested in another event company, Rugged Races, which hosted events where players encountered extreme obstacles. Herjavec made two successful investments in art-related products. Identifying himself as a "redneck from Croatia," he bet on ChordBuddy, a simple device for learning how to play the guitar, offered by a man from a small town in Alabama who was seeking money to build a factory in order to keep jobs in America. He also invested in a more sophisticated invention: Lumio, an elegant "book" that opened into a luminous lamp, developed by Max Gunawan, who had emigrated from Indonesia. An earlier Kickstarter campaign for Lumio had been greatly successful: its initial goal was $60,000, but within a month it had garnered almost ten times that amount. The bidding, from all five Sharks, was intense, and Herjavec ended up with a deal of $350,000 for 10 percent equity.

The biggest category reported on for the first nine seasons was niche items. Six of them were simple but compelling household or health care products: ReadeREST; Scrub Daddy; Buggy Beds, a system that detected bedbugs, which five Sharks invested in; Lollacup, a spill-proof sippy cup (Cuban and Herjavec); Squatty Potty, a device that elevated a toilet seat to facilitate defecation (Greiner); and Simple Sugars, exfoliating sugar crystals that helped solve skin problems (Cuban).

The most successful investments reveal the nature of some but hardly all of the key dimensions of relatively small-scale American capitalism in the early twenty-first century. Although there were some exceptions, by and large these enterprises represented the world of committed, visionary inventors and entrepreneurs who relied on sweat equity, personal savings, and support from friends and family members instead of skills and knowledge gained in business school or funding from outside investors. Successful pitchers were more likely to be lone wolves than members of teams. Although the Sharks often made clear the limitations of building a company around a single product, most of the companies sold just one product or, as in the case of Scrub Daddy, Lumio, and Breathometer, additional products very closely related to the original one.

The show's summary of nine years of episodes revealed that people representing a quarter of a million enterprises had applied for appearances in 199 episodes. Almost 800 contestants had appeared, one in twenty of them younger than twenty-one years old, two-thirds of them male. Slightly over half of the pitches resulted in deals, though it was unclear if that figure represented all deals agreed to on air or only those finalized later on. The Sharks had offered $125 million for deals, with Cuban investing $32 million. Of the top ten enterprises with the highest cumulative sales, none came from the first three seasons, and Greiner captured six, Corcoran two, and Herjavec and John one each. Four of the top ten were clever items to wear: weird sweaters and other items by Tipsy Elves; two lines with a social mission, socks by Bombas and women's apparel by Grace and Lace; and curlers for people with long hair by Sleep Styler. Two of the top ten sold food: Cousins Maine Lobster and Bantam Bagels. Then there were three niche items for the home: Squatty Potty, Scrub Daddy, and FiberFix, a repair wrap stronger than duct tape. The last of the top ten was Simply Fit Board, an exercise device.[12]

What are we to make of these patterns, which reveal the specificity of what the show represents? Scrub Daddy, a winner in season four, has had the greatest sales—$170 million, or likely an average of about $35 million a year; number ten on the list was Grace and Lace, with sales averaging $4 million annually. Although we do not have enough data to fix on accurate valuations, it is likely that the ten most successful enterprises have valuations ranging from $4 million to $50 million or more—although it is hard to know what percentage of equity the contestants or the Sharks still own.[13] Moreover, there are other ways of measuring financial success, and the more dramatic *Shark Tank* successes are those where a major corporate entity eventually bought out a company pitched on the show.

Valuations and sales of this order are hardly insignificant, but it is difficult to imagine any of these companies gaining the heft and value that made the Sharks themselves so wealthy. Although the Sharks are worth $40 million to $3 billion plus, the pitchers and audience seem interested in entrepreneurship on a more modest level. Even so, the appeal of the show's Sharks remains aspirational. For most pitchers, sales in the hundreds of thousands or single-digit millions seem to be the goal, at least in the short term. And focus on the most successful pitches makes it clear that the most successful products occupy specific niches, which may make the businesses difficult to scale up. None of the top ten enterprises are in the service, technology, energy, transportation, consumer durable, federal government, or health care sectors, to name a few prominently missing. The version of entrepreneurial capitalism that *Shark Tank* presents hardly matches the version seen on Wall Street or Sand Hill Road, the Main Street of Silicon Valley. *Shark Tank* may fulfill the American dream for some lucky few, but it does so in highly personal, at times idiosyncratic, and relatively modest ways. There are many varieties of capitalism, yet *Shark Tank* features mostly small-scale, homegrown, startup entrepreneurship rooted in familial and friendship relationships. If millions of Americans feel overwhelmed by large-scale and highly technical enterprises, especially in the wake of the Great Recession, then *Shark Tank* offers comfort because it focuses on smaller-scale and easier-to-understand initiatives, giving them a sense of control in face of seemingly overpowering forces.

Eager to compare *Shark Tank* with other pitching venues, on Saturday, January 13, 2018, I entered the world of aspiring young entrepreneurs as a judge for a high school competition. Most of the participants had learned about pitching from watching *Shark Tank*, even though a high school pitching competition is very different from a reality TV one. A thousand high school students and more than one hundred adults (judges, organizers, officials, and teachers) participated in a three-day event held at a Marriott hotel in the East Bay suburban town of San Ramon, California. This was the 2018 Northern California Career Development Conference, a regional high school competition whose winners would go on to the statewide finals in Anaheim in early March. Those victorious in Anaheim would proceed to Atlanta in late April for the International Career Development Conference, where 18,000 high school students, their parents, advisers, alumni of the program, and businesspeople would gather.[14]

This event, and others like it elsewhere, takes place under the aegis of DECA, a.k.a. Distributive Education Clubs of America, a nonprofit organization that promotes student career development. One of ten organizations under the umbrella of Career and Technical Students Organizations, DECA brings together high school, college, and business students and professionals at conferences, workshops, and competitions that focus on business. DECA boasts 200,000 members in 3,500 high schools and 15,000 in 275 institutions of higher education throughout the United States and abroad, including in China, Spain, Mexico, and Germany. Its website announces that "the United States Congress, the United States Department of Education and state, district and international departments of education authorize DECA's programs," with corporations and foundations also lending their support. Since its founding in 1946, DECA claims, it has "impacted the lives of more than ten million students, educators, school administrators and business professionals. . . . Their strong connection with our organization has resonated into a brand that people identify as a remarkable experience in the preparation of emerging leaders and entrepreneurs."[15]

At the NorCal CDC, I encountered a highly organized but sprawling set of competitions, including Knowledge Tests, Professional Selling and Consulting, and Team Decision-Making events. They involved a wide range of fields, including business administration, entrepreneurship, financial literacy, accounting, and management, in sectors ranging from automotive services to entertainment and hospitality. The meeting rooms were abuzz with activity, with judges and organizers reconnecting or meeting each other for the first time and students networking and nervously preparing. At the end of the day, adults could return to their homes or schmooze with peers, while students could take a bus to a discount mall eight miles away and, when they returned, go to a DECA dance or a game room before the late-night curfew.[16]

As one of four judges in a tiny corner of a vast room, I had the task of role-playing a less insulting and more encouraging Shark as individual students pitched their projects in the category of Entrepreneurship Event. Unlike on *Shark Tank*, the students did not choose their own enterprises or even know in advance what they would be pitching. The enterprises were assigned—in the morning, the opening of a vinyl record store; in the afternoon, the launch of a small pet-grooming business—and the students received information about them just ten minutes before they were due to pitch. A junior in the business administration program from California State University, Chico, was our competition's wrangler. He handed me an instruction sheet that provided questions to ask the aspiring entrepreneurs and the direction to conclude my role-playing by thanking the student without offering any evaluation, and then he showed me to my seat at a table. To the students, he passed out three pages of instructions that detailed the project they would pitch, complete with demographic data and the criteria on which they would be judged, such as "21st Century Skills" and "Performance Indicators." After the students had ten minutes to prepare, he delivered to me a student who introduced herself—unlike the judges and pitchers on *Shark Tank*, neither of us knew anything about the other—and then presented her pitch. After the pitcher left, I had what seemed like a minute to assign scores within the constraints of a highly structured set of numerical parameters and to hurriedly jot down some evaluative comments.

Truth to tell, it took me a while to figure out the nature of my responsibilities. Initially I did not realize that all the students had to follow the same set of directions or that I had to ask a prescribed set of questions, and watching hours of *Shark Tank* had ill prepared me for what I had to do. Yet in each case I did one thing I assume most of the judges did not do: I asked the pitchers what they had learned from *Shark Tank*. Most responded with a good deal of information. And in each case I did something I was specifically instructed not to do: I gave the students who had appeared before me a sense of how they might do even better.

Because the conference occurred very shortly after President Donald Trump said that the United States should not welcome immigrants from "shithole countries," it was hard to avoid experiencing the conference through the lens of citizenship, immigration, and national identity. From what I can determine from a list of the conference winners, based solely on their names, those whose families came from China and India were among the most successful contestants, and Middle Eastern Muslims, whites, and Latinxs also did well. Based on an estimate of what I saw of the 1,000 students present, it looked likely that less than 1 percent were African American. Of the fourteen students with whom I role-played, it was clear to me that there was one white (an upper-middle-class male), one Muslim young woman, six Asian Americans, and six Latinxs.

A week after the conference, thinking back to what I had witnessed, I remembered my experience in high school as the winner of the Connecticut American Legion Oratorical Contest, where I delivered a well-rehearsed speech on the glories of the American Constitution and then had to answer a question about a specific section of it. In contrast, the students at the DECA conference encountered a tougher situation: under pressure and time constraints, they had to devise a strategy in response to a surprise scenario. With remarkably few exceptions, the students impressed me with their poise, intelligence, and ability to perform under pressure. At the conference, I had encountered ambitious, articulate young entrepreneurs, many of whom validated a vision of America as the magnet of talent.

I also wondered what ideology undergirds these competitions. My guess is that in the 1950s, DECA's vision of distributive education involved providing high school students with practical introductions to specific trades—for example, as a high schooler, I took a class that taught me how to set type manually, and I tried to sell shares in the company I developed in the local Junior Achievement program. At some point, probably in the 1980s or 1990s, the organization shifted to its current focus of preparing entrepreneurial leaders.[17] That is how the students I encountered presented themselves as they revealed that they knew how to write business plans and convince a pretend investor that they knew what they were doing.

In important ways, my first experience as a judge in a high school entrepreneurial competition showed how this world draws inspiration from *Shark Tank* even as it differs in crucial ways from the television program. Though like "reality" television high school competitions are highly scripted, they nonetheless value education over entertainment. Omnipresent on television, an explicit and broad vision of the American dream and American capitalism is absent there. While Sharks could sometimes humiliate pitchers, my role as a judge was to be helpfully supportive. The student pitchers are much more diverse than the ones who have appeared on *Shark Tank*, reflecting the nation's future rather than its past. Whereas *Shark Tank* envisions a world of free-market individualism, the DECA event reminded me of the importance of public-private partnerships that involve the cooperation of governments, nongovernmental organizations, and corporations.

In mid-January 2019, I returned to San Ramon to serve as a judge in another high school pitching competition. Little was significantly different from the first competition, but this time I determined that I would later interview some of the students there who had watched *Shark Tank*. The resulting conversations underscored the prevalence of entrepreneurial passion and served as a reminder that the television show represents just one of many approaches to entrepreneurship. I had already talked with dozens of adults who frequently watched the show. I learned from them why in season ten (and earlier) the producers brought on guest Sharks and famous contestants to keep ratings high. After all, while in 2015 over 8 million Americans watched *Shark Tank*, in 2018, during season ten, the audience was bouncing between 2.8 and 4.5 million. Talks with adult viewers revealed a pattern: someone discovers the show, becomes fascinated with it for a time, and then gets bored. As with almost any formulaic show, it is hard to make changes to *Shark Tank* that inventively recapture and sustain attention. Yet one night when watching the show with friends who had never seen it, I saw that even sophisticated skeptics loved to talk to the screen and critique a pitch or a valuation. And I learned from conversations with inveterate watchers that what they experienced was vastly more entertaining than it was educational.

I began my calls to high school students I'd met through DECA by reaching out to Anushka Nair and Alizah Nauman, two ninth graders from Irvington High School in Fremont, California. I started with them because they were among the most impressive of the members of the nine teams that had pitched their proposals to me. They made it clear that *Shark Tank* inspired them to strive for success; one of them reported to me that when watching the show, she said to herself, "I can do it, too. This could be me." But they also took away from the show practical lessons—about how to speak in public, how to value a company, how to convince someone to trust you, and how to present a product or company in a credible way.[18] Another conversation, with Piram Singh, a senior at Washington High School, also in Fremont, demonstrated what it means to become a serial entrepreneur. At age thirteen, he had spent two weeks at the Business Academy for Youth at the Haas School of Business at the University of California, Berkeley. There he discovered, he told me, that he had a "passion for getting into a customer's head, a passion for ideas." By the time he graduated from high school, he had raised money for and patented several inventions, including one to enhance the shopping mall experience and another that attached to a shower head and helped conserve water. Knowing what it takes to be a serial entrepreneur, he remarked, he would "go for it and if does not work, start over again."[19]

Finally, there was Mikey Paine, a junior at Washington High School. Like other students I talked to, he watched *Shark Tank* with family members who talked back to the screen by offering their judgments about products and pitches. Like many of his peers, he understood that the show, 75 percent entertainment by his measure, relies on dramatic techniques to sustain the attention of viewers and hardly presents an accurate representation of real-world interactions between pitchers and investors. Yet he had gleaned much from watching, including how to learn from failure, what makes a presentation effective, and why multiple rounds of investment can cause problems with dilution. Like other high school students I talked to, Paine had an entrepreneurial mindset that led him to apply what he learned from DECA and *Shark Tank* to his own life. With Justin Morgan, he developed *Success HS*, "the #1 global podcast for high school success!" In describing their podcast, following advice you might hear from professional investors, they declared that there is no "recipe for success," though they hastened to add that their podcast was "a source of knowledge to create value and success, and improve your life and mindset for high school and beyond!" One episode featured Singh, who discussed "his new inventions, the strong roots of his community, and having the courage to be yourself and stand out from the crowd." He talked movingly about how being Sikh both made him feel like an outsider and motivated him to succeed. Emphasizing the importance of passion, he described his commitment to social entrepreneurship, especially water conservation in the developing world. At the end of our own talk, Paine stepped back to ponder the larger meaning of what he had learned. Getting an MBA or working for a consulting firm were decent options, he remarked, but the "beauty of America was visible in *Shark Tank*," because it represented "something bigger" than oneself.[20]

Iterations of *Shark Tank*'s pitches are pervasive in American culture, from competitions at business schools to more amateur performances in grade schools. Depictions of early-stage entrepreneurial investing also suffuse popular culture. And among the most influential examples of both media representations and the centrality of pitching in contemporary life is *The Social Network* (2010), the fictionalized movie version of Mark Zuckerberg's development of Facebook.[21] *The Social Network* and *Shark Tank* offer up carefully crafted stories of shifting alliances, exploding tempers, and unexpected twists in the plot, but what we see in a theater on the big screen is different from small-screen *Shark Tank* episodes. The movie version of the creation of Facebook at Harvard College and in Silicon Valley offers stories fueled by drugs, alcohol, sex, and legal maneuvers. Betrayal

Sharks Everywhere

A would-be entrepreneur can look to sources other than reality TV to understand the process of developing an enterprise. The challenge, of course, is sifting through the competing advice. Near the end of his book *The Hard Thing about Hard Things: Building a Business When There Are No Easy Answers*, the Silicon Valley venture capitalist Ben Horowitz tells readers that the "first rule of entrepreneurship" is that "there are no rules."[1]

This is hard to square with the advice of Simon Sinek, whose TED Talk, "How Great Leaders Inspire Action," has racked up more than 40 million views and been translated into forty-seven languages since it was first broadcast in September 2009.[2] Sinek begins by asking how some exceptional people can achieve what seems to "defy all of the assumptions." As with many inspirational speakers or writers, what he says is more evocative than instrumentally specific. He draws three concentric circles and labels the center one "Why?"; the next, "How?"; and finally the outermost ring, "What?" Together these three questions, but especially "Why?" comprise what he calls "the Golden Circle." Focusing on the example of Apple cofounder Steve Jobs, Sinek asserts that most entrepreneurs began with "What?": "We make great computers. They're beautifully designed, simple to use, and user friendly. Want to buy one?" In contrast, at Apple Jobs started with "Why?": "Everything we do, we believe in challenging the status quo, [and we do so] by making our products beautifully designed, simple to use, and friendly. We just happen to make great computers. Want to buy one?" Because Jobs took this route, Sinek insists, success followed.

Sinek elaborates on these themes in his 2009 book *Start with Why: How Great Leaders Inspire Everyone to Take Action*. He tells the story, the outlines of which will be familiar to those like me who read inspirational how-to books, of how one day, no longer loving his work, he found himself "in a very dark place" because his "Golden Circle was out of balance." The novelty of launching his own business had worn off, and he had become depressed and paranoid. Realizing that he had forgotten his "why"—the reason he did what he did—he cast his eyes on his past and remembered that his why was to inspire people "so that together, we can change our world." Recapturing his why restored his "passion to a degree multiple times greater than at any other time" in his life. Sinek tells stories of how other people, both ordinary and exceptional, also discovered the power of why, and he celebrates those "who wake up feeling fulfilled by the work they do" because they focus on their purpose. For entrepreneurs, Sinek's argument about the importance of why suggests that they should—in addition to conveying to investors, employees, associates, and consumers the importance of discipline, clarity, and consistency—use charisma, which derives from a focus on why, to inculcate trust.[3]

Though Sinek claims that he grounded his theory in biology, by stepping back we can realize two things. First, his arguments are remarkably similar to those in inspirational books such as Napoleon Hill's *Think and Grow Rich* (1937) and Norman Vincent Peale's *The Power of Positive Thinking* (1952): focusing on and having faith in purpose as the key to leadership, prosperity, and creativity. Second, the timing of Sinek's talk was crucial for its impact. He delivered it almost exactly one year after the collapse of Lehman Brothers, when the dark clouds of the Great Recession still hovered over the land.[4] Sinek offered those in his audience a chance to rely on their own vision to realize their dreams in perilous times.

Ben Horowitz and Simon Sinek introduce perspectives and experiences very different from those portrayed on *Shark Tank*. Horowitz is a modern version of the entrepreneur as organization man—a principal in the Silicon Valley venture capital firm Andreessen Horowitz. Founded in 2009, just when the nation began to emerge from the Great Recession, the firm made early bets on Twitter, Skype, Groupon, Facebook, and Lyft. Yet Horowitz could insist there were no rules except one because, like similar firms, Andreessen Horowitz placed many bets that did not work out so well, even though on paper they looked like equally good bets. In contrast, Sinek, who consults for organizations, offers simple rules wrapped in an inspiring albeit familiar and often-elusive vision that relies on the charisma that the Golden Circle inspires.

On television, the Sharks proceed differently. They believe there are rules for successful entrepreneurship that rest on individualistic opposition to the institutional expertise of others—except what the Sharks themselves offer through strategic partnerships. Like most venture capitalists and angel investors, to some extent they follow the same strategy that Ben Horowitz does: make many bets, because you can win big even if only a small percentage provide triumphant results. Strikingly, the Sharks' advice to entrepreneurs typically insists that they can make it on their own even as the Sharks' own career history reveals them as organization men and women. A look at the results of the Sharks' various investments reveals more about the television entertainment than about the realities of the American and world economies.

The Sharks as Investors and Entrepreneurs

There is remarkable variety in what happens after a *Shark Tank* pitch is filmed: some never air; some products that receive investments ultimately flop; some ventures win in the studio but Sharks and pitchers fail to come to terms on them later; some of those go on to success anyway while others fail; some enterprises that the Sharks turn down nonetheless go on to have some degree of success; and deals that contestants reject on the show, especially ones that are eventually very lucrative, despite a lack of support from Sharks. On *Shark Tank* as in life, the difference between success and failure, between pitchers who make deals and those who do not, comes down to sometimes-predictable and sometimes-inexplicable combinations of performance, product, chemistry between investors and pitchers, timing, and plain and simple luck. Moreover, what happens with consummated deals reveals the extensive business empires the Sharks have built, replete with accountants, lawyers, managers, and public relations teams that support them as they close deals, help build businesses, and venture out as investors, consultants, and motivational speakers. Together these varied outcomes reveal not only the varieties of American business experiences in the early twenty-first century but also some aspects of entrepreneurship in the same years.

Sometimes Sharks and contestants strike a deal on air and then seal it after airing, but before long the venture fails. This underscores that what we see on television is only part of the story, and one that often suggests more-promising outcomes than those delivered.[5] The revealing difficulty I encountered in researching failed products backed by Sharks is that Sharks are so typically boastful that they usually do not want to talk about their failures. Thus, in a 2012 article in *Forbes* titled "Shark Tank—Their Best and Worst Deals," the Sharks focused on the former but finessed the latter. Daymond John talked about two of his triumphs but made no mention at all of deals gone wrong. Barbara Corcoran, without mentioning the Body Jac by name, said her worst deal was "investing in a fast-talking cowboy selling exercise equipment who needed to lose 50 pounds. Instead, he lost my $50,000." Then, in typical fashion, she went on to talk extensively about a great success. Lori Greiner remarked that she liked all the deals she had agreed to and all the partners she had done them with and that "things [were] progressing really well for most." She then proceeded to tout the one she was most proud of before briefly and elliptically saying, "As for the worst, I can't say yet." Having sort of expressed caution, she ended by insisting that in the upcoming season viewers would see "a lot of exciting follow ups with several of my deals." Robert Herjavec, having touted a triumph, insisted, "There is no worst—I tend to look forward not backwards."[6]

Toygaroo fits the category of invested-in flops. It was a subscription service for toys whose pitch aired during season two on March 25, 2011. Recognizing how toys cluttered homes and how quickly children tired of them, it offered families a way to frequently get new toys and get rid of old ones: the company sent a family a box of toys each month (or, for a higher price, more often); subscribers then returned them; the company cleaned them; and then sent them out to another household. On the show John expressed concern that the pitcher, Nikki Pope, owned only 10 percent of the company; when she was pressed about the reason for this, Pope's remarkable vagueness should have set off alarms. On air, Mark Cuban and Kevin O'Leary, two of the toughest Sharks, agreed they would together invest $200,000 in exchange for 35 percent of the company. Apparently in the end Cuban was the only investor who finalized the deal, even though Pope focused her hopes on O'Leary because of his extensive experience with toy companies. A little over a year after the episode aired, the company declared bankruptcy. "I don't think that the 'big name' investors we got really came through with what I had hoped," said Phil Smy, Toygaroo's former chief technology officer, as he seemed to shift blame to a Shark. "Cuban's personal role was extremely limited. We did have frequent contact with 'his people.'"[7] One moral of this and other stories: keep your failures hidden and remember that on-screen, as in Garrison Keillor's Lake Wobegon, "all the women are strong, all the men are good-looking, and all the children are above average." Both Cuban and O'Leary briefly admitted that Toygaroo fit the category of invested-in flops without acknowledging publicly that they did anything wrong. Cuban said this was "the only failure I have had."[8]

An example of a project that was successful even though a deal made on-screen collapsed is Smart Baker, a business pitched in March 2012 during season three. Daniel Rensing, a tech professional, and his wife, Stephanie Rensing, a recently laid-off schoolteacher passionate about cooking, had developed a series of baking-related products: an apron conveniently printed with a conversion chart, towers for displaying cupcakes, and parchment paper precut to fit standard pan sizes. Seeking $75,000 for 25 percent of their company, they accepted Corcoran's offer of the same amount of funding but for 40 percent equity, with a 5 percent royalty on sales until she got her initial investment back. But the deal soon collapsed when Corcoran and the Rensings could not agree on a business strategy. Nonetheless, without the funding and business acumen of a Shark behind them, but with the help of the *Shark Tank* effect, they prospered. In the year before their appearance on the show, they had sales of $140,000, with $100,000 in profit. After their episode aired, sales quickly grew to $500,000, and though estimates vary, their company appears to have eventually achieved sales between $1 million and $2 million, and their website now features an even more robust range of baking products.[9]

If one might argue Corcoran missed the boat on Smart Baker, other examples appear to confirm how shrewd (or lucky) the Sharks are. One useful example is How Do You Roll, offered by Yuen and Peter Yung, two brothers from Austin, Texas, who were franchising their model of a sushi restaurant where customers assembled their own rolls. When they appeared on the show in 2013, they had already sold fifteen franchises. The deal they struck with O'Leary, $1 million for 20 percent equity, soon fell through because he insisted on control of the company's board of directors, even though on air he'd seemed to indicate that he would seek profits but not control. In the short term, the company experienced explosive growth as it expanded in the United States and abroad. Then came a dramatic downturn, and it is not clear if the company still exists, except perhaps in Texas.[10]

The juxtaposition of Smart Baker and How Do You Roll is instructive. On-screen, How Do You Roll involved a dramatically higher valuation, a remarkably slicker presentation, a considerably more ambitious business plan, and more robust managerial expertise. But Corcoran found the presentation's "too buttoned up," while both and Cuban and John expressed concern about the challenge of running a restaurant. In the end, Smart Baker's modesty seemed to work out better than How Do You Roll's sky-high ambition, polished slickness, and commitment to a dangerous rate of growth.

Then there are examples of business success without the help of Sharks, where the Sharks never made an offer but aspiring entrepreneurs nonetheless achieved varying degrees of success. This category proves that results do not always bear out the Sharks' claim that their involvement is crucial to the success or failure of a business and underscores the extent to which entrepreneurial results rest on many factors. Several pitches fall into this category, although the Sharks probably would not regret failing to invest in these enterprises if they had only modest success. One example involves two African American women, Melissa Butler and Rosco Spears, who came on the show offering the Lip Bar, a line of lipsticks made from natural ingredients and available in a range of bold colors. The Sharks mocked them and turned them down, citing less-than-stunning sales, powerful competitors, and weak messaging in the presentation. Yet there was an audience for these lipsticks. "In a society where little brown girls aren't often shown their beauty through mainstream media," a reporter for an African American fashion magazine later remarked, "Melissa and her team strive to turn the anomaly into the norm—one bold and beautiful campaign at a time."[11] By 2018, they were successful enough to have secured coveted shelf space at 142 Target stores across the nation.[12]

The Lip Bar founder Melissa Butler and her creative director, Rosco Spears, used a varied and vivid display to attract investors in their company on the February 6, 2015, episode. They failed on television but succeeded in the marketplace because of their product's vibrant colors and compelling images.

The final category of deals Sharks missed out on involves enterprises that eluded them because contestants turned down offers on the show—and sometimes these ventures became especially lucrative later on.[13] Several stand out. One of the most dramatic negotiations between Sharks and entrepreneurs involved Coffee Meets Bagel, an online dating site offered to the Sharks in season six on January 9, 2015, by three sisters, Arum, Dawoon, and Soo Kang. Their product was in an already-crowded market that included not only dating sites that were capacious in their reach, such as Match, OKCupid, Tinder, and eharmony, but also niche sites for a specific kind of user, such as JDate for Jewish singles, Adam4Adam for gay men, and OurTime for singles over fifty years old. Every dating app had a distinctive approach, and Coffee Meets Bagel deployed several: it used Facebook data to identify compatible matches, insisted on proceeding deliberately, and limited the number of matches per person per day. The Kang sisters claimed that these strategies, along with a brand name that suggested informality rather than potentially exploitative sexual relations, made their app more woman-friendly than its competitors.

On the show, their proposal did not seem to be going anywhere. All five Sharks declared themselves out: the financials (many subscribers but no profits) and valuation ($500,000 for 5 percent) were problematic even though the business model was impressive, especially given the company's explosive growth. Then Cuban, who had exited early because the sisters were not willing to reveal precisely how many subscribers they had, appeared to jump back in when he asked, "If I offered you $30 million for the company, would you take it?" It was the largest offer ever made on the show. But the sisters rejected it, citing their hopes for the future. A closer look reveals that Cuban's offer may well have been hypothetical or at least exploratory, something that quickly became clear when, citing the relationship between risk and reward, he once again declared himself out. Over time, Coffee Meets Bagel's value far exceeded what Cuban had offered. While it's difficult to verify its precise valuation, if estimates are anywhere near accurate, the site was a big prey that eluded the Sharks.

Copa Di Vino was another, even more notorious offering that the Sharks could not capture, albeit for very different reasons. James Martin first appeared during season two, on March 20, 2011, to offer his single-serving wine in a glass. The next season, a little over a year later, he appeared again, and on both occasions the Sharks, though hungry for success, failed to close a deal. On the first iteration, O'Leary offered to purchase 51 percent of the intellectual property (principally the patent), which he would offer to many wineries for $600,000, leaving Martin with a 49 percent share of

On April 13, 2012, James Martin made his second appearance on *Shark Tank*, again offering the Sharks a stake in Copa Di Vino. Martin's display acknowledged that his second chance with the Sharks was dicey, depicting himself as a "dead man walking." As it turned out, the poster correctly predicted his fate: once again, in an especially tempestuous, drama-filled episode, Martin and the Sharks failed to reach an agreement.

that piece of his business and freeing him to focus on other aspects of his enterprises. Visibly sweating, Martin turned him down. O'Leary, a wine connoisseur, replied that he would drink a $1,000 bottle of wine that night, because he "was *weeping* for the opportunity lost. . . . *This* was your moment. You turn around, it's gone."

However, Martin's moment was not gone, because in a then-unprecedented move, he was invited to appear on the show a second time to offer the Sharks, in his words, "that elusive second bite of the apple." "Agonize no more, this time we're going to make a deal," he told O'Leary as he presented what he said was a $1,000 bottle of wine divided into Copa Di Vino glasses for the Sharks. Discussions proceeded about the proper valuation of the company, with Cuban, Herjavec, and O'Leary joining together for a bid of $600,000 for 30 percent of the entire company. When Martin hesitated, John and Cuban warned him not to blow his chances once again. Herjavec cautioned, "James, you've done something nobody in the tank has ever done. You've been given the American dream to come back." Martin continued to hesitate because he found the valuation too low, and, with a visibly cool flair, he opened one of the small containers of wine. Cuban declared himself out, remarking, "You screwed around . . . and there's nothing more that I hate than playing games." Herjavec dramatically declared himself out as he walked off the stage. "Cheers," Martin replied, arrogantly raising a glass and walking away. Cleverly, O'Leary responded with his own riposte by serving glasses of the expensive wine to his colleagues. Later on, recalling what had happened, Martin said the Sharks needed him more than he needed them, but they lost out because they were too greedy. Herjavec's analysis was different and surely reflected his peers' judgment. He said that Martin forgot his place; he thought he was the Shark, "but we're the Sharks." By the spring of 2015, sales of Copa Di Vino, available in forty-five states, had hit $15 million.[14]

The most successful lost opportunity was DoorBot, a video doorbell that enabled homeowners to view and communicate with visitors. In response to an ask of $700,000 in exchange for 10 percent equity, only O'Leary made an offer, which the pitcher Jamie Siminoff turned down. The other Sharks balked because they believed competition would erode the company's market share and price. However, after taping, guest Shark Richard Branson decided to invest in the company. The product was renamed Ring, and Amazon purchased the company in 2018, reportedly for $1 billion.[15] Four and a half years after the episode aired, a reporter for CNBC asked O'Leary to discuss his regrets about successful enterprises that had eluded him. O'Leary, who in this case probably gave voice to the views of the other Sharks, responded, "I never cry over spilled milk because I've learned on 'Shark Tank,' over 10 years, I'm going to see 10 great deals right after his, and I did."[16] This comment successfully captures key aspects of the Sharks' entrepreneurship: a focus on present and future opportunities and not on past failures, because they believe the world out there is filled with lucrative possibilities; an apparent refusal to learn from their mistakes; and what strikes me as arrogance.

The variety of successful and failed projects on *Shark Tank* reminds us of key elements of contemporary entrepreneurship as well as both the problems and the possibilities of the Sharks' approach. For pitchers, evaluating their company correctly, pitching it convincingly, and negotiating successfully on the spot are all important. In most situations the powerful Sharks shape outcomes, but not always. In venture capital and angel investing, picking winners is difficult. Luck is among the factors that make the fate of an enterprise difficult to anticipate accurately. In the short run, the *Shark Tank* effect is powerful, but in the long run, timing, planning, access to skilled professionals, and adequate financial resources that the Sharks provide are vital. For any wealthy person who invests in myriad ventures, including the Sharks, it is inevitable that there will be successes and failures, as well as some ventures that land somewhere in between. Some products do not easily fit into existing categories and present distinctive challenges. Generally speaking, over the long term the Sharks surely can claim to have done well, despite any missteps.[17]

Out of the Water in *Beyond the Tank*

Beyond the Tank, a follow-up show that aired in the spring of 2015 and in the first half of 2016, not only helps us understand what happens after episodes air but also provides some limited insight into how the Sharks manage the companies they invest in.[18] This is so even though *Beyond the Tank* is more about drama and entertainment than it is about the "reality" that reality TV supposedly delivers. Compared with *Shark Tank*, and even more decisively with what surely goes on during the filming of *Shark Tank* that television viewers never see, *Beyond the Tank* reveals relatively little about how negotiations or enterprises actually work. Moreover, the follow-ups provide all-too-superficial glimpses into execution, which is less compelling and dramatic than pitching.

The episodes typically begin with a breathless opening that lasts a bit more than a minute and reminds viewers what happened with a particular pitch on the original show and then provides information about what occurred later on. "For entrepreneurs making it into the tank," Cuban emphatically announces as viewers watch pitchers enter the tank on the original show, this "is the American dream." What immediately follows is a series of snippets in which each of the six principal Sharks briefly appears, offering moments of hope and warnings to aspiring entrepreneurs. First are celebratory scenes of victory after an entrepreneur gets a deal, and then Greiner asks, "But what happens next?" Now, with a deal struck, O'Leary announces, "the *real* work begins." Corcoran says, "Some entrepreneurs have life-altering success," and John adds, "And some don't." "It's your job to run the business," Herjavec remarks as a series of tense moments when Sharks engage successful pitchers flashes across the screen, followed by boisterous celebrations.

Following this general introduction, virtually all of the episodes of *Beyond the Tank* focus on common business challenges, especially how fledgling companies handle growth. The good news is that the *Shark Tank* effect almost always kicks in for companies that appear on the show, and they experience an increase in sales. The frequently experienced bad news is that websites sometimes crash and some companies cannot handle explosive increases in demand—even though the months between filming and airing should have provided pitchers and their Shark allies with ample time to prepare for surging demand. Soon enough winners also face other challenges as they struggle to manage growth. Revenues might increase without adequate or commensurate growth in profits. A common question is whether to expand the brand by developing additional, usually related products. For example, should Neal Hoffman, who presented the Chanukah Kit and Mensch on a Bench, move into other Jewish holidays or add additional Jewish characters? Should Cousins Maine Lobsters expand their brand beyond food trucks by opening a restaurant in Los Angeles, or should Mo's Bows add a full line of men's clothing to its successful line of bow ties? Sharks usually advise caution in making such moves and often insist that inexperienced entrepreneurs keep public attention on their products in other ways.

Also instructive on *Beyond the Tank* are the several instances where a Shark works with a pitcher who failed to get a deal or whose on-air deal later broke down during negotiations. Although the Sharks are notoriously reluctant to work with pitchers who have MBAs, Cuban nonetheless agreed to a deal with Nick Taranto and Josh Hix, who developed their idea for Plated, a company that sells chef-designed food kits for home delivery, while at Harvard Business School. The deal they struck with Cuban on the show eventually broke down, supposedly because Taranto and Hix wanted to up the already-robust valuation agreed to on air. But when Nick later ran into O'Leary at a conference, their meeting resulted in another deal. Plated, which also was funded by venture capital, was enormously successful, and Albertsons eventually acquired it for $300 million.[19]

As a way of reminding viewers of what they too can aspire to, *Shark Tank* emphasizes the close, albeit carefully staged, personal relationships between Sharks and contestants. And nowhere is this more prominent than in *Beyond the Tank*'s follow-ups on many pitches that focused on family.[20] Historically, firms controlled by wealthy families played significant roles in the corporate world, just as they do today, but on *Shark Tank* we see family businesses that are more modest in scale, though the relationships are just as complicated. The pitch that most prominently dramatized the importance of family, and did so on many levels, was Bubba's Boneless Ribs. Al "Bubba" Baker, an African American man who had played football for the NFL for thirteen years, appeared on the show with his daughter Brittany. He explained that he had developed boneless ribs when his wife refused to eat traditional ones because they were too messy. Baker and John struck a deal, $300,000 in exchange for 30 percent of the company. On *Beyond the Tank*, John traveled to the small Ohio town where Baker had his restaurant to see Baker, who was seeking help in finding a new company that would ready the ribs for market. The meeting grew tense because a visibly frustrated John felt he had done a lot for Baker and Baker had let him down.

Baker invited John to his house for some barbecue in order to build trust with him. After meeting three generations of Baker's family, John joined them in a game of touch football. Later, back in the house, Baker raised a glass to toast "family." John responded with a dose of schmaltz, invoking memories of Thanksgiving dinners and noting that the Bakers' get-together showcased "something I don't think that we highlight enough in the world, about great family units that support each other." He went on to say he trusted Baker's family. Later, John said, "When I hang out with his family, it makes me more and more excited [about the business]." In a voiceover, Baker said, "One of the reasons I work so hard is for my family." Soon Baker went to New Jersey to visit the Rastelli Food Group factory. Seated at a table with members of the Baker family, one of the Rastellis remarked, "You are a beautiful family ... and we're a family business."[21]

So what do we have here? Aside from a few gestures and linguistic turns, there's no mention of race or of John's family. John, an African American Shark, goes to Avon, Ohio, a small town where only 2.3 percent of the population is black. Two African Americans—Bubba Baker, a six-foot, six-inch former defensive lineman, and Daymond John, at five feet, seven inches the shortest of the male Sharks—have a tense meeting, and then Baker invites John to meet his family. What ensues on the show is a sentimental celebration of families, both Baker's African American family and the Italian American family behind the Rastelli Food Group. Hosannas to family and, especially, family-based capitalism provide drama that overshadows any potential lessons about how capitalism works.

Perhaps more than *Shark Tank*, *Beyond the Tank* focuses on highly staged dramas rather than material showcasing how businesses can or should operate. Episodes often feature heart-wrenching stories about life-threatening health problems or economic reversals caused by external circumstances, especially the Great Recession. Producers also heighten drama by lacing episodes with connections between problems an entrepreneur faces and those a Shark has encountered. No example is more compelling than John's relationship with Moziah Bridges of Mo's Bows, an African American boy who at age nine developed a fashionable line of bow ties with the help of his mother and grandmother. No Shark agreed to invest in his enterprise, but Daymond John promised to mentor Mo. On *Beyond the Tank*, John took Mo to his old neighborhood so he would understand where John came from, and he talked with Mo about how the dynamics of his past relationship with his mother paralleled what Mo was encountering in his own life.

Beyond the Tank almost always ends with an emphasis on success, more so than do most small businesses. True to their frequent embrace of clichés and passionate insistence that Americans have an abundance of opportunities, even when their investments fail, the Sharks invariably remain confident about the future. Indeed, the rhetoric that captures such hopes evokes the vitality of the American dream. Usually this confidence about the future remains implicit on *Beyond the Tank*, but on occasion it bursts into view.[22]

Unlike Real Sharks, Those on *Shark Tank* Only Appear to Swim Alone

Shark Tank's mythic emphasis on one-on-one relationships often collides with the truth that larger organizational networks are vital to entrepreneurship.[23] While some aspiring entrepreneurs do act alone or with a few associates, often family members, the Sharks themselves preside over complicated enterprises and rely on scores of people. In 2018, O'Leary had thirty-four companies in his *Shark Tank* portfolio.[24] Once a year Herjavec invites successful contestants to meet with him and talk about where they are currently and what challenges and opportunities they see for the future. But only rarely on *Shark Tank*—and somewhat more frequently on *Beyond the Tank*—do we get a glimpse of later interactions with pitchers or of the corporate teams on which Sharks rely. Nonetheless, the glimpses we do get are instructive.

On *Beyond the Tank*, there are often vague references to a Shark's "team" or "advisers," but sometimes there is more specificity. At the follow-up meeting for Tipsy Elves, which sold outrageously ugly sweaters, Herjavec had by his side a vice president for operations and a business development manager. When meeting with the Red Dress folks who run an online women's clothing boutique, Cuban brought along a director of web services and a senior financial adviser. When Herjavec went to DreamWorks Animation to seal a deal that allowed the slipper company Happy Feet to feature DreamWorks characters on their slippers, accompanying him was his vice president for marketing and public relations, who, we learned, frequently met with successful pitchers. Similarly, when John connected with the college friends who developed AquaVault, portable containers that keep your belongings safe at the beach or the pool, at his side was one person who was in charge of entertainment and lifestyle for his enterprises and another who was in charge of production and manufacturing. Nonetheless, though these associates appeared on screen and sometimes spoke up, the Sharks dominated the conversations.

Once, Daymond John was so impressed with a pitcher that he brought him into his corporate office, an action that complicated the show's emphasis on individualism and provided a capacious view of a Shark's operations.[25] As an engineering student at George Tech, Patrick Whaley had developed a weighted shirt for athletic training, but after he was shot during a mugging, he found that the shirt helped him regain his strength during physical therapy. This inspired him to launch his company, TITIN, in order to sell his invention commercially. He raised $117,000 on Kickstarter, and then on the show he made a deal with John for $500,000 in exchange for 20 percent equity. Sales increased exponentially after the episode aired, and John upped his investment to $1 million. Soon after, he recommended that Whaley move from Atlanta to New York and work in his office on the sixty-sixth floor of the Empire State Building. This, John insisted, would put Whaley into continual, on-the spot contact with John's people who were handling production, shipping, public relations, advertising, design, billing, and marketing. John showed Whaley a sophisticated test lab/gymnasium he had set up, where athletes work out and designers focus on improving products. John then introduced Whaley to a design engineer and his team of about six people, as well as to a social media expert. Impressed with John's setup, Whaley moved to New York and apparently achieved considerable success.

The episode featuring TITIN provides a window into the work of entrepreneurial organization men and women as it reveals how at least one Shark, and probably the others in different ways, builds organizations to manage the companies they invest in on the show, as well as other enterprises they hold a stake in. A November 2015 article on Business Insider spoke of how "the show and its responsibilities have become integral aspects of each of the Sharks' careers, despite their other businesses," with some of the investments reportedly bringing in "millions of dollars in profit every year." Sharks, the reporter noted, "have teams dedicated to helping them manage their 'Shark Tank' investments, and will stay in regular contact with their entrepreneurs during crucial parts of the year." Surely with some exaggeration, Aaron Krause, the founder of Scrub Daddy, Greiner's most successful investment, reported that Greiner "has been available via phone or email for valuable insight at all times of the day, including the middle of the night," and makes "herself personally available to each of her entrepreneurs."[26]

Yet exactly how the Sharks operate remains somewhat unclear—

especially the extent and structure of their operations; the relationship between *Shark Tank*–related ventures and unrelated ones; and the nature of their involvement with entrepreneurs they discovered on the show. Nonetheless, some things are knowable. Carrying out due diligence between coming to a verbal agreement on air and signing a formal, legally binding contract is obviously a crucial step in which accountants, lawyers, and others play prominent roles.[27] In Greiner's case, her husband Dan's involvement gives her enterprises a family twist. Trained as an accountant, he resigned from his job as a corporate controller to handle, as a reporter for *Forbes* put it, "the parts, the shipping and packaging, and the inventory and accounting issues to make a business that carries some 112 products work so smoothly while it's accomplishing such meteoric success."[28] With the other Sharks, operations seem more impersonally corporate, since they rely on their own organizations and on outside ones. For example, John works with the brand management company Vector Management and the prominent global talent agency William Morris Endeavor.[29]

The Sharks' websites provide abundant, though meticulously shaped, evidence of how they use organizations to promote their achievements and visions and thereby extend their personal and corporate brands.[30] Media scholars Susan J. Douglas and Andrea McDonnell have noted that TV personalities rely on what they call "the celebrity production industry," which business scholars Eric Guthey, Timothy Clark, and Brad Jackson describe as a "a well-oiled publicity machine, in fact a network of interlocking publicity and media engines acting in tandem." Moreover, business celebrities, like the Sharks, who rely on their prominence as authors of best-selling books and as consultants, operate in ways that both underscore and "smooth over some of the key cultural and ideological tensions" that contemporary capitalism represents.[31] The celebration of entrepreneurship and the American dream in troubled times on reality TV shows such as *Shark Tank* simultaneously evokes the benefits of entrepreneurial capitalism and reminds us of contemporary social and economic fissures.[32] At times, the Sharks and other business celebrities seem to step over the line between giving sensible advice and hyping impossible-to-fulfill dreams when they promise that reading their books, listening to their talks, following their advice, or even investing with them will bring quick and abundant riches.

To explore all this, we can begin with Greiner's website, which reports that her products have grossed more than half a billion dollars in sales. Using typical get-rich-quick language, one page of the site announces, "I'll Make You MILLIONS!" Greiner herself says, just below this headline, "One of my favorite things about being a Shark ... is helping to make the American dream come true for people across our country." Greiner's work on *Shark Tank* is only one part, and probably well under half, of what she does.[33] In addition to hosting her QVC show, *Clever and Unique Creations*, she is the founder of For Your Ease Only, Inc., a company that helps entrepreneurs develop and market products, and gives talks as a motivational speaker—for a fee that usually ranges from $50,000 to $70,000. In my judgment, more than any other Shark, Greiner presents herself as an individualistic entrepreneur, crucially helped by her husband but otherwise acting alone—without the help of lawyers, accountants, or operations managers. She does this even though a 2012 article on Business Insider revealed how she relied on others, such as a floor manager and makeup artist.[34]

With his website, Herjavec presents a somewhat different entrepreneurial face to the world, one that barely hides the corporate dimensions of supposedly individualistic entrepreneurship. *Shark Tank* figures prominently in his life and probably more so in his self-presentation, but other aspects of his world also command attention. Prominently there is the Herjavec Group, the cybersecurity firm he founded in 2003. Like his peers, Herjavec offers his services as an inspirational speaker; according to his website, he "leverages his life and business experiences as he navigates his presentation, giving audiences practical and tangible tools they can incorporate into their own professional aspirations."[35] Then there is his passion for exotic and expensive racing cars. In his books, he is remarkably more revealing about his life than the more circumspect Greiner, but they both have relatively little to say about how they manage their *Shark Tank*–related businesses.

Corcoran's website leads in many directions. You can connect to a recommended real estate agent in several cities. To see if you are an entrepreneur, you can take her Entrepreneur IQ Test. You can find out what products and services she has endorsed, such as Zebit (a service promising to reduce the stress employees experience about their finances) and OnDeck Capital (a company that loans money to small businesses). Or you can contact her about a speaking engagement; she gives talks on topics such as her rags-to-riches story, how to lead a company to greatness, and what it's like behind the scenes on *Shark Tank*.[36] Her site also informs people about investing along with her as a venture capitalist. In 2014, with Phil Nadel she established Forefront Venture Partners, an operation open to investors who can put in as little as $1,000 for a single deal. On AngelList, a website linking investors and job-seekers with startups, the company says— perhaps with some exaggeration—that it's "one of the largest and most successful" syndicates on the site and has "a portfolio of many notable, high-growth start-ups." Among the companies in which Forefront Venture Partners has invested are Wevorce, which specializes in consummating amicable divorces; HigherMe, which matches employees with employers; and VetPronto, which brings veterinarians to your home.[37]

With O'Leary, John, and Cuban we encounter business empires with more ambitious reach, more complicated structures, and different compositions. O'Leary's enterprises fall into many categories, but he has two offerings different from those of any of the other Sharks. Beginning in the summer of 2015, he developed a series of mutual funds that follow, the website says, his mother's lesson to invest conservatively for the long term. And as an oenophile, as he reports on Facebook, he has developed his own line of wine, O'Leary Fine Wines, which "show an immediate return on investment with ample dividends of flavor for years to come."[38]

The website of John, "the People's Shark," is the one that most fully invites aspiring entrepreneurs to learn from and work with him. If you book him to give a speech, "he will reveal how you too can live the American Dream" and inspire audience members with his "rags-to-riches success story of sacrifice, hard work, and perseverance." You can also hire him as a consultant for your company and learn from the "free Shark resources" on his website, such as "Identifying Your Target Market" and "A Step-by-Step Guide to Product Validation."[39] John also plays to his distinctive strength as an expert in branding. As "arbiter[s] of culture and style," he insists, he and his company the Shark Group do not simply have "our finger on the pulse—we dictate the beat."[40] The Shark Group offers entrepreneurs the opportunity to work with its branding, marketing, social media, licensing, product development, and manufacturing teams. Aware of the power of popular culture, it offers to connect entrepreneurs with celebrities, popular icons, and tastemakers. His support team is extensive and includes a president of the Shark Group and the head of its speaking bureau, as well as people from Ortner Management Group, Stan Rosenfield and Associates, William Morris Endeavor, FUBU, Mark Burnett Productions, ABC, Sony, and CNBC.[41] The websites of Greiner and Corcoran rarely if ever mention gender, and although John's websites make little if any mention of race, they do feature younger, hipper, and more racially and ethnically diverse people than the other Sharks' sites.

Cuban's enterprises are by far the most extensive and varied, and the structure of his ventures is surely the most elaborate. His website, MarkCubanCompanies.com, leads to more than seventy-five non–*Shark Tank* companies in which he has invested, ranging from the ones he is most associated with and in which he is a major player (the Dallas Mavericks NBA team; Landmark Theatres; AXS TV, which makes live music events available on television; the distribution company Magnolia Pictures) to emerging ones in which he is, presumably, one of many investors (CommitChange, which connects donors with charities, and Condition One, which is developing immersive video technologies). An inquiring mind can find out more about almost fifty movies and television shows with which he has been involved: more than two dozen on which he was a producer, usually for Magnolia Pictures; some on which he was an actor; and many TV shows on which he made an appearance, not only *Shark Tank* but also *The Simpsons* and *The Late Show with David Letterman.* You can also buy items from the Mark Cuban Collection, such as T-shirts that say "Future Shark" or "I'm an ENTREPRENEUR, You're a WANTENTREPRENEUR."[42]

The six principal Sharks rely on varied business models for their own enterprises. Corcoran's is probably the simplest; free from major obligations from a pre–*Shark Tank* career, she focuses on building out from what the television show provides. Greiner and Herjavec have major pre–*Shark Tank* enterprises that probably command more time (though in Herjavec's case, carry less visibility) than the TV show. O'Leary and, even more so, John and Cuban have multifaceted empires that necessitate elaborate corporate structures and ample managerial skills. According to data available on Wikipedia, their net worths start at multiple tens of millions for Greiner and Corcoran; increase to Herjavec's at $200 million, John's at $300 million, and O'Leary's at $400 million; and finally jump to Cuban's at $3.3 billion. It is likely that the higher the Shark's net worth, the lower the percentage of wealth stemming from *Shark Tank* investments. Even at the lower end, other sources may well account for most of the income, although the visibility of *Shark Tank* can make it difficult for the public to conceive of the Sharks having other sources of income.

However, there is a serious issue that the Sharks in their boastfulness never address. A study of factors that predict a company's success concluded that "if you had a full-time mentor who was not part of the company's management team, and who had actually run both a start-up and a larger business, the success rate increased from less than 25% to over 80%."[43] If this is true, then one has to wonder about the *Shark Tank* model. Given all their commitments, it is hard to imagine that the Sharks and members of their teams can be considered "full-time mentors" to the entrepreneurs whose ventures they invest in. In the end, the reality outside the tank reminds us of both the promises and pitfalls of contemporary entrepreneurship. The Sharks' multifaceted successes as contemporary versions of a 1950s organization man hardly hide the challenges that more individualistic aspirants face, sometimes less successfully than *Shark Tank* would have us believe.

There is a yawning gap between how the Sharks portray themselves and are portrayed, on the one hand, and how they operate their enterprises. Some evidence to the contrary aside, on the television shows and in business magazines and on social media, the Sharks appear to be Lone Ranger investors and entrepreneurs who sometimes join with one or more peers who somehow seem to disappear in post-*Tank* appearances. The wannabes they place their faith and funds in may well come in and remain on teams, often ones composed of friends and family members. But when the Sharks make public appearances, typically they are not joined by lawyers, accountants, operations managers, vice presidents for this or that, or even administrative assistants. Usually hidden from view are the complicated bureaucratic structures, ranks of support staff, experts from inside and outside their firms, and meetings where strategies are debated and decisions made. In practical and specific terms, Sharks help less-seasoned business executives gain access to people who can assist in solving production or distribution problems, help with cash flow, arrange licensing deals, identify additional ways of spreading the word about a product or service, and provide entry into new venues, such as big-box stores.

Most kinds of real sharks, hammerheads excepted, do not swim in schools. The Sharks who cruise and bite on television do swim in schools — sometimes with other Sharks but more often with a wide variety of managers, consultants, accountants, and other support staff. Thus, while O'Leary says "I was born to work for myself" and insists on being "in charge of [his] own destiny," in the acknowledgments of one book, not unlike what Ken Langone did even more fully, he thanked "the hundreds of people" he had worked with, including business partners, colleagues, investors, members of his management teams, "TV compatriots," family members, and the writers and publishers who made the book itself possible.[44]

Corcoran went by herself to Maine to celebrate the success of Cousins Maine Lobsters. Greiner appeared at a big-box store to shine a spotlight on her products. John walked around his old neighborhood with Mo of Mo's Bows. At a conference, O'Leary encountered someone who lost on the show and then struck a new deal with him. Herjavec was pictured promoting Natural Grip, wraps that protect weight trainers' hands. Cuban was shown tossing a football with a pitcher who convinced him to invest in Rent Like a Champion. However dramatic and appealing these images are, what they capture is the enterprising entrepreneur and investor as an individualist, not as a modern organization man or woman. It is ironic that the Sharks, whose on-screen performances as individualistic entrepreneurs parallel the advice they offer to aspirants, off-screen become organization men and women—not exactly as William H. Whyte portrayed the white, male version in 1956, but organization men and women nonetheless.

Outside the Tank

A look at how the Sharks operate on-screen and off does not provide a fully accurate picture of the broader worlds of American entrepreneurship. Multiple efforts underlie, reflect upon, and amplify what appears on the show. These range from multibillion-dollar global corporations to grade-school imitations of the reality TV show, with coverage by old and new media in between. All of this, along with the entrepreneurial activities more centrally related to the activities of pitchers and Sharks, offers windows into some elements of contemporary American enterprises. If large corporations undergird and profit from *Shark Tank*, media coverage and imitation competitions make it possible to gauge its impact and understand the many ways it appeals.

A discussion of *Shark Tank*–related enterprises begins at the top with the powerful corporations that launch, support, and broadcast episodes. The relationships are complicated enough to keep hundreds of lawyers busy and this historian puzzled but hard at work: The Japanese company Sony owns the franchise. Two sprawling American corporations air the program. The Walt Disney Company owns ABC, which offers new episodes. Beginning in 2013 multiple weekly rebroadcasts have been shown on CNBC, part of NBCUniversal, which is owned by Comcast.[1] Down the broadcasting lines are YouTube and Hulu, each owned by behemoth corporations, which together make the work of this researcher both easier and more time consuming and enable anyone around the world to watch almost any *Shark Tank* episode at any time. If large multinational corporations profit from reality TV, so too does Mark Burnett. Over time he has come to hold commanding positions at or near the top of a rapidly shifting and complicated web of business organizations that include the Hearst Corporation, MGM, and United Artists Media Group.

CNBC specializes in shows like *Shark Tank* as it deploys the motto Get Yours, presumably encouraging viewers to succeed in their pursuit of the American dream. As if to build on an assumption that there is a clear line between legitimate and illegitimate enterprises, the cable network developed reality TV shows on both sides of that line. *American Greed* (2017), about highly problematic get-rich-quick schemes, features clearly illegal ventures. On the other side of the line between the kosher and the *traife* are abundant offerings. First, there are shows that focus on the working, middle, and upper middle classes. *Billion Dollar Buyer* (2016) features Tillman Fertitta offering small-business owners the chance to improve and then sell their products. On *The Profit* (2013), Marcus Lemonis decides whether to work with and invest in businesses that are struggling to make a go of it. When he does, he enters the fray with gusto, focus, and dramatic force. *Back in the Game* (2019) features New York Yankees star and successful businessman Alex Rodriguez helping athletes navigate the challenges they face after they stop playing on the field, court, or ice. *Undercover Boss* (2012), originating on CBS and rebroadcast on CNBC, is an Emmy Award–winning show in which corporate executives disguise themselves and work at low-level jobs in the companies they normally run from on high. An episode culminates when the boss, no longer disguised, meets with the underlings he or she encountered and rewards them with the fruits of paternalistic capitalism—a pattern more common on reality TV than in actual reality. Further along the class-defined chain of success is *Blue Collar Millionaires* (2015), which combines reality TV and documentaries and features people who have risen from humble origins.

Then we move to the top of CNBC's ladder of riches, shows that feature the fruits of the American dream. *Jay Leno's Garage* (2015) presents the retired late-night TV host exploring the pleasures of owning and driving expensive automobiles. *Filthy Rich Guide* (2014) focuses on how billionaires spend their fortunes: for example, in the premiere episode, entrepreneur Charles Shaker runs up a $500,000 bar tab in Monte Carlo. *Secret Lives of the Super Rich* (2013) features an inside look at the lifestyles of the super wealthy, not only the usual yachts, mansions, specialty automobiles, and extravagant collectibles but also bizarre indulgences, such as an apartment decorated wall to wall with dead animals.

In addition to the many corporations directly involved in the production and distribution of *Shark Tank* are those that report on and analyze it. The media plays a critical role in amplifying the reach of *Shark Tank* and provides windows into its popularity and how viewers respond to it.[2]

Much of what dominates the coverage of *Shark Tank* in the *Wall Street Journal* and the *New York Times* are either human interest stories or articles that use *Shark Tank* as a model or metaphor for intense competition.[3] The *Wall Street Journal* uses episodes (which are often mentioned only briefly) to illustrate more general themes, such as the impact of the Great Recession, the competition for tech talent, or the problematic nature of Donald Trump's pre-presidential business deals. Like other business publications, it also reviews episodes to mention lessons that viewers can learn. On offer are the inside scoop and "secrets," which are actually available to anyone who reads the books by Sharks, surfs the web, or watches the show.[4] Then there are stories that provide contrasting assessments of a show's value. In a September 2013 roundtable discussion on a range of issues, one participant remarked that the program was among his "guilty pleasures." "In a weird way," he said, "I find it to be a reasonably accurate caricature of the corporate decision-making process for funding new ventures, in which the sharks use both analytics and intuition to evaluate a proposal."[5]

As if to prove that its coverage was fair and balanced, exactly one year after the 2013 roundtable the *Wall Street Journal* published a well-informed critique of the show. The article's anonymous author noted that in a university class he taught on entrepreneurship, students did not recognize "where reality stops and entertainment begins." The episodes were "shockingly devoid of positive lessons for real-world entrepreneurs," the writer said, and instead perpetuated "destructive startup myths." The author also pointed out that the show's formula featured a series of sped-up pitches and decisions rather than the more deliberative considerations that took place in the real world, and that the show emphasized appealing ideas rather than "the entrepreneur's ability to create value via effective execution."[6]

Another rare example of extended criticism (however ambiguous) in any media outlet was a September 2017 *New York Times Magazine* article by Jaime Lowe on *Shark Tank* as a show about "trickle-down economics if trickle-down economics actually worked, a Potemkin village dedicated to the wonders of capitalism." Lowe had grown up in a household where President Ronald Reagan "was a hated capitalist pig." Her experience working for a venture capitalist's daughter, who benefitted from her father's nepotistic favoritism, extended her youthful education and convinced her that "American capitalism was a fallacy built on the concept of equality" in which privilege was passed on from generation to generation. She knew that venture capitalists, most of them white men, usually invested in companies that reaped "ungodly returns" for investors at the same time that they destroyed middle-class jobs. Yet Lowe enjoyed *Shark Tank*'s "comforting, inclusive form of capitalism in action," even though, or perhaps because, she knew it presented an inaccurate picture, an "equal-opportunity forum" that miraculously "[recast] a brutal economic system in its best light" by dramatizing "a romantic vision of our economy, depicting it as a bootstrap meritocracy." She ended her smart essay, which bristled with unresolved tensions, by remarking, "Even if 'Shark Tank' is propaganda—the selling and marketing of the American dream—the fantasy feels real. I get to imagine the country as it could be but never really was."[7]

In contrast to skeptical criticism stands "'Shark Tank': A Celebration of the American Dream—and of Capitalism," published in the *National Review* in 2013. This essay hyped the show as one that embodied an egalitarian and inspirational vision. The author was Lee Habeeb, vice president of content on a Christian radio network. "The American Dream is a co-star ... along with another co-star called the free enterprise system," wrote Habeeb, "which allows for such dreams to happen in the first place. Indeed, it may just be that capitalism itself is the biggest star of all on 'Shark Tank.' And there is nothing more American than that."[8]

Especially striking but hardly surprising is how extensively major business publications such as *Forbes* and *Entrepreneur* cover *Shark Tank*.[9] These magazines regularly run profiles of Sharks and contestants and have also published advice on how to get on the show, how to develop a compelling marketing strategy, and how to build a successful business. They breathlessly offer lists such as "Killer Quotes from *Shark Tank* Stars," "Golden Tips" for startups, and "13 Best *Shark Tank* Episodes of All Time." The vast majority of the stories are celebratory; rather than addressing the broader conditions that shape business, they extol generic values such as ambition, grit, and vision.[10]

Writing in *Forbes* in the fall of 2016, journalist Emily Canal offered a notable exception. Surveying 237 of the 319 business owners who accepted deals on air during the show's first seven seasons, she found that 43 percent of the deals collapsed, often because a Shark changed the terms significantly enough that the agreement was no longer attractive to the aspiring entrepreneur. In the other 57 percent of cases, the deal was consummated, sometimes with Sharks securing modifications than enhanced their position. Mark Cuban was the most reliable one; he closed 87.5 percent of the deals he struck on air. In contrast, Barbara Corcoran, Lori Greiner, and Robert Herjavec ultimately completed about half their on-air deals. Yet all was not lost for the pitchers who failed to walk away with deals. The publicity generated by merely appearing on the show could bring bountiful results, a factor that helped make it possible for 87 percent of those who exited empty-handed to continue operating their business. Similarly, success was often possible even for businesses whose on-air deals were not later consummated.[11]

Later, in the fall of 2018, Canal, now writing in *Inc.*, offered the results of her systematic study of the first nine seasons, which used somewhat different metrics. Looking at more than 250 pitchers who appeared on *Shark Tank*, including those that failed to secure a deal, she showed that appearance on the show significantly boosted revenues, especially in later seasons. This made sense because as the show had become "a cultural mainstay and ratings increased, so too did its promotional oomph and the returns of founders who braved its turbulent waters."[12]

The most recent and comprehensive analysis of the show appeared on a relatively new business and tech news site, the Hustle. Journalist Zachary Crockett relied on the research of angel investor and *Shark Tank* fan Halle Tecco to examine the patterns that held for the show's first ten seasons. In 222 episodes, there were 895 pitches; 56 percent of them resulted in a deal, though it was not clear if that figure represents all on-screen deals or only those that were fully consummated. Sharks invested $143.8 million in those ten seasons; Cuban struck the most deals and invested the most money. However, he was by far the wealthiest Shark, and his commitments to *Shark Tank* entrepreneurs represented only 1 percent of his net worth, while Greiner's amounted to an estimated 22 percent of hers. The most common categories invested in, at 55 percent, were food, fashion, and lifestyle. The fact that less than a quarter of the deal makers were women while 36 percent of American business owners are women (although only 2.2 percent of venture capital deals are made with women) means that female entrepreneurs "were under-represented even in the manicured landscape of reality television." Moreover, women gave up more equity and secured less capital than men.[13]

An article pondering the meaning of *Shark Tank*'s success appeared in *Inc.* at the end of July 2015. The headline writer had a field day, calling the show "the new 'American Idol'" and claiming that it had turned "America into 'Shark Tank' nation." Below the headline, the journalist Graham Winfrey cited four reasons for the show's success. First, Mark Cuban brought celebrity status and new energy to the screen. Second, the program, Winfrey said inaccurately, was "completely unscripted" and "a *real* reality show." Third, inspiring viewers to imagine what they might invent, proposed innovations were infectious, especially when it came to simple consumer products. Finally, unlike *Survivor* and *Keeping Up with the Kardashians*, the program appealed to "everybody ... because entrepreneurship is a core American value." The article ended on an upbeat note with a quote from a supervising casting producer: "It's not a guilty pleasure.... It's a pleasure."[14]

Most online-only news sources that cover the business world offer material similar to what appears in print: features covering the Sharks and pitchers, as well as lists, especially those offering how-to advice gleaned from episodes and from the Sharks themselves.[15] Business Insider, a business news site launched in 2009 that has both global reach and an American focus, has published well over 1,000 stories on the show, and they fall into the usual categories of lists, recaps, and praise.[16] It also offered at least one article critical of *Shark Tank*. It focused on Scott Jordan, who in 2012 successfully pitched his tech-enabled line of clothing but exited empty-handed because he was unwilling to give away the amount of equity the Sharks insisted upon. Several years later, he told a reporter that appearing on *Shark Tank* was, "to say the least," an "idiotic" way to raise money. He did not think all the time it took to prepare was worth it because so few of the applicants ever appeared on air, and those who did could hardly be sure they would secure a commitment from the Sharks. Instead, Jordan advised, it was better to pitch one's idea to friends and family or draw on home equity. "There are lots of business lessons to be learned" from the show, he concluded, "but do not believe that what you see on TV is what is happening."[17]

Sites such as Facebook, Tumblr, YouTube, Instagram, and Twitter, podcasts, and fan discussion boards offer hundreds of thousands if not millions of posts about *Shark Tank*.[18] Especially striking is how intensely personal most posts are. Speaking from the gut, often rushing and not worrying about spelling or grammar, viewers focus on personalities, performances, and products. Abundantly present are inside-dopesterism, listiness, not-so-secret secrets, how-to advice, intense personalism, celebrity fawning, and human interest stories. Despite a few outliers, much of the coverage of *Shark Tank* focuses appreciatively and chattily on entrepreneurship in ways that highlight the role of celebrities, the abundance of opportunity, and importance of risk-taking. The vast majority of the posts are by armchair second-guessers who evaluate pitches, products, and investment decisions. They describe their watching as an indulgence in a guilty pleasure and relish being sideline spectators who talk back to the television program as they offer their own judgments.

Striking among all the postings on social media and websites was how ordinary people used these platforms to associate themselves and their dreams with *Shark Tank*. Successful pitchers celebrated past appearances and the successes they brought, and future pitchers called attention to their upcoming appearances. Sometimes pitchers told of an apparent defeat turned into a victory. For example, on the show, Kevin O'Leary talked of how the two African American women behind the Lip Bar, which offered brightly colored lipsticks made from natural ingredients, would be crushed like the cockroaches they were. Yet one of the entrepreneurs, Melissa Butler, appeared on several websites in a promotional video that told how "The Lip Bar Went from a *Shark Tank* Rejection to a $400k Brand." This was a case of someone who, according to the words that streamed across the bottom of the video, wanted to "give women the courage to be who they are."

Similarly redolent of aspirations the program prompted were postings that revealed a connection between a Shark and a celebrity-seeking fan. "I met Mark Cuban backstage while they were shooting a 'Shark Tank' episode!" a fan enthusiastically posted on Instagram. "Mark seemed to be quite approachable," she continued, and she concluded by quoting some of his aphorisms, such as "Every no gets me closer to a yes." "Who's a fan at @SharkTankABC?" wrote a young woman who posted a picture of herself with Corcoran. "Look who I ran into while skiing?♥ #SharkTank." Aspiring entrepreneurs often use the program's official Facebook site to pitch their ideas. Again and again, "financial strategist" Louie Frias made an appearance: for example, he posted a picture of himself standing in front of a sign for a *Shark Tank* open call at the Consumer Electronics Show in Las Vegas and hyping RescueMeTonight.com as the "app of the year." Stories of inventions people have developed and hope to promote on the show are quite common. "I have a successful lemonade stand and am looking to expand. I'm seeking 1 million dollars," joked someone who well understood some of the exaggeration the show and its pitchers relied on.

The abundant attention lavished on personalities and products stands in contrast to the general lack of evidence that watching the show has enabled viewers to learn about entrepreneurship specifically or the economy more generally. It is not difficult to imagine that a frequent viewer, or even an occasional one, could obtain a sophisticated education about valuation, negotiation, risk, and learning from mistakes. To be sure, while some commenters claimed that "the show is the real life not practice," others saw artifice and staging that were more valuable as entertainment than as information. "Have to say it's great, comedic gold even," remarked one observer. "Haven't jeered this hard for a long time." Yet relatively rarely did anyone point to something specific that they learned. More frequent were remarks that echoed the inspirational more than the practical. "Dude. Fantastic story and completely inspirational" was how one person responded to a pitcher who lost out on the show only to have Herjavec turn to him later on. "Congrats u guys are making America great again," responded another, using a political reference common after 2016.

Despite the frequency with which Burnett and the Sharks sling around invocations of the American dream, rarely do postings on these sites mention such a theme. There are exceptions. In response to a tweet by Cuban, a woman wrote, "Me and my 8yr old son watch it every night I want him to see how you the sharks make the American Dream come true with hard work every day!!" In contrast, in 2016 "Latverian Diplomat" admonished Cuban on the Primetimer forums for asserting "that hard work alone separates success from failure. . . . This is just not how life works," especially since Cuban "owes most of his fortune to being in the right place at the right time, even though what he sold (broadcast.com) did not pan out for the company (yahoo!) that bought it." He no doubt worked hard, the commenter allowed, "but he is just as easily the poster boy for being lucky."[19]

If explicit and extensive critiques are relatively rare, spoofs and jokes are somewhat more frequent, making it clear that followers of the program can be critical. "Thinking of going on shark tank show to pitch my notebook of 93 poems," wrote one person on Twitter. On Tumblr, "justdickingabout" posted a list of "failed business ventures," albeit not specifically linked to *Shark Tank*, that included stapler rentals, sparkling milk, and insect pornography. A stand-up comedian reported that his wife watched so much of the show that when he asked her to go upstairs "and fool around," she said she was too tired and "so for that reason, I'm out." Another comic used Tumblr to try out his routine. "Good evening Sharks!" posted Nick Alexander. "I'm a standup comedian looking for an investment of 2 free drinks for a ten minute share of my comedy routine."

Fans are critics, especially on class and gender issues. Although those who post almost never discuss race or poverty, they do focus on class by commenting on the privilege of some pitchers. Gender dynamics come in for even more commentary. An especially compelling discussion emerged in response to the proposal for the Caddy Girls, an unsuccessful pitch for a service, not very different from Hooters, that provides male golfers with sexy female caddies. Among the most pointed responses was one from "Miss Scarlet," who was disappointed that none of the Sharks remarked on the proposal's bad taste and inappropriateness. "Every time I think the world is moving the slightest bit away from stuff like that," she remarked, "I see something like this.... A lot of women claim that this is actually part of the feminist movement, because these women are making their own decision to do this and feel 'empowered' by it." However, she "completely" disagreed, noting that she "actually had a female professor in graduate school argue with me that this is the 'new feminism' and women have 'this power' and should 'use it.' Puke."

Finally, there are remarkably few—one might say virtually none at all—references by commenters to the wider business and economic world beyond the confines of the show—to the stock market after the waning of the Great Recession, to the challenges posed by shifts in the economy, outsourcing, and globalization, or, aside from specific innovations, to the disruptive power of new technologies. Like many treatments of entrepreneurship, *Shark Tank* has a tendency to make its existence self-contained, largely isolated from external forces, and responses to the show reflect that. To be sure, there are some relatively rare exceptions, including occasional expressions of skepticism about social entrepreneurship and a few critiques of the outsourcing of American jobs, which stand in contrast with the way the Sharks often urge pitchers to manufacture abroad. Nonetheless, like much contemporary scholarly and popular writings on entrepreneurship, viewer comments give little sense of the connections between the micro and macro levels.[20]

Some of the new media sites that focus extensively on early-stage venture funding and *Shark Tank* are uncritical, while others stand back and implicitly critique the show.[21] *Shark Tank Fan Podcast* is the most popular and affectionate of the fan outlets. The hosts, who come across as good old boys, discuss the program in a gee-whiz, informal fashion and focus on personalities of both Sharks and pitchers. With a mixture of skepticism and appreciation, they chattily rehash each episode as they review what the contestants offered and how the Sharks responded. Only at rare moments do they move beyond a casual review to make an evaluative comment.[22]

While it doesn't directly discuss *Shark Tank*, the podcast *The Pitch*, which appears on Gimlet Media, a podcast network founded in 2014, offers some implicit criticisms in the way it seeks to distinguish itself from the show.[23] Begun in 2015, the program features real entrepreneurs pitching their ideas to real investors, just as *Shark Tank* does, but early on it developed a commitment to gender and ethnic diversity.[24] *The Pitch*'s pace is slower and tone more conversational than *Shark Tank*'s, and the investors act more like teachers or advisers than humiliating judges. Two features prominent on *Shark Tank* are notably lacking on *The Pitch*: explicit invocations of the American dream and the presence of celebrities. Moreover, compared with many of those on *Shark Tank*, most of the offerings on *The Pitch* strike me as less niche and cutesy, and with more potential to make the big time.

Then there is Jeremy Alexander, who hosts a popular show called *Shark Tank Breakdown* on his YouTube channel. Animated, articulate, and well-informed, Alexander offers sharper but not very critical evaluations of an episode. On his YouTube channel home page, this self-described "entrepreneur, creator, nice guy" informs viewers, "I like to share my journey as I build my business and this channel by posting the occasional vlog [video blog]."[25] Like some people who talk about *Shark Tank* in media such as podcasts, Alexander is an entrepreneur who is trying to build a career and make a living by responding to episodes of *Shark Tank*. With him and others, we find ourselves in a world of aspiring, adventuresome, market-testing entrepreneurs who use the far more successful Sharks to launch their own businesses.

Knockoff imitations of the show attest to its power and sometimes offer criticism of its clichéd conventions. On November 1, 2014, *Saturday Night Live* presented a spoof of *Shark Tank*.[26] Men dressed as terrorists made a pitch for ISIS with an idea that would "revolutionize the world" as they sought $400 million for 1 percent interest in their enterprise. "Who's ready to invest in crushing the West?" they asked the panel of four imitation Sharks. The faux Cuban began the questioning, inquiring how they arrived at such a high valuation. When told they were making $5 million per day by stealing oil, he responded, "Wow, that is interesting." "It's taking a lot of courage to look you in the eye," commented the faux Corcoran, "and I like that about you." She went on to point out that though the pitchers said they represented ISIS, their brochure said ISIL; "I need a unified brand," she said, at which point faux O'Leary insisted he needed numbers, not a pamphlet. When the terrorists revealed a map of a huge region "of unusable land" that they controlled, Mr. Wonderful's stand-in asked why they could not easily develop a competing brand—proof that the *SNL* writers had nailed O'Leary's approach. Faux John, on the other hand, responded to the news that the pitchers were willing to make FUBU "the official retailer of the Islamic State" with "I'm listening" and a gleeful smile. Faux Cuban declared himself out, saying, "Genocidal regimes are a very tricky business." When faux Corcoran said she had a problem with the company's logo, the terrorists revealed a new one, featuring Geico's gecko. Insisting it would take more than a revised logo to win him over, faux O'Leary declared himself out. Faux Corcoran complimented them on their numbers and savviness but declared herself out because of everything they stood for. Only faux John was still in, and he told the ISIS representatives he knew he could make money from this deal—by bringing onstage representatives from Homeland Security so he could collect the $30 million bounty. Just then three pretend officers came on the stage and took over.[27]

As skillfully as *Saturday Night Live* cracked the show's codes, what more fully conveys *Shark Tank*'s impact and captures key elements of its ideology are the hundreds if not thousands of school and college competitions that imitate it. Schools have developed *Shark Tank*–style competitions for children as young as eight, who came to be known as "kidtrepreneurs."[28] Typically, a teacher engaged in a business-oriented school organization, such as a Young Entrepreneur Club or a STEM Center, helps students prepare to pitch their innovations to local business owners and educators. The students begin their preparation by watching episodes of *Shark Tank* and then develop proposals; compared with those on the show, student proposals are often more community focused—for example, students have pitched a pantry for the homeless filled with hygienic products and a trip to an animal shelter. Although real funding is sometimes at stake, ranging from a hundred dollars to several thousand, the more apparent goal is educational.

School-based *Shark Tank* imitators teach basic economic concepts such as the relationship between supply and demand, how to determine a reasonable valuation, and the importance of developing a sound business strategy. However, more prominent is a focus on pedagogical innovation and student skills: these competitions teach students how to work together on projects, make effective presentations, and solve problems. Many of the participating schools are in the suburbs, but tech entrepreneurs have also sponsored inner-city programs modeled on the ways entrepreneurs in Silicon Valley foster innovation to give "struggling students confidence by exposing them to repeated failures."[29]

Some *Shark Tank*–style competitions exist at the intersection of corporations, government, schools, and foundations. The key federal legislation is Every Student Succeeds, the comprehensive 2015 law that governs K–12 public education. The act established pilot programs that allowed schools to experiment with performance-based assessment, which some advocates envisioned as variations on *The Apprentice* and *Shark Tank* in which students demonstrate what they've learned in front of a panel of judges.[30]

On November 1, 2014, *Saturday Night Live* presented a send-up of *Shark Tank* in which four actors portrayed aspiring entrepreneurs from the terrorist organization ISIS. In its skillful mimicry, the skit attested to the cultural resonance of *Shark Tank*. Here, in the skit's dramatic ending, law enforcement officers arrest the ISIS members so that the faux Daymond John can collect the bounty offered for their capture.

Among the indications of the power of *Shark Tank* specifically and of entrepreneurship generally is the proliferation of *Shark Tank*–style competitions, including in elementary schools. Here, a fifth grader in Corpus Christi, Texas, pitches his product at his school's Entrepreneur Quest competition. Apple White / Alamy Stock Photo.

A prime example of nonprofits and corporations joining with schools to promote entrepreneurship was the Social Innovation Series launched by the software company SAP and GENYOUth, a nonprofit organization that promotes physical health for students and sponsors a student social entrepreneurship program called AdVenture Capital. The Social Innovation Series was a six-city series of one-day workshops in which teenagers with an idea for solving a problem in their school met with SAP employees who helped them prepare a presentation; at the end of the day, the students pitched their idea to a panel of judges, also from SAP, and asked for funding to implement it. "It really brings out that entrepreneurial spirit kids naturally have—the want and need to think big we kind of lost as adults," remarked a spokeswoman for SAP.[31]

Another example of a *Shark Tank* imitator that revealed the intertwined connections between schools, business corporations, and foundations was a conference in Boise, Idaho, in September 2016. The conference was held by America Succeeds, a nonprofit organization that aims to increase schools' focus on business practices, and was sponsored by the J. A. and Kathryn Albertson Family Foundation, a charitable organization built by the family behind the nation's second-largest grocery chain. "Our nation is at a crossroads in the history of public education," representatives of the program announced. "Presidential politics notwithstanding, preparing our students to succeed in the global economy remains our nation's highest calling and most vexing challenge." At the invitation-only meeting, the main event was a competition modeled on *Shark Tank* in which philanthropic Sharks, such as representatives from the Gates Foundation, heard from organizations offering breakthrough innovations designed to overcome "the obstacles that lie between the unacceptable status quo and educational excellence for all kids."[32]

The ideology of entrepreneurship underlying such endeavors is only partially hidden in the language of partnerships, pedagogy, and global competition the nonprofits and corporations use. Yet at key moments, the larger implication of these programs becomes clear. In May 2015, *Money* magazine reported on a class modeled on the *Shark Tank* that James Kindle taught to middle school students at Sullivan Community School in Minneapolis. "I want to give my students a taste" of the American dream, Kindle remarked, "while teaching persuasive language, entrepreneurship, and financial literacy skills."[33]

Even more pervasive and ideologically inflected than what I witnessed in San Ramon at DECA meetings are *Shark Tank*-like competitions at colleges and universities. From struggling community colleges in small towns to Yale University's School of Management, hundreds if not thousands of institutions of higher education hold competitions based to varying extents on the TV show. These are often sponsored by an organization, such as the Emerging Entrepreneurs Club at Catawba Valley Community College in North Carolina; by an academic unit such as the Program in Entrepreneurship and Innovation at Lake Forest College in Illinois; or by a department or school of business. The judges range from owners of local small businesses to major corporate or governmental figure; the competitions are often sponsored by local business owners or successful alumni; and the prizes can go as high as $10,000.

Key to the proliferation of *Shark Tank* imitators is the dramatic explosion of programs, majors, minors, institutes, departments, and schools of entrepreneurship whose title includes the word *innovation*. An especially impressive, if ultimately and unintentionally ironic example of a *Shark Tank*–style competition was the Deac (short for "Demon Deacon," the school's mascot) Tank Competition at Wake Forest University, sponsored by the Center for Innovation, Creativity, and Entrepreneurship.[34] With an impressive set based on the television show's, the event featured Michael and Laura Dweck, cofounders of Basic Outfitters, a company offering men's clothing, even though when they appeared on *Shark Tank* they failed to make a deal because the Sharks chastised them for sitting on too much inventory and having already bargained away too much equity.

Like K–12 competitions, those at colleges and universities often lie at the nexus of government, foundations, higher education, and corporations. For example, at Penn State an annual competition modeled on *Shark Tank* is part of "the Inc.U development and entrepreneurial initiative," which supports local businesses and is underwritten by the Pennsylvania Technical Assistance Program and funded by money from the federal Economic Development Administration.[35] Prominent on the national scene is Future Founders, which supports nationwide *Shark Tank*–style competitions. In December 2016, it sponsored its second annual U.Pitch competition, an elevator pitch competition for college students, held at a Luxury Collection Hotel in Chicago and featuring Daymond John as one of those judging which of six finalists from colleges around the nation would take home a portion of the $10,000 prize. Future Founders touts itself as a nonprofit organization "that believes every youth can become an entrepreneur" and creates "experiences that inspire and empower [students] to create their own opportunity. We believe this leads to a generation more determined, hopeful and equipped as they engage the future." Having served over 33,000 students, from those in elementary schools to those in college,

Future Founders is supported by marquee corporations such as Motorola, Blackstone, Capital One, Bank of America, Ford, and Accenture.[36]

What frames and inspires these *Shark Tank* knockoffs are the challenges of achieving the American dream in a world transformed more by worldwide competition than new technologies. "As new centers of power emerge in the global economy," read the announcement of Long Island's Farmingdale State College, "the capacity of our region and state to 'grow our own' innovative products and services, startup companies and good quality jobs continues to gain in importance." In that context, key "to sustaining and enhancing our nation's leadership in science and engineering" was "fostering entrepreneurial talent" on the local level, a project in which colleges and universities play a critical role. Specifically, Farmingdale's Dare to Risk Entrepreneurship competition encouraged "student entrepreneurs to self-identify" and provided them with "tools and resources to develop their fledgling ventures."[37] The emphasis on competing globally occurred in the content of struggles to sustain the American dream. Pitch competitions "are like the American dream," one supporter on a Dolphin Tank competition, the playful name the Michigan Women's Foundation gave to its competitions, said of their appeal. "Everyone has a dream, and pitch competitions let you talk about your dream and share something you believe will make a difference. It's just so much fun, energizing and inspiring to hear people articulate what they are dreaming about."[38]

On old and new media, the responses to representations of entrepreneurship, from those on the award-winning television show itself to more amateur grade-school iterations, both elide and reveal many dimensions of early-twenty-first-century American entrepreneurship. Labor unions are out of the picture in most renderings, even more so than they are in reality. Poverty is portrayed as something people can overcome with grit and determination. The federal government makes an appearance infrequently, principally but not very prominently in its role in granting patents or approving drugs. Globalization shows up not as unskilled labor or inexpensive goods coming into the United States but as highly skilled immigrants who become pitchers and as opportunities for sales or manufacturing abroad.

Compared with what the show itself features, especially puzzling is how few commentators mention the Great Recession or the American dream. In addition and not unrelated, it's striking how rarely posters on websites and writers in a wide range of media offer critical assessments of the show. Early on, the working title of this book was *TV Capitalism: How Television Teaches Americans about How the Economy Works*, but as I did more research, I realized two things. First, *Shark Tank* is about entrepreneurship, a specific and historically situated form of capitalism. Second, the show is minimally about education and overwhelmingly about entertainment—which I realized as I saw how personalism and listiness dominated responses. The producers and Sharks may want to teach audience members about the vitality of the American dream, and it is certainly possible that viewers learn about this despite how little they reference it. Surely the impact of the Great Recession shaped people's responses, even though there is little evidence for this in responses and commentary. Entertainment has subliminal power, a way of embedding its messages so deeply in the culture that they need not be referenced. Moreover, reality TV evokes responses that are reassuring rather than critical because that is what often unreal media does.

Shark Tank in all its iterations, but especially on the show itself, gives an expansive if often glossy and overly optimistic picture of American enterprises. Billionaires are present in *Shark Tank* and the corporations that make it possible, as well as in the hopes of third graders. There may be a gap between the least wealthy Shark and the most successful pitcher, but the promise is always on the horizon that the investment and wisdom of a Shark will soon close that gap. There is some bathos and pathos, but more hope and triumph. Failure is less present on the show than in reality: almost a third of all new businesses fail in the first two years and half in the first five. The fallout of the Great Recession colors some episodes, but there are more happy endings than sad ones. Unpredictability plays a larger role in reality than on reality TV. In short, *Shark Tank* captures vivid and varied dimensions of the world we live in, but what it shows is an incomplete and abundantly rosy prospect of what the pursuit of the American dream can bring. There is almost no evidence of illegal enterprises on the show, although sometimes Sharks suspect that is in the offing from pitchers.

Although Mark Burnett is connected to national and global corporations, *Shark Tank* itself betrays remarkably little presence of major enterprises. There's almost no mention of Wall Street banks, Fortune 500 companies, private equity firms, or hedge funds. Nor are there glimmerings of industrial-scale farms, extractive industries such oil or coal, or extensive domestic factories and warehouses. Practical applications rather than basic research loom large. Big-box stores appear not as powerful institutions but as venues where customers can find niche products. New technologies, online shopping ones especially, show up not as disruptive forces but as spurs to sales of pitched products.

Some scholars assert that new media, especially online, opens up arenas for critical and interactive discussions. This can be so even though audience involvement in the form of podcasts, fan sites, and other responses relies on unpaid labor; powerful corporations often promote and benefit from such exchanges; and the relationships between producers and consumers range from the adversarial to the reciprocal. At its most robust, this line of argument, as seen in the work of media studies scholar Henry Jenkins, highlights the fact that fan responses can be participatory, creative, collaborative, and even oppositional.[39] "The power of participation," Jenkins writes, "comes not from destroying commercial culture but from writing over it, modding it, amending it, expanding it, adding greater diversity of perspective, and then recirculating it, feeding it back into mainstream media."[40] Along somewhat similar lines, in an influential essay cultural theorist Stuart Hall discusses three ways those viewing media might respond: adhering to the dominant or preferred readings advocated by the powerful, finding more mixed or negotiated responses, or crafting entirely oppositional analyses.[41] Scholars claim that new media provides low-cost or no-cost open spaces where people are free to express and debate their opinions, where activism and criticism are abundant.

However, an examination of the most prominent coverage of *Shark Tank* in new media reveals a more complicated, less adversarial, and even reciprocal picture. Probing and often oppositional responses clearly occur when intensely involved fans engage with programs like *Survivor* or *Big Brother* that are not produced the way *Shark Tank* is and that rely on carefully selected amateur contestants whose narratives unwind over a season. In contrast, a structured reality television show like *Shark Tank* takes place in a studio, relies on a small number of highly skilled performers backed by a vast production team, and features self-contained episodes. This difference may help explain why the evidence shows that most people who track *Shark Tank* through Facebook, Twitter, Instagram, podcasts, and blogs are more casual viewers than fully engaged fans, people who revel in platitudes rather than engage in protests, critical analysis, or interactive exchanges. These platforms overwhelmingly feature hyped attention to *Shark Tank* rather than vigorous and meaningful debate or exchanges that are reciprocal and capacious.[42] As second-guessers, most armchair spectators take pleasure not in careful analysis and robust criticism but in displaying how smart and engaged they are. The media scholar John Fiske calls this "enunciative productivity" and says that fans create a "culture with its own systems of production and distribution" that makes up a "'shadow cultural economy' that lies outside that of the culture industries yet shares features with them" as they develop their own socially shared identity as viewers and at the same time signal their membership in a specific community of fans.[43]

Although there are some exceptions, members of *Shark Tank*'s audience seem engaged individualistically rather than collaboratively, communally, or reciprocally.[44] What usually dominates the responses of viewers and discussants is not adversarial challenges or even highly creative playfulness but fascination with personalities, lists of favorites, the pursuit of how-to advice, and the subjectivity of personalism. As the media scholar Annette Hill has argued, those who watch reality TV participate in an "experience economy" in which corporations sell "interaction and emotional engagement" through "an emotional identification with performers and their 'journey' through the competition."[45]

Ironically, some writers in traditional print media and the business press are more likely to look critically at *Shark Tank* than are their new media counterparts.[46] As the sociologist Joshua Gamson has remarked in a different context, for "conventional news operations . . . maintaining a reputation as independent pursuers of facts remains more critical for sales than celebrity information and images." The situation is different for writers who have cozy relationships with industry publicists and rely on them for access and information. "Giving in to publicists' power," Gamson notes, "undermines the bases of many journalists' professional identities: access to investigation is largely blocked, the possibilities of writing a textured or nuanced story impeded, interpretation and analysis discouraged, the integrity of free and creative expression compromised." The result is that information is often presented "in a standardized, controlled, packaged form."[47]

In the end, the vast majority of viewers are people who watch in order to be entertained rather than educated. Perhaps at some deep but not readily apparent level, the power of neoliberalism has anesthetized them, preventing them from understanding the connections between what they see on *Shark Tank* and the transformation of the social and economic worlds swirling around them. This could go a long way toward explaining why they so rarely refer to the American dream or the Great Recession. Perhaps the format of social media also discourages more thoughtful responses. Yet it is also possible that, as powerful and entertaining entertainment, *Shark Tank* promotes not only escape but also pleasure, guilty or not. The notion that fans of reality TV are "suckers who watch uncritically," television critic James Poniewozik astutely notes, "misses a key point: no one more strongly believes that 'reality TV isn't reality' than its fans," who talk back to the screen and second-guess the producers by trying to figure out what is going on behind the scenes.[48] *Shark Tank* provides soothing reassurance and problematic escape, as well as pleasurable and exciting entertainment. Although some of the responses to it are trite and fawning, others reveal the power of well-informed and skeptical critiques.

Enterprising Organizations

A variety of organizations undergird and represent American entrepreneurship. However, none does so more completely than Babson College in Wellesley, Massachusetts, whose primary purpose is to provide students with an education in the full range of business and management. Its faculty's research, its students' achievements, and the breadth of its extracurricular efforts reveal what an enterprising organization encompasses. On September 21, 2018, I made the first of several trips to Babson so that I could begin the process of getting to know institutions that focus significantly on entrepreneurship. My visit to this unfamiliar territory introduced me to the robust complement of strategies that institutions deploy to foster entrepreneurship. The Babson College library made it easy for me to read academic and popular publications on the subject. The institution's curriculum enabled me to see what a state-of-the-art education in the field is like. Its extracurricular and outreach activities, some of them supported by foundations, provided ample evidence of the college's emphasis on innovation, disruption, and ingenuity. The campus was alive with ventures that promised that there was money to be made and social benefits to be achieved through entrepreneurship. The history of Babson College both anticipated and presented in full flower what has happened in other locations. To be sure, other institutions of higher education

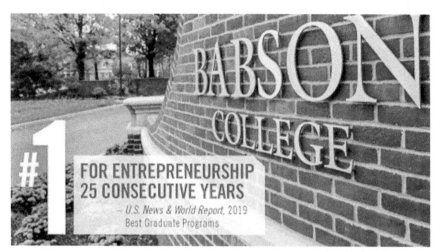

In its curricular, extracurricular, and outreach efforts, Babson College robustly represents the full range of entrepreneurial efforts. Here, an image posted to the college's Twitter account on March 20, 2018, advertises Babson's achievements in entrepreneurship education. @babson, March 20, 2018, https://twitter.com/babson/status/976102681436655616.

also have significant entrepreneurial ecosystems and cultures. However, I focus on Babson here because it concentrates more on entrepreneurship than any other college or university.

Disseminating Entrepreneurial Culture

On campus and elsewhere I could catch glimpses of the powerful and varied ways the word about entrepreneurship is spread. Magazines and their accompanying websites that hype the field include *Entrepreneur* (1977), *Inc.* (1979), and *Fast Company* (1995). They resemble other, more general business-oriented outlets in their celebratory emphasis on lists, personalities, and how-to advice. Book publishers also play prominent roles in the field's promotion. I like to joke that for writing my books, I earn six cents an hour, perhaps an accurate figure. However, if I'd chosen a different, more lucrative path, I could have called this book *TV Entrepreneurship!!: 37 Steps to Riches and Happiness* or *You Too Can Become a Millionaire Entrepreneur: How I Gave Up Being a Professional Historian and Discovered a Path to Wealth.*

Textbooks, including those published by Babson faculty members, are another important outlet and echo many of the themes articulated elsewhere in this book.[1] Like others who advocate the importance of entrepreneurship, their authors emphasize risk, tenacity, initiative, opportunity, and innovation. Speaking in a more mundane and practical mode, a stu-

143

dent wrote this on the top of the title page of my copy of the 2010 edition of a textbook on entrepreneurship: "Figure out the max I can produce $$." The authors of another widely used textbook took the high ground in the first sentence as they offered celebratory exaggerations. "Entrepreneurship," they boasted, "is the most powerful force known to mankind! The 'entrepreneurial revolution' that has captured our imagination during the last decade has now permeated every aspect of business thinking and planning." The American economy, they continued, "has been revitalized because of the efforts of entrepreneurs, and the world has turned now to free enterprise as a model for economic development. The passion and drive of entrepreneurs move the world of business forward" as "they challenge the unknown and continually create the future."[2]

Babson is a particularly concentrated site for entrepreneurial culture, but it has parallels elsewhere. For example, the University of Central Florida in Orlando has its Center for Entrepreneurial Leadership, which supports a full panoply of enterprising activities in imaginative ways, including helping dozens of students a year launch their companies by linking them with relevant community members, organizing pitch competitions, and every few weeks hosting an event that features students' innovative work. The University of Central Florida's program asserts that "*entrepreneurship leadership capabilities* are essential to creating value, making a difference, and experiencing personal and professional fulfillment" in ways "that enrich our lives, our economy, and our society."[3]

Student interest in entrepreneurial education has grown dramatically even as not only the Sharks but also many academics (including professors in traditional fields in business schools) have called into question the legitimacy of formal education in entrepreneurship. Yet the Darden School of Business at the University of Virginia tells students, "Whether you plan to start a new business or become a catalyst for innovation within an established firm, [our course of study] provides you with the skills and knowledge to become an entrepreneurial leader who will responsibly pursue creative destruction." A program at Smith College emphasizes that "being entrepreneurial is a mindset." Its Conway Center for Innovation and Entrepreneurship lends support to people at the college "who are attracted to opportunities, innovation and value creation," those who are "calculated risk takers" who can "thrive in an ambiguous environment."[4] Similarly, in the summer of 2018 an article about the National Association for Community College Entrepreneurship claimed that "despite a dwindling economy," programs that are members of the association can provide "the secrets to entrepreneurship success" and offer training in "new and innovative forms of entrepreneurial development" that will enhance job growth and economic development.[5]

The entrepreneurial vision also emerges when we look at how thousands of innovation labs (or iLabs), accelerators, and incubators on campuses foster startups and early-stage enterprises. Using a limited-term model, they bring together students, professors, and investors.[6] They are a relatively recent phenomenon whose prominence spread as the Great Recession intensified. Like the innovation centers at Babson, they are supported by corporations, foundations, universities, and government agencies to help launch new ventures. We can locate one origin of this approach in 2005 when the computer scientist, essayist, and venture capitalist Paul Graham launched Y Combinator in Cambridge, Massachusetts, and Silicon Valley; later he closed up shop in Cambridge and consolidated operations in the Bay Area. Another foundational moment came a year later when Techstars, a seed accelerator, was born in Boulder, Colorado. In 2010 it launched Global Accelerator Network (GAN) in conjunction with President Barack Obama's Startup America, a federal effort to foster high-impact entrepreneurship. "We believe," GAN's website announces, "that people will have healthy, fulfilling lives when they have access to economic opportunity and meaningful social connection."[7] Another key institutional moment occurred with the emergence of design thinking, a method for creative problem-solving, at Stanford's d.school. Its website describes this as the university's "place for explorers & experimenters," a "hub for innovation, collaboration, and creativity." As early as the 1950s, people at the university produced the intellectual foundations for a full array of programs based on its principle of creative problem-solving for executives, students, teachers from kindergarten to graduate and professional schools, aspiring entrepreneurs, and those involved in government, nonprofit, and corporate organizations. "Newfound creative confidence," the promotional material for Stanford's d.school claims, "changes how people think about themselves and their ability to have impact in the world."[8]

Private foundations are major players in the field of entrepreneurship, with Blackstone, Kauffman, and Lemelson (which all have some personal or institutional connection to Babson) among the most important ones with significant national and international reach.[9] Funded by the Blackstone Group, the world's largest investment firm that focuses on alternative opportunities, such as those made possible with hedge funds and private equity investments, Blackstone Charitable Foundation commands attention. It is "committed to inspiring entrepreneurship globally" by "leveraging the resources and intellectual capital of Blackstone," the website claims. "The Foundation empowers entrepreneurs, generates job growth, and supports the communities in which we live and work," its promotional material announces using typically boastful language.[10]

Blackstone's LaunchPad particularly drew my attention because of its reach and how it reveals issues that reverberate through other locations of entrepreneurial activity. It serves as the point of entry for many corporations seeking partnerships with higher education programs by connecting students, mentors, and resources. Built on the belief that skills are better learned through experience than through formal education and that in order for students and America to flourish in a competitive world, education needs to break out of traditional bounds, LaunchPad aims to greatly expand education well beyond the confines of specific programs and courses. LaunchPad's programs are now available to three-quarters of a million students in universities around the world, and its supporters claim, using familiar, even utopian language, that they can transform education by building "inclusive communities, align[ing] the interests of college constituencies and provid[ing] the necessary opportunities for both venture creation and skills acquisition to positively impact students' trajectories well beyond graduation."[11]

Based in Kansas City, Missouri, the Ewing Marion Kauffman Foundation is among the most important nonprofits in the field, though entrepreneurship is but one of its principal focal points. Founded in 1966, it now has an endowment of about $2 billion. Among its programs are those that focus on entrepreneurship through education, websites, global networks, and research into the ways innovation fosters economic growth. Much of what the foundation articulates is familiar enough: optimistically exaggerated claims that focus on empowerment, innovation, and creativity. Yet at least two of its programs stand out. The first is its 2003 Kauffman Campus Initiative, an ambitious effort to "make entrepreneurship a campus-wide experience, to help schools become more entrepreneurial, and to ensure that thousands of students on diverse campuses ... begin to see their own knowledge and resources from a more entrepreneurial perspective."[12] Then there is its emphasis on inclusion. Mr. Kauffman himself, the website claims, "believed it was a fundamental right for anyone who had a big idea to be able to bring it to life." This invocation of Kauffman's vision undergirded the foundation's relatively recent emphasis on a commitment to "break down barriers" that had left "too many" "out of our economy," an effort that addressed how "lackluster productivity" had dragged down American "wages and living standards." The foundation's programs involve "working together with communities and collaborating organizations to level the playing field for entrepreneurs that have been systematically left behind due to demographic, socioeconomic, and geographic barriers," including ones that adversely impacted women and minorities.[13]

Social Entrepreneurship

Although social entrepreneurship, which does good by doing well, has deep historical roots, in the 1990s it emerged as a self-conscious but not centrally organized phenomenon. In 1997 the British writer Charles Leadbeater, at one time an adviser to Prime Minister Tony Blair, authored *The Rise of the Social Entrepreneur*. He asserted, using typical neoliberal language, that with the weakening or even disappearance of the "welfare state," which "was designed for a world of male full-employment and stable families," developed nations were no longer able "to respond effectively to a growing array of social problems—mass long-term joblessness, drugs, family break-up, illiteracy." With radical reforms impossible to achieve and only tinkering with social welfare on the table, he said, what was needed was "a long wave of social innovation to develop a new philosophy, practice and organisation of welfare" that would "create social capital by encouraging people to take greater control of their lives."

Citing the examples of hospitals and churches that developed treatment programs for AIDS patients and people struggling with drug addiction, Leadbeater focused on putting existing "under-utilized resources . . . to use to satisfy unmet social needs." This involved deploying "entrepreneurial skills for social ends," bringing together government agencies and private sector volunteer organizations. As "driven, ambitious leaders," social entrepreneurs created "impressive schemes with virtually no resources." They relied on "a culture of creativity" that promised to deliver "services far more effectively than the public sector" in large measure by setting in motion "a virtuous circle of social capital accumulation" that helped "communities to build social capital which gives them a better chance of standing on their own two feet."[14]

Leadbeater offered an intellectually and organizationally bold version of social entrepreneurship, which some American companies matched in ambition while others were more private and modest. Among the relevant exemplars helped by appearances on *Shark Tank* are Bombas, a company that makes athletic socks, which was founded by Babson alumni and linked sales to charitable offerings; Grace and Lace, a women's clothing operation that devoted some of its profits to supporting an orphanage in India; and Hungry Harvest, which innovatively linked problems facing farmers, sales to the well-to-do, and nutritious food for poor urban dwellers. "So-

Bombas, a sock company developed by Babson alumni, is a successful example of social entrepreneurship: for every pair of socks sold, it donates a pair to organizations that help the homeless. In their pitch, which aired on September 26, 2014, cofounders Randy Goldberg and David Heath used a large visual to remind the Sharks that "one pair purchased = one pair donated."

cial entrepreneurs create ventures that further societal goals," one news article on social entrepreneurship claimed, before going on to mention foundations that promote sustainability, small-scale economic development efforts in the Third World, or world peace.[15] Social entrepreneurs and wealthy philanthropists improve the lives of millions. But their work also highlights the weakening of government-sponsored social welfare systems and the related emergence of volunteerism and self-determination.

Entrepreneurship Central

All these varied endeavors in support of entrepreneurship are vividly on display at Babson College. Compared with the liberal arts colleges where I have taught, such as Scripps and Smith, Babson has a more focused and practical mission, and it emphasizes entrepreneurship education. When I arrived at Babson on that fall day in 2018, I first met with Debi Kleiman, the executive director of the college's Arthur M. Blank Center for Entrepreneurship. I then caught a bite to eat in the building housing the Franklin W. Olin Graduate School, where I discovered several events taking place: By coincidence, that day was the beginning of an alumni reunion, announced as "Back to Babson: You Never Graduate from Good Times." As luck would have it, the annual Young Entrepreneurs Conference was also taking place that day. This event was presented by eTower, a residential program that houses undergraduates "passionate about developing business ideas through the network of peers living" there and is touted as "the heart of entrepreneurship in action at the College." The conference brought together "founders from all over the world" for "4 hours of non-stop value" and included the appearances of several successful alumni. "Get ready for the biggest and best event of the year!" the announcement broadcast boastfully.[16] I also learned that the conference featured a talk by Adam J. Bock, who teaches entrepreneurship at University of Wisconsin–Madison and who has founded a series of life sciences companies. At Babson he was going to "lead students through his 'Innovation Marketplace' to explore why some innovations succeed and others fail."[17]

The Arthur M. Blank Center for Entrepreneurship sponsored Bock's talk. Gradually it dawned on me that the center specifically and the college as a whole represent so many elements of contemporary entrepreneurship— the center is funded by and named for a man who, with Ken Langone and Bernie Marcus, founded Home Depot; Babson fostered the careers of several students who have appeared on *Shark Tank*; its faculty once included Jeffry A. Timmons, one of the key founders of the academic field of entrepreneurship; Babson has global aspirations; and above all, it is an institution whose curriculum and extracurricular activities underscore its aim to be, as its website states, "the preeminent institution in the world for Entrepreneurial Thought & Action."[18]

Babson College both recapitulates key elements of the history of entrepreneurship and provides a window into what higher education in the field looks like elsewhere, almost always in less concentrated form. As much as any institution of higher education in the United States, Babson has pioneered entrepreneurship as a field and has capaciously developed a focus on it. Looking at the school allows us to glimpse what such commitments mean at other colleges and universities and, even more broadly, in American culture.

In 1919 Roger W. Babson, a serial entrepreneur who made his fortune as an economic forecaster, founded the Babson Institute.[19] Almost from the start, he insisted that the institute's education be distinctive, focusing not on lectures but on learning by doing. The college's historian, John R. Mulkern, writes of an initial "one-year intensive training program that immersed students in a simulated business environment … and drilled them in the routines and demands of real (as opposed to theoretical) executive work."[20] Students learned by making sales pitches, examining case studies, going on field trips, and participating in a group conference that resembled what might take place in a corporate boardroom. They had to punch in on a time clock when they entered and left several buildings on campus. In addition, the college's website reveals, students were "assigned an office desk equipped with a telephone, typewriter, adding machine, and Dictaphone. Personal secretaries typed the students' assignments and correspondence in an effort to accurately reflect the business world." Roger Babson, the site concludes, "prepared his students to enter their chosen careers as executives, not anonymous members of the work force."[21]

Over time, many things changed. The college's governance became less autocratic, especially as Babson himself grew older and after he died in 1967. Tuition, initially quite high, fell in line with American norms for private universities. Recruitment of students focused less exclusively on sons who were preparing to take over the family business. The institution grew in size and ambition. The curriculum shifted from an exclusive focus on business to include the liberal arts, and the college went from offering only certificates to bestowing degrees (including graduate ones). The most significant changes began to take hold in the late 1960s. In 1969 male-only Babson Institute became the four-year, coed Babson College and emphasized a capacious view of management that led to careers in private corporations as well as nonprofit and public-sector organizations.

However, from my perspective, the most important change was the emergence in the 1970s of a focus on entrepreneurship. At Babson and in higher education more broadly, entrepreneurship grew in importance in the curriculum in the 1970s and early 1980s partly in response to crises of growth in employment in large and well-established firms. The chronology of events confirms the judgment that those years were critical. At Babson this involved the creation in 1977 of the Academy of Distinguished Entrepreneurs, which honored entrepreneurs from around the world, and a year later the establishment of the Center for Entrepreneurship Studies, apparently the world's first such center. In 1979, almost a decade after the college's first course in entrepreneurial studies was introduced, Babson began offering a major in the field. In 1981 came the Babson College Entrepreneurial Research Conference (BCERC), a prominent meeting of scholars from around the world. The year 1984 saw the establishment of the Price-Babson Symposium for Entrepreneurship Educators (SEE), as well the first undergraduate business plan competition, which was followed three years later by a parallel competition in the MBA program. The ensuing years witnessed the establishment of additional ventures, including the Hatcheries, the Babson College Seed Fund, and the Babson Venture Accelerator Program.[22] These innovations helped keep Babson in its top position in the *U.S. News and World Report*'s ranking of entrepreneurship education programs for a quarter of a century, although in the ranking of MBA programs overall it fell far short of first.

Babsonian Entrepreneurship

From the 1970s on, Babson College committed itself to fostering an entrepreneurial vision that would permeate as many aspects of the institution as possible. Key administrators and faculty members hoped that Babson would not just teach entrepreneurship but also embody it by becoming an agent of change that spread the gospel of entrepreneurship widely. Over time and through different college leaders and constituents, the capaciousness and impact of what entrepreneurship meant for Babson as an institution varied. At its fullest, it involved much more than programs and courses. Fritz Fleischmann, a German-born scholar of American literature and at times a senior administrator at Babson, offered a sense of what it meant to think of entrepreneurship at Babson not just as a central element of the curriculum but as what he called "a way of life." This involved, he wrote, "looking at knowledge holistically and at education as a life-long process that challenges us to reflect on our learning in each stage and connect the different parts." A lofty goal, to be sure, but one he brought down to earth when he insisted, "[It] means living on a construction site; it means that you not only lay out the road, that you maintain the signs and the ditches, but that you are willing to rip it all up from time to time and do it over." With its emphasis on applying values from the world of innovative businesses holistically, this vision promised creativity, passion, risk-taking, teamwork, and the breakdown of boundaries between constituencies on and off campus.[23]

Of course, this sounds at the least optimistic and at the most utopian. Babson College was indeed more successful than institutions that had difficulty integrating entrepreneurship into the well-established disciplinary structure of the curriculum. Yet it should not surprise us that even at Babson there were gaps between institutional aspirations and reality. Some faculty members, especially in the humanities, dissented, although others aligned their commitments with those of the college, in part by making business culture central to their work as teachers and scholars. Nonetheless, there is something unusually optimistic and transformative about the ways people at Babson apply the elements of entrepreneurship developed in business in an institutionally global way. Sometimes "global" means a capacious but vague embrace of everything, and sometimes it means something more literal. And for Babson, thinking globally did involve a problematic venture abroad. In 2016 came an announcement that Babson Global was involved with a college of business and entrepreneurship in Saudi Arabia, the first in the kingdom to offer degrees in entrepreneurship. "The Crown Prince of the Kingdom," the announcement proudly stated, "agreed to lend his name to the college, which has been re-branded 'Crown Prince Mohammad Bin Salman College of Business and Entrepreneurship.'" This cooperative venture, the official statement continued, was "a vital step toward creating an entrepreneurship eco-system in the region that is consistent with King Salman's vision to promote the intellectual development of Saudi citizens."[24] This new venture came when freedom of speech and women's rights were precarious in Saudi Arabia and a little over two years before the CIA concluded that it was highly likely that the crown prince had ordered the assassination of the *Washington Post* journalist Jamal Khashoggi.[25]

As president of Babson from 1974 to 1981, Ralph Sorenson played a crucial role in putting entrepreneurship front and center. Two professors teaching there at the time said he was "the very first college or university president in the world to create a vision and make a strategic commitment to entrepreneurship as a field of education, research, and community outreach."[26] Those words appeared in the dedication to the seventh edition of *New Venture Creation*, a book that, beginning with its first edition in 1977, played a prominent role in defining entrepreneurship. So too did one of its authors, Jeffry A. Timmons, whose pioneering work began in the late 1960s under federal support connected with the War on Poverty.[27] The other author of the seventh edition was Stephen Spinelli, who on July 1, 2019, returned to Babson as its president.

"We are in the midst of a silent revolution, a triumph of the creative and entrepreneurial spirit of humankind throughout the world," Timmons wrote in his 1989 book *The Entrepreneurial Mind* soon after he joined the Babson faculty. He believed "its impact on the 21st century [would] be equal to or exceed that of the Industrial Revolution on the 19th and 20th."[28] That potentially transformative faith reverberated in much of the writing in the field, at Babson and much more broadly. "Students and faculty see the world as it really is," promotional copy for Babson College insisted; they "conceive innovative solutions to its complex human, financial, and environmental challenges."[29] In the best-selling *The Portable MBA in Entrepreneurship*, William D. Bygrave, the Frederick C. Hamilton Professor of Free Enterprise Studies at Babson, rejected Joseph Schumpeter's characterization of entrepreneurship as involving creative destruction. He offered a more all-encompassing definition, one that, by lumping together all small businesses, enabled him to claim that entrepreneurs were responsible for the majority of new jobs in America: they were, he said, the people who saw opportunity and created "an organization to pursue it." He insisted, "This is the age of entrepreneurship," with entrepreneurs "driving a revolution that is transforming and renewing economies worldwide. Entrepreneurship is the essence of free enterprise because the birth of new businesses gives a market economy its vitality."[30] This was an unintentionally ironic statement given that one of the origins of modern entrepreneurship studies, at Babson and nationally, was Timmons's work on federal government-sponsored projects to alleviate poverty among African Americans and poor rural whites. It was also ironic given that contemporary entrepreneurship has resulted in large, monopolistic corporations, such as Google, Amazon, and Microsoft, which may well stifle innovation.

At Babson College today, Heidi M. Neck is the Jeffry A. Timmons Professor of Entrepreneurial Studies and faculty director of the SEE program, which Timmons first developed. She is also one of the authors of a leading textbook in the field, *Entrepreneurship: The Practice and Mindset.* Countering those who see entrepreneurs as narrowly focusing on business, start-ups especially, Neck and her coauthors insist that the biggest category of entrepreneurs are "the drivers of positive change, the ones who use energy, passion and ideas for forces of good, and the ones who will ultimately shape the world in which we live" by contributing to "employment, societal wealth, personal wealth, innovation, economic development." Though only with difficulty can some people see the possibility of entrepreneurship in the midst of economic or natural adversity, it is precisely "this sort of turbulence that often pushes us into creating new opportunities for economic progress." Completing the neoliberal promise, she insists that "anyone—regardless of background, ethnicity, social class, gender, sexual orientation, country, or education—can become an entrepreneur if given the opportunity."[31]

Entrepreneurship is one of ten academic divisions at Babson—and a large one at that, employing as it does twenty-five full-time professors and an equal number of adjuncts/practitioners. Moreover, the college insists that everyone in these categories have entrepreneurial experience. Undergraduates can focus on topics such as the role of founders, social venturing, family venturing, and technology. Among what is distinctive about the college's curriculum is that all undergraduates in their first year must take Foundations of Management and Entrepreneurship. Co-taught by faculty from the Management Division and the Entrepreneurship Division, this award-winning, two-semester, twelve-credit course "provides a year-long immersion into the world of business . . . rooted in theory" but teaching "practical skills and capabilities" in fields such as marketing, accounting, and organizational behavior to teams of students who "invent, develop, launch, manage, and liquidate a business." The college requires that every team devote eighty hours to community service and loans each team $3,000 in seed money to develop a startup. At the end of the year, if they have made a profit, they return the seed money to the college and donate the rest of what they earned to a nonprofit organization.[32]

At Babson, even more expansive than the curriculum are the cocurricular opportunities, coordinated by the Blank Center, another element that connects the college to the larger world of business innovation. The Blank Center's efforts reflect Arthur Blank's own focus on entrepreneurship. As with Langone, who was the grandson of Italian immigrants, the immigrant experience and ethnicity shaped Blank's life: prejudice against Jews dashed his hopes of being a medical doctor, which led him to turn to business instead. Unlike Langone's memoir, the one coauthored by Blank and Bernie Marcus, who along with Lagone dreamed up and founded Home Depot, did not explicitly explore the meaning of success in America or whether they were self-made individuals. But it did talk about what they learned from their experiences in the retail business. Offering many stories but little analysis, they emphasized what entrepreneurship professors now teach at Babson (but perhaps little of what Blank absorbed as a member of Babson's class of 1963): provide leadership for a team, emphasize customer service, focus on merchandising and branding, dominate a market, invert the pyramid so that customers and employees are at the top, counter conventional wisdom, do the right thing by giving back to the community, and focus on shareholder return. In addition, of course, they acknowledged the importance of developing an "entrepreneurial spirit."[33]

Largely under the aegis of the Blank Center, Babson provides a vast array of programs for students and for off-campus audiences in the Boston area, nationally, and around the world. Hundreds of campuses have iLabs, launch pads, or accelerators—and Babson has its own, the John E. and Alice L. Butler Launch Pad, which, like others, connects students, faculty, alumni, and entrepreneurs. Like many of its peers, Babson also arranges internships. It hosts an annual event, Rocket Pitch, where students from Babson, Olin, and Wellesley Colleges practice offering investors a piece of the action. Every spring, the Blank Center sponsors another pitch competition titled the B.E.T.A. (Babson Entrepreneurial Thought and Action) Challenge. There are also specialized programs that zero in on women, global entrepreneurs, social entrepreneurs, educators, and those with interest in food, family businesses, or fashion.

A clear picture of an entrepreneurial vision emerges when we look at the vast array of entrepreneur-supporting organizations, including colleges and foundations. At a time when political divisions are so painfully powerful, they seem to remain apolitical. They usually avoid explicit statements of political ideology or mention the importance of government action as a way of healing the world. They sometimes pay too little attention to the failure rate of new enterprises and even more rarely consider the social costs of creative destruction or whether the world really needs another gadget. Instead, what they broadcast is an optimistic view of the possibilities for innovation, positive social change, and achievement.

We can catch a glimpse of both such expansive visions and the success of Babson graduates from information on their appearances on *Shark Tank*. Many colleges take pride in their students and alumni who appear on *Shark Tank*, and Babson is no exception.[34] There are at least seven such cases. One that we have already encountered is the sock company Bombas, founded by brothers Andrew Heath and David Heath, respectively graduates of Babson's graduate and undergraduate programs, who secured an investment from Daymond John. An example of social entrepreneurship, so far the company has logged over $50 million in sales and donated more than 8 million pairs of socks. The serial entrepreneur Jamie Siminoff, class of 1999, represents one of the biggest prizes that the Sharks were not astute enough to catch when he pitched his enterprise. His company Ring (offered as DoorBot on *Shark Tank*) produces Wi-Fi-enabled video doorbells that connect to smartphones. Siminoff's pitch on the November 15, 2013, episode didn't result in a deal, though Kevin O'Leary made an offer that Siminoff did not accept. Amazon eventually acquired the company for about $1 billion.[35]

Siminoff appeared on *Shark Tank* in early October 2018 as a guest Shark, the first former contestant to return as a Shark. In an article he wrote for *Entrepreneur*—whose headline called him a "self-made billionaire"—Siminoff insisted, "I owe a lot of my American dream to *Shark Tank*." After identifying all the obstacles his company faced, he focused on the three "keys to success": hard work; a mission—in the case of Ring, reducing crime; and luck, which in his case included the boost that his appearance on *Shark Tank* provided. He ended the article by saying it was "a duty and an honor" to return as a Shark and "assist others in achieving their dreams and furthering their missions to hopefully make an impact on the world."[36]

The publicity his company received from Siminoff's appearance on *Shark Tank*, as well as the help he now offered others as a guest Shark, again reminds us that claims of being "self-made" cannot hide how other people and institutions help us achieve our goals. Moreover, the fact that a hugely successful entrepreneur rejected by the Sharks in late 2013 returned as a panelist almost five years later reminds us of the gap between television entrepreneurship and the real thing.

Conflicting Visions of Entrepreneurship

If the work of institutions such as foundations and universities provides one way of evaluating *Shark Tank*, then media representations of startups, popular and academic books on entrepreneurship, and analyses of the show by knowledgeable investors offer other insights into how the television show reflects and distorts reality. An examination of these varied sources corrects the impressions with which *Shark Tank* leaves viewers. Implicitly and sometimes explicitly, they all qualify, critique, and contextualize the perspectives Mark Burnett and the Sharks have offered over many seasons and in hundreds of episodes. Compared with the reality TV version of entrepreneurship, the varied and extensive literature on the topic, some of it more ideological than others, offers a more trenchant investigation into the ingredients of successful business innovation. It recognizes more fully the multiple and relevant contributions of early-stage investing and pays less attention to evocative myths that center on the American dream. Comparative materials give lie to the tropes of *Shark Tank* and the superheated, celebrity culture version of entrepreneurship it represents. They help us see the problems with and limitations of reality TV's offerings.

Shark Tank jostles with the outsize and distorting attention commanded by Silicon Valley as a central location of transformative business enterprises. Nowhere is the power of mythology clearer than in the popular HBO show *Silicon Valley* (2014), which features a bunch of geeks who work at an incubator and develop a data compression algorithm.[1] The episodes reference all the familiar tech stereotypes: A small group of white, Asian, and Asian American young men along with a few women (a character remarks early on that the sex segregation in tech is like that in a Hasidic wedding). Two competing investment proposals, millions outright in exchange for the technology or less money in exchange for equity—with a valuation of $1 billion on the horizon for the company. Funding rounds, legal roadblocks because of theft of intellectual property, and shifting alliances. Fascination with innovative consumer technologies and Eastern religions. Outsourcing to Asian nations and competition with China. A shift in workplace sites from a live-work suburban home to a glitzy office with all the accoutrements that seem to eliminate any distinction between work and play. Disruptive technologies that will supposedly make the world a better place. "You're like an artist, an entrepreneur, an iconoclast," two programmers from a competing firm tell a character early on.

Different from what the HBO series *Silicon Valley* offers is what appears in scores of books on entrepreneurship that combine inspiration and advice, some of it over the top in its evocations. Among the most popular are Gary Vaynerchuk's *Crushing It! How Great Entrepreneurs Build Their Business and Influence—and How You Can Too* (2018) and Jay Samit's *Disrupt You! Master Personal Transformation, Seize Opportunity, and Thrive in the Era of Endless Innovation* (2015). In *Happier? The History of a Cultural Movement That Aspired to Transform America* (2018), I explored how academics in the fields of happiness studies and positive psychology policed the border between books based on research and how-to books offering inspiration. Yet when I think about the varieties of books that viewers of *Shark Tank* might turn to, I realize how even more imprecise, permeable, and shifting this border is.[2] Indeed, it is hard to imagine greater variety among the authors of these books. There are a small number of academics who sustain their careers as ivory tower researchers, and there are professors who also work as consultants, executives, or investors—including some who remain based in universities, some who go round and round in revolving doors between the business world and academia, and some who abandon ship to join the business world. Then there are consultants, executives, and investors who become professors and those who sustain their original careers; and there are those who start out as inspirational writers and become consultants. And finally, there are a small number, perhaps close to zero, of inspirational writers who do nothing but write books. Rarely is there a professor of entrepreneurship who neither blogs, podcasts, nor consults; or a nonacademic author of a popular book who neither consults, speaks, podcasts, blogs, nor invests professionally.[3]

The study of entrepreneurship is now an immense field, with at least seventy-one journals, thousands of books, and thousands of university courses.[4] Until the 1940s, most theorists assumed that entrepreneurship-driven change was rare because corporations stifled change, capital was expensive, and people preferred stability over innovation. Joseph Schumpeter challenged this view, and his work remains influential in shaping how writers approach entrepreneurship. Central to his capacious vision in *Capitalism, Socialism, and Democracy* (1942) was the idea of a "gale of creative destruction" as a transformative process driven by entrepreneurs and which involved the "industrial mutation that incessantly revolutionizes the economic structure from within, incessantly destroying the old one, incessantly creating a new one." To some extent Schumpeter pessimistically predicted that corporate power with its specialized research would stifle innovation considered central to fundamental economic change.[5] Institutionally, in the development of entrepreneurship as a field of study, an important moment came with the establishment at Harvard in 1948 of the Research Center in Entrepreneurial History, which Schumpeter helped found.

In the 1950s, the work of writer and consultant Peter Drucker was both transformative and part of a more widespread appreciation of the appetite for innovation both inside and outside major corporations. An émigré like Schumpeter, Drucker placed the entrepreneur in a central position in the drama of capitalism's transformation because he understood the tremendous power of technology, the way automation underwrote the power of what he called "knowledge work." By the mid-1950s, innovation in the context of transformed industrial relationships was emerging as central to his vision. "Unshackled from the routine, repetitive, and highly specialized tasks of industrial labor," the historian Angus Burgin wrote as he underscored the importance of Drucker's contribution, "people would be freed to adopt an 'entrepreneurial' approach ... and organizations could focus on harnessing technological changes for profit without worrying about their social and cultural effects."[6] In the early 1960s economists at the University of Chicago echoed Drucker's optimistic analysis, with Gary Becker offering a capacious celebration of the power of innovation and entrepreneurship.

Most business schools moved more slowly in placing entrepreneurial innovation in a central position in their courses of study. References to the word *entrepreneurship* in the wider world began to accelerate in the late 1940s. Mentions in the *Harvard Business Review* started ticking up in the early 1970s.[7] In the early 1960s, just as Drucker and Chicago school economists were more fully embracing entrepreneurship, the dominant approach among business historians was quite different. Influenced by the postwar quest for the security the organization man seemed to offer and represented by the work of historian Alfred D. Chandler, historians of business and MBA programs tended to focus on the management of large, established corporations. Then in the 1970s, as employment in Chandlerian corporations stagnated and the general economic outlook looked bleak, business schools began to focus more on entrepreneurship—albeit grudgingly—when students made clear they wanted more courses on how to start a business.[8] In 1990, Howard Stevenson coined an important definition when he remarked that entrepreneurship is a process by which individuals "pursue opportunities without regard to the resources they currently control," a process that involves innovation in product, market, and/ or business model.[9] This distinguished entrepreneurship from administrative and strategic management, which is about allocation of resources and not the pursuit of opportunity.

What dominates current scholarship on entrepreneurship is an emphasis on how individuals deploy cognition and creativity.[10] Prominent is the work of Scott Shane and Sankaran Venkataraman, who in 2000 defined "the field of entrepreneurship as the scholarly examination of how, by whom, and with what effects opportunities to create future goods and services are discovered, evaluated, and exploited" by "the set of *individuals*" who do the discovery, evaluation, and exploitation. Entrepreneurship, they insisted, "involves the nexus of two phenomena: the presence of lucrative opportunities and the presence of enterprising individuals."[11] Their approach and that of others reminds us that it is not Schumpeter but those influenced by Austrian economists who have so powerfully shaped the field. The focus on the cognitive ability of entrepreneurs to identify opportunities has resulted in an emphasis on micro-level developments rather than attention to the complex histories and cultures of capitalism, a narrower perspective seen in episodes of *Shark Tank*.[12]

Student demand for classes in entrepreneurship came well before significant increases in scholarship on the subject. And it was only in the 1990s that significant numbers of academics took the concept seriously in a sustained way. Clayton M. Christensen's influential *The Innovator's Dilemma: When New Technologies Cause Great Firms to Fail* (1997) celebrated the transformative possibilities of what he called "disruptive innovation" due to changes in technology and market structure. Even when "well-managed companies . . . have their competitive antennae up, listen astutely to their customers, [and] invest aggressively in new technologies," some of them nonetheless stumble. So he advised corporate leaders to embrace "principles of disruptive innovation" that would enable them to solve the innovator's dilemma of failing despite doing all the right things. Customers and investors control how money will be spent, he argued. Over time, as companies grow, it becomes increasingly difficult for them to access newer markets that will dominate the future. It is impossible to analyze markets that do not yet exist. Organizations' capabilities "exist independently of the people" who work there. And in the long run, the supply of technology is unlikely to be capable of meeting the demands of markets.[13]

In the twenty-first century, a series of other well-respected writings by scholars, journalists, and experienced investors have offered a rich and full sense of the field of entrepreneurship and especially startups. Discussing these writings, even briefly, helps explain the lay of the land against which *Shark Tank*'s advice can be judged. It is possible that the Sharks know of at least some of these approaches, and at times, they do seem to draw on some of their insights, though without acknowledging their origins. Yet were *Shark Tank* about education rather than entertainment, the Sharks would point viewers to the fact that they can learn from sources other than a reality television show.[14]

I begin with the story that made the greatest impression on me. I remember not being able to sleep one night in mid-May 2015 after I read Tad Friend's "Tomorrow's Advance Man: Mark Andreessen's Plan to Win the Future," a feature in the *New Yorker* on the venture capital firm Andreessen Horowitz.[15] Though it's not quite how Friend pictured the company operating, I envisioned a bunch of guys with access to huge amounts of capital sitting around a table and saying: "We have disrupted the newspaper, taxi, and hospitality industries. What's next?" To be sure, some of my disquiet stemmed from the fact that one of principals in the firm was Ben Horowitz, who is no relation to me but has the same name as my computer scientist son. When I read Horowitz's *The Hard Thing about Hard Things* (2014), I encountered a world of entrepreneurship very different from that offered on reality TV. Self-help and management books, Horowitz says, are problematic because "they attempt to provide a recipe for challenges that have no recipe," "really complicated, dynamic situations" such as building a high-tech corporation, helping people get out of trouble, or motivating colleagues when a situation turns grim. He recognizes that "the hard thing isn't setting a big, hairy, audacious goal" or writing a business plan but making difficult choices, such as those involving hiring and firing. The difficult moments, he says, make you "[wake] up in the middle of the night in a cold sweat when the dream turns into a nightmare." Denouncing what he calls "the positivity delusion," he insists, as I discussed in chapter 5, that the "first rule of entrepreneurship" is that "there are no rules," a view that the Sharks and authors of most inspirational books do not share.[16]

A more confident, even utopian, and often-elusive book is Peter Thiel's *Zero to One: Notes on Startups, or How to Build the Future* (2014). A libertarian and successful venture capitalist, Thiel suggests that miraculous technologies in the future will be a force that makes it possible to accelerate innovation and growth dramatically, from zero to one "in a world of gigantic administrative bureaucracies both public and private." Like the Sharks and Ben Horowitz, he insists that it is impossible to teach entrepreneurship because "no authority can prescribe in concrete terms how to be innovative." Yet, implicitly contradicting the way Sharks and authors of inspirational books celebrate the heroic individual, Thiel concludes that successful startups involve not lone individuals but small groups of people working together. Calling Ayn Rand's heroes "unreal" as he seems to go against his own libertarianism, he insists that founders need to avoid exaggerating their individualistic power. "To believe yourself invested with divine self-sufficiency," he notes, "is not the mark of a strong individual, but of a person who has mistaken the crowd's worship—or jeering—for the truth."[17]

Less ideological and more practical than Thiel's book is Eric Ries's *The Lean Startup: How Today's Entrepreneurs Use Continuous Innovation to Create Radically Successful Businesses* (2011). Written by a Silicon Valley serial investor and entrepreneur, this wildly popular book, which implicitly critiques *Shark Tank*'s approach, emphasizes the role of product development in entrepreneurship. Having noted that most startups fail, Ries criticizes the "mythmaking industry" that is "hard at work to sell us" the narrative that "through determination, brilliance, great timing, and—above all—a great product, you too can achieve fame and fortune." There is, he insists, "something deeply appealing about this modern-day rags-to-riches story" that makes "success seem inevitable if you just have the right stuff. It means that the mundane details, the boring stuff, the small individual choices don't matter." In contrast, he recommends that those involved in startups, a category that he insists can include someone working in a garage as well as very large organizations, learn how to manage in the "context of extreme uncertainty." At every point, they have to use "innovation accounting" to scientifically test every "element of their vision" in order to "turn ideas into products, measure how consumers respond, and then learn whether to pivot or persevere."[18]

In *Venture Deals*, serial investors Brad Feld and Jason Mendelson carefully discuss negotiating strategies with far more nuance than what episodes of *Shark Tank* reveal. Feld and Mendelson focus on financing startups through venture capital, although what they write is also relevant for other funding options. Of the books under consideration here, this one is the most technical, containing as it does virtually none of the rhetorical hyperbole found in the others. "We know much of this material is dry," the authors note at the end, before going on, in a rare flourish, to remark that they hope it "has been helpful to you as you work to create an amazing new company."[19] They discuss key players, starting with entrepreneurs and venture capitalists, before explaining the roles of others, including lawyers and mentors. They present the types of funding available, principally from a wide range of venture capital firms but also from crowdfunding. Interested readers will find lucid discussions of key terms that are of little interest outside the world of startups: phrases like *financing round negotiation, term sheets,* and *capitalization tables*. At crucial moments, it is as if the authors are taking the reader behind the scenes of what happens after a contestant makes a pitch on *Shark Tank*.

The Founder's Dilemmas by Noam Wasserman (2012) explores the challenges entrepreneurs face, especially in the early years of a company's history. If *Shark Tank* offers an entertaining and anecdotal window into young businesses, most of them consumer oriented, Wasserman provides a careful examination of what startups face based on data of thousands of companies, with deeper attention to several hundred startups, principally in the life sciences and technology sectors. Given the importance of "the entrepreneurial activity we so often acclaim as the very heart and soul of the economy," he notes, a careful study of what happens in early stages of a startup is vitally important. "If entrepreneurship is a battle," he says, "most casualties stem from friendly fire or self-inflicted wounds," especially as founders face dilemmas in balancing wealth and control.[20] The most significant decisions, which are often made in a haphazard manner, involve relationships with friends, family members, and strangers; problems surrounding roles and decision-making; and the challenge of forecasting the long-term consequences of decisions. While Ries is an experimenter skeptical of excessive planning, Wasserman recommends relying on "systematic planning" and "dispassionate reasoning" rather than problematic gut feelings and incautious optimism, which inevitably lead to overestimating one's own abilities and underestimating the amount of resources necessary.[21]

The puzzles Wasserman's research reveals contradict the dreams *Shark Tank* and inspirational literature promote. He shows that, though there are superstar exceptions, the average founders would have greater earnings had they invested in open market assets rather than in privately held ventures. Few company founders achieve both wealth and control. Indeed, it is often the person who replaces the original founder who gains the greatest financial rewards.[22] Founders, he cautions, can counter the dilemmas posed by the tension between the pursuit of control and the pursuit of wealth by having more and varied resources at the outset (including financial, social, and human capital); by learning how to anticipate problems; by moving beyond a sense of inspiration to focus on specific challenges; and by relying on "scientific study and the wisdom of the experienced."[23]

A number of useful conceptual tools that experts have recently developed and entrepreneurs deploy also underscore the superficiality of what viewers see on *Shark Tank*. The Business Model Canvas, first presented in 2008 by Alexander Osterwalder, places "value propositions" at the center of plans that entrepreneurs use strategically as they wrestle with the decisions about partners, resources, customers, costs, and revenue.[24] Developed by two professors at the international business school INSEAD early in the twenty-first century, the Blue Ocean Strategy advocates creating new demand by focusing on non-customers whom other companies have ignored and focusing on innovation in the attributes of a product that these neglected customers value most. This approach relies on a ERRC (Eliminate, Reduce, Raise, Create) grid.[25]

In his *The Illusions of Entrepreneurship: The Costly Myths That Entrepreneurs, Investors, and Policy Makers Live By* (2008), another example of contemporary writing, Scott A. Shane counters commonly held myths about entrepreneurs and entrepreneurship. He dismantles the familiar picture of the entrepreneur as a lone genius who builds an immensely successful, technologically focused enterprise. More typically, he points out, the entrepreneur is "a married white man in his forties who attended but did not complete college. He lives in a place like Des Moines or Tampa, where he was born and has lived much of his life. His new business is a low-tech endeavor, like a construction company or an auto repair shop, in an industry where he has worked for years." He relies on a "sole proprietorship financed with $25,000 of his savings and maybe a bank loan that he guarantees personally. The typical entrepreneur has no plans to employ lots of people or to make lots of money. He just wants to earn a living and support his family" and be his own boss. Generally speaking, those who launch new businesses have little cultural capital, are neither especially innovative nor ambitious, are more likely to fail than succeed, and work harder and earn less than they would have as employees. More broadly, Shane presents evidence that the United States is less entrepreneurial now than it was in the early twentieth century and is less entrepreneurial than poorer and more agricultural countries like Peru and Uganda.[26] What limits the explanatory power of Shane's work is that he makes the common mistake of failing to distinguish between those who launch small businesses that do not grow significantly and the smaller number of entrepreneurs whose work is broadly transformative.

Despite illuminating works such as these, there is much that we still do not know about entrepreneurship. Definitional uncertainty remains. Moreover, historical and comparative dimensions of entrepreneurship remain less than fully explored, despite how some historians and economists have flirted with—though never fully committed to—exploring these topics. Though we know about the development of the concept, we are far from certain about when and how the American economy became more or less entrepreneurial over time. Nor can we be confident that we adequately understand how entrepreneurship in the United States compares with entrepreneurship in other nations, both developing and developed ones, now and in the past.

Though much of the work by popular writers, entrepreneurs, and scholars is not very explicitly ideological, there are two books—one by a liberal academic in the 1970s and the other by a conservative nonacademic in the 1980s—in which there emerged influential and pointed arguments about the importance of the entrepreneur.

As a writer, teacher, and developer of academic programs, Jeffry A. Timmons was a transformative figure in entrepreneurial studies; in fact, Michie P. Slaughter of the Kauffman Center for Entrepreneurial Leadership called him "the premier entrepreneurship educator in America."[27] Timmons, whose work at Babson College is discussed in chapter 7, taught at Northeastern University soon after he earned his doctorate at Harvard Business School, and then he went back and forth between teaching at Harvard Business School and Babson. He began his exploration of entrepreneurship with his 1970 dissertation, "Entrepreneurial and Leadership Development in an Inner City Ghetto and a Rural Depressed Area." In the title of his early November 1971 essay in the *Harvard Business Review*, which was based on his research, he asked, "Black Is Beautiful. Is It Bountiful?" He answered that rhetorical question in the essay's subtitle: "Research Offers Encouraging Evidence That the Key to Development of Minority Enterprise Lies in Motivational Training." In the essay, he reported on an "entrepreneurial training program" he had directed for African Americans in inner-city Washington, D.C., that explored solutions to the "dilemma of poverty" that was producing "much of the unrest and despair so prevalent" in American cities. Drawing on the work of the psychologist David C. McClelland, who had sat on his dissertation committee, Timmons emphasized the importance of "the achievement motivation that provides the fuel for the personal drive and inner energy of the active entrepreneur" and which in turn relies on an "intense competitive spirit" and "high standards of personal excellence."[28]

In a 1969 book, McClelland and his coauthor, David G. Winter, had described the Black Power movement as psychologically "a rather emphatic assertion that one is an agent, rather than a pawn to be oppressed, or 'helped,' or otherwise pushed around by white people. As such, it is part of the psychological transformation needed to bring about improved economic performance." He noted that since "the Black Power philosophy may not appeal as much to middle-class Negroes," it was possible they would "find some alternative means of becoming proud of themselves and their community, if they are to think of themselves as capable of improving their own position, rather than just creeping slowly forward as retreating whites let them."[29]

Timmons began his research in the summer of 1967 when he worked with about 100 current and aspiring businesspeople, half of them African Americans from the District of Columbia and half of them whites from a depressed rural community in Oklahoma, in seminars sponsored by the Economic Development Administration of the Department of Commerce and hosted by a company McClelland had founded and directed. The seminars relied on "active learning by discovery": they took participants through a series of exercises in which they analyzed their own motivations, discussed "actual cases of new business development," and then amplified their "own personal goals and plans of action." Timmons concluded in "Black Is Beautiful. Is It Bountiful?" that the project accelerated the development of enterprises, helped create new jobs, encouraged investments, and promoted business planning and entrepreneurial activity. All this built a sense of greater optimism, self-respect, and confidence among participants, which he hoped would "supply the spark for self-determination, dignity, and freedom which most blacks and other minorities seek."

But Timmons had to temper such hopeful conclusions with the acknowledgment that, by itself, such training would not change the basic structures that shaped power relations in America. However, as he explained in what he wrote, he found a glimmer of hope elsewhere. After finishing his research, he began working with Alexander Dingee and Leonard Smollen from MIT's Sloan School of Management, who were "applying the concepts and findings of entrepreneurial training to a systems approach for new venture development."[30] In addition to teaching, they were, respectively, the executive director and associate director at the Institute for New Enterprise Development. Working at MIT, they had developed expertise under their own grants from the Office of Economic Opportunity, a federal agency that originated in 1964 as part of President Lyndon Johnson's War on Poverty.

In the *Harvard Business Review* article, Timmons reported on programs supported by the federal government's Community Development Corporations and Minority Enterprise Small Business Investment Companies, which provided expertise, financing, and infrastructure to promote entrepreneurship in economically depressed communities. He celebrated "black capitalism." Having despaired of the possibility of the nation overcoming the tragic consequences of poverty and racism, he nonetheless ended the article with the positive conclusion that black could be both beautiful and bountiful. "The *will* and the *commitment* of local ghetto residents" to gain the necessary "knowledge and resources to launch new enterprises," he asserted, would enhance their "self-determination and self-respect." Combining all this "with a systematic approach to new-venture creation" could "prove to be a major contribution toward solving the perplexing problems and challenges of poverty."[31]

Timmons's dissertation, handed in just under a year before his article was published, revealed more. A key phase of his research in the nation's capital took place from December 1967 to September 1968 in the Shaw and Langdon neighborhoods. This meant that he was well aware of, if not actually present during, the riots that occurred a few blocks away following Martin Luther King Jr.'s assassination in early April 1968. This surely helps account for the sense of urgency he expressed in his dissertation, at key moments using more dramatic language than he did in his published article. He spoke of the "fear of reprisals and genocide reminiscent of the Nazi era." "In fact," he said, "to some observers of clashes between the police and Black Panthers in recent months this genocide has already begun." Another sign of the sense of urgency he felt was his insistence that it was desirable and possible to eliminate "the fundamental causes of poverty and economic stagnation."[32]

The dissertation reveals that Timmons felt the right approach to entrepreneurship in underserved communities was poised between the federal government's programs funded during the Great Society and McClelland's emphasis on psychological motivation. Though he acknowledged the importance of federal programs that provided financial and technical resources for entrepreneurs, Timmons insisted that it was impossible to "simply buy our way out of the community development problem" by what he called "work and give-away programs." Rather, he stressed that emphasizing the "need for achievement motive," which provided "fuel for the personal drive and inner energy of the active entrepreneur," was more cost effective. It would encourage "an intensive competitive spirit" and foster "individual responsibility for tackling challenging problems that lead to the attainment of excellence." Using neoliberal language that would become increasingly prominent in the ensuing decades, even as he wrote under the auspices of a federal government program, he emphasized the importance of "personal energy, commitment and charisma for initiating and leading new enterprises." In the very last sentence of his dissertation, Timmons called "entrepreneurial training" the "missing link" that "could prove to make a major contribution toward solving the problems and challenges of poverty left unanswered in the 1960s."[33]

Neither in his *Harvard Business Review* article nor in his dissertation did Timmons mention the spring 1968 riots that took place in the neighborhood he had studied and in more than one hundred other cities nationwide. Nor did he explore the ways in which entrepreneurship was often not up to the challenge of bringing about transformative social changes. Yet it is one of the ironies of history that what he learned from his study of African American entrepreneurship in Washington, D.C., soon morphed into a more generalized theory of entrepreneurship in a way that underscores how government-sanctioned concern for the problem of poverty in the 1960s transitioned in the 1970s and beyond into support mostly for white entrepreneurs rather than specifically African American ones. Indeed, it was Dingee, Smollen, and Timmons who authored the first edition of *New Venture Creation: A Guide to Small Business Development.* According to one source, it was also in 1977, perhaps not coincidentally the year the first edition on *New Venture Creation* was published, that Babson College president Ralph Sorenson "made entrepreneurship the explicit focus" of education at Babson College.[34] Now in its tenth edition, with different authors and the new subtitle *Entrepreneurship for the 21st Century, New Venture Creation* remains in a towering position as an influential book in the field.

At the outset of the 1977 edition of their six-hundred-page book, the authors of *New Venture Creation* noted that antiwar protests, the civil rights and women's liberation movements, the energy crisis, unemployment, and threats to world peace and the environment all reflected "a need for creative leadership in solving extremely complex problems." Many members of the younger generation, they observed, were "questioning the ability and capacity of larger, established institutions—private and public alike—to cope with these and other" problems.[35]

Having set themselves the ambitious goal of equipping students to solve these problems, they quickly shifted the focus of their book away from the social justice issues they mentioned to what they called "economic entrepreneurship." The first edition was important because it laid out in great detail the ways in which entrepreneurs fostered "new venture creation," a term Timmons had used in his article "Black Is Beautiful," even as the three authors acknowledged that "the first origin of the book" was Timmons's dissertation and the work of the Institute for New Enterprise Development in developing "new businesses in economically depressed areas." They provided extensive sections of the book for readers to write down what they thought, offered elaborate guides to "self-paced exercises, small group projects and experientially based techniques," called on readers to examine their own motivations, and advocated for "new venture simulation."[36] Ironically, they modeled all this on what Timmons had developed for inner-city African Americans and poor rural whites.

In the book, Timmons, Smollen, and Dingee relegated the importance of a product or service to a secondary position, talked of how to generate business plans, and provided information on sources of funding, including venture capital. They also stressed the importance of "realistic self-appraisal and goal setting," warned against "extreme independence and self-reliance," which work against team cooperation, and, echoing McClelland, emphasized that "a high level of achievement motivation" plays a crucial role in success. They asserted that "the key to the creation of successful enterprises—large and small—is the right combination of people, a viable idea, and seed capital." Above all, it was the people on "the entrepreneurial team" who provided "the *single most important ingredient*." Writing decades before *Shark Tank*, they anticipated its portrayal of entrepreneurs and business when they criticized how the "mass media" often portrayed "in a shallow way the ease and genius with which [business ventures] made their founders wealthy."[37]

If Timmons developed his ideas about entrepreneurship as a positive response to aspirations among African Americans, conservative writer and investor George Gilder approached entrepreneurship through a negative reaction to the women's liberation movement. Between 1973 and 1986 he wrote four books in which he claimed that assertive women were a threat to male dominance in business and more generally menaced "not only the sex roles on which the family is founded but also the freedoms at the very heart of free enterprise."[38] The 1980 publication of Gilder's *Wealth and Poverty*, a defense of both the male-dominated nuclear family and supply-side economics, coincided with the presidential inauguration of Ronald Reagan, for whom Gilder had once written speeches.[39] Gilder's earlier books had not done well, but *Wealth and Poverty* sold more than a million copies, and Gilder suddenly "became the intellectual darling of the Reagan administration," as Susan Faludi wrote in *Backlash*, and himself "went from poverty to wealth."[40] Gilder opposed social policies that he believed undermined families headed by a male breadwinner. Similarly, he asserted that poverty stemmed from misguided social welfare policies that weakened people's commitments to faith, family, and work.

In contrast, he insisted that wealth came from pathbreaking technological advances created by bold entrepreneurs. He criticized those on the Left such as John Kenneth Galbraith who thought that what best represented America was the power of large, well-established corporations characteristic of a mature economy. Such an analysis, Gilder said, overlooked the transformative power of insurgent, technologically oriented entrepreneurs, who were aided by a cut in taxes on capital gains and who, he hoped, augured a future in which "politicians can comprehend the value of free men and free wealth." It was bold entrepreneurs who were "fighting America's only serious war against poverty" by creating job-generating new businesses. He said that "the potentialities of invention and enterprise," especially in small companies that echoed the promise of Schumpeter's creative destruction, were "greater than ever before in human history."[41] For Gilder, capitalism, dependent on a belief in God, was not rapacious but altruistic.

Four years later, in his book *The Spirit of Enterprise*, Gilder offered a fuller celebration of entrepreneurship, one focused less on antifeminism and more on religious faith. Here he found fault not with ambitious women but with entitled elites, complacent and shortsighted organization men, wrongheaded government bureaucrats, and unduly pessimistic academic economists. Creators of new computer-related technologies and of new service sector jobs had launched, he wrote, "a profound and far-reaching economic revival in the late 1970s" that proceeded to "overthrow establishments rather than establish equilibriums." Like others, Gilder didn't distinguish between the huge number of small-business operators and the smaller number of bold entrepreneurs; instead, he celebrated "an immense class of entrepreneurs and aspiring businessmen—perhaps 30 million in the United States alone—who comprise a near majority of working citizens." "Mostly outcasts, exiles, mother's boys" spurred by lower capital gains taxes (and he hoped a flat tax that he claimed would eliminate job killing loopholes), they were selfless innovators who created wealth, "leading the world economy into a new age of growth and prosperity." Inspired by religious values, they understood "the deepest truths of giving and sacrifice, the miraculous powers of commitment and faith." It was "the spirit of enterprise" that infused "the most modern of technological adventures," led by "bullheaded, defiant, tenacious, creative entrepreneurs." Entrepreneurship was, he wrote in the book's final sentence, "the saving grace of democratic politics and free men, the hope of the poor and the obligation of the fortunate, the redemption of an oppressed and desperate world."[42]

Whereas racial issues inspired Timmons, gender and class compelled Gilder—a fact laced with irony. Class privilege marked Gilder's life. He was the great-great-grandson of Charles Lewis Tiffany, founder of Tiffany and Company, and the great-grandson of the designer Louis Comfort Tiffany, and his grandfather Richard Watson Gilder had edited the prestigious *Century Magazine*. When his own father was killed in action in World War II, Gilder and his mother were left in relatively modest circumstances. However, his father's Harvard roommate, David Rockefeller, the grandson of John D. Rockefeller, fulfilled his promise that if his roommate was killed in the war, he would help oversee young Gilder's upbringing. Rockefeller paid for Gilder's education at Exeter and Harvard. In the acknowledgments to *Wealth and Poverty*, before going on to extol the generosity of capitalists, Gilder said the book was "most deeply a tribute" to David Rockefeller and his wife for "their unending love and generosity to me."[43]

Yet the implication of the book was that people like Rockefeller paled in comparison with the new-money folks whose ambition and inventiveness Timmons so admired. Indeed, in *Wealth and Poverty*, Gilder said that the Rockefeller family "was in steady decline ... dissipating [assets] in collapsing securities or failing companies at home and abroad, incarcerating [them] in foundations, and selling off or donating to nonprofit institutions, or even to government, some of their principal holdings of land and personal property," as the Rockefellers had done with "their venerable Westchester" estate. David Rockefeller and his children, he concluded, "had neither the motivation nor the available money to sustain the manorial symbols of family power."[44] Soon after *Wealth and Poverty* was published, the *New York Times* reported that Gilder earned $50,000 a year—about $142,000 in today's dollars—directing programs for the International Center for Economic Policy Studies, which "promot[ed] conservative economic ideas" and was "funded by family foundations and corporations, one of the most generous of which [was] Mr. Rockefeller's Chase Manhattan Bank."[45] There is abundant irony in all this. The Rockefeller fortune, built on entrepreneurial success that history had overtaken, early on funded Gilder's education and later helped sustain his work.

After the publication of *Wealth and Poverty*, Gilder built paths forward based on the promise of new technologies. He developed and participated in EduComm and Telescom conferences, which celebrated innovation, as did his 2009 book, *The Israel Test*. An investor in new technologies, he was hailed in a 2018 article in *Forbes* as a "technology prophet" predicting "big tech's disruption."[46]

All these works on entrepreneurship, especially those by academics, professional investors, and entrepreneurs, offer information helpful to those seeking funding and publicity, even as they present perspectives that contradict and complicate the examples seen on *Shark Tank*. Scholars of entrepreneurship and entrepreneurs themselves challenge commonly held assumptions, some of which are visible on *Shark Tank*. Television's emphasis on innovation and creative destruction, as the historian Nan Enstad has shown, overlooks the manipulation of corporate law and legislation by powerful corporate interests.[47] It also turns out that the popular focus on a small number of tech greats, such as Steve Jobs and Bill Gates, distorts reality because startup ventures in technology are important but hardly the only or typical ones. In addition, *Shark Tank* gives an inaccurate picture of the full range and power of other funding sources. In early 2018 Kevin O'Leary claimed that the program was "the number one venture capital platform firm on *earth* today."[48] Yet by the end of season nine the Sharks had offered about $125 million, a figure presumably greater than the amount actually invested. As a comparison, Andreessen Horowitz, one of the nation's leading venture capital firms, which launched shortly before *Shark Tank* first aired, often invests more than $100 million just in one company and in 2016 created a single fund with $1.5 billion to invest.

Angel investors like those on *Shark Tank* and venture capitalists hardly encompass the full range of possible funding sources. Most entrepreneurs are not lone geniuses whose ideas come from their fertile imaginations. Rather, they often work in teams and/or are supported by family, friends, and others in their social networks. Though many are educated white men, there is more diversity among their ranks than we see on television. Nor are they all barely out of their teens. Many of them are "use innovators": people, including those employed by corporations, who develop significant expertise in an area in ways that lead them to launch innovations. Successful entrepreneurs are more apt to manage risks than to pursue especially risky opportunities.

Shark Tank also provides little insight into the challenges of execution and securing later rounds of funding. A substantial majority of entrepreneurs fail rather than succeed, including those replaced in their own company by a chief executive officer brought in from the outside. It is very difficult for a founder to end up both rich and in control. On a risk-adjusted basis, most aspiring entrepreneurs like those seen on *Shark Tank* can earn more in the stock market than by putting their funds into what they are pitching. And compared with some scholars, the Sharks pay too little attention to government and globalism.[49]

The gap between what *Shark Tank* portrays and ideas about entrepreneurship expressed by sophisticated and well-informed writers, academics, and investors came home to me when I was researching this book. A serial entrepreneur who wishes to remain anonymous provided a vivid and dramatic evaluation. "My main complaint," he wrote, "subsuming all others, is that [*Shark Tank*] betrays no experience of real life in the world of capital and venture. The difference between the Sharks and real businesspersons is the difference between professional wrestling and college wrestling. One excites the money lust and *Schadenfreude* of the mass market, providing thereby an occasion to advertise luxury goods that counterfeit social elegance; the other is for gentlefolk, connoisseurs of sporting arts, who celebrate the beauty, skill, and resolution of victor and vanquished alike." Like dramatic works on big business, he continued, *Shark Tank* revealed "an utter cluelessness of what it's like, how people talk, what they want, how they decide," instead offering "gladiatorial face-offs of obsessive, amoral greedheads who rise or fall mostly by scheming." Drawing on his experience as both an investor and a pitcher, he insisted that "real venture capitalists, institutional or angel, and real entrepreneur/supplicants are a lot tougher negotiators than the Sharks, but they don't talk tough or dismiss counterparts with a sneer. They gently disappoint supplicants as one declines any unattractive invitation, citing other priorities and simulating a practiced regret that one is unable to attend." Then he ended on a final note: "*Shark Tank* wins for fantasy, vulgarity, and boredom. Real investors win for prudence, courtesy, diligence, rapacity, and betrayal."[50]

A private investor with decades of experience, including as an angel investor, also weighed in. *Shark Tank*, he said, is 80 or even 95 percent entertainment, and he worried that the program might unwittingly encourage audience members to detour from sensible career paths by leading them to underestimate the risks involved in bold but perhaps ill-conceived ventures. As I learned when I attended professional pitch events, in the real world, unlike what's portrayed on-screen, investors pay scant attention to personal stories, relying instead on analysis, and rarely make take-it-or-leave-it offers that are decided upon in less than an hour. Professional investors, my source correctly insisted, focus more on the macro environment. The terms they negotiate are more complicated, the deals structured in more sophisticated ways. *Shark Tank*'s producers bring into the tank consumer products because they assume that viewers will understand a cupcake better than a complicated new technology, so *Shark Tank* ends up depicting a "microscopic sector of the world" of possible investments. In the real world, many presenters work in large corporations for a decade or more before striking out on their own, rather than working in their garage for a few months or years. Nor does the show help its audience members understand the importance of a management team, even though the Sharks themselves rely on an ecosystem filled with members of their own staff. Having said all that, my source also acknowledged that *Shark Tank* serves at least two useful functions: it promotes a "can-do attitude," and it opens doors that most contestants could not open on their own.[51]

My third exchange was with someone with extensive experience in entrepreneurship. After reading a draft of this book, he wrote that he "found the stories of the Sharks fascinating and the story of how the show was developed riveting. The details on how they orchestrate and coach the sharks and contestants [were] fascinating." Then, as he read on, he told me, "I began to get angry and upset." It struck him that the Sharks represent "what is so wrong with this made for TV, VC setup": they have "a little skin in the game when they invest, but NO DOWNSIDE!" Any potential downsides are countered by the publicity their investments buy them and the fact that "their investments are partially offset by their salaries." Rather than true angel investors, they are actors whose "end game is to promote themselves and the idea that anyone can come up with a great idea and get rich, ignoring the work that goes into succeeding." That is why people watch: they love the idea of "getting rich quick" with "the possibility of a spectacular and humiliating crash."[52]

In the end, the juxtaposition of *Shark Tank* with advice and evaluations from scholars and businesspeople underscores some of key aspects of the reality TV program, including problematic ones. The episodes offer ample examples of how to and how not to pitch an investment to investors. The Sharks correctly emphasize the importance of approaching investors with a reasonable valuation, but the show features much that real-world investors would take issue with, including the yardsticks that the Sharks use and the harsh tactics they often deploy. Obviously in the real world negotiations proceed in slower and more subtle ways, and the deck is not so unfairly stacked against supplicants. The show can also help audience members appreciate the importance of customer acquisition costs, although many astute observers of and participants in entrepreneurial activities do not emphasize the centrality of salesmanship as robustly as do the Sharks.

While the Sharks only implicitly focus, on the air and in their writings, on whether a pitcher can be coached and taught, it is not difficult to understand the importance of teaching and coaching when watching the show. Although the lines are often blurred between formal and informal training, there is nonetheless disagreement over the value of formal education for entrepreneurs. The Sharks—even those who benefitted from relevant formal education, like Mark Cuban, Lori Greiner, and Kevin O'Leary—usually minimize its importance, and they are especially skeptical of graduate schools of business. Their general antipathy to expertise and advocacy for gut instincts reflects their rhetorical opposition to the organization man in well-established corporations and resembles other anti-elitist impulses prevalent in post–Great Recession America. In sharp contrast, academics, entrepreneurs, and some who are both believe that is possible to teach entrepreneurship in colleges and universities, especially when curricular and extracurricular efforts are integrated. Moreover, critics note that *Shark Tank* represents a specific and very small sector of entrepreneurial investing: angel investing, mostly in niche consumer products, at a startup's early stage, by a wealthy individual in exchange for equity. It turns out that, though *Shark Tank* may be popular and entertaining, it offers a distorted and highly problematic picture of how contemporary entrepreneurial capitalism works.

Writings and teachings about entrepreneurship by scholars, businesspeople, and popularizers have some of the same problems that the reality TV show does. By and large there is widespread, unquestioning acceptance of the fundamentals of contemporary entrepreneurial capitalism among these folks. Widely shared is an apolitical vision of enterprise as, not greedy or exploitative, but exciting and creative. The focus on startups and the individual can too easily divorce the treatment of enterprise from broader considerations about the nature and dynamics of capitalism. The resulting disconnections minimize the consideration of larger socioeconomic forces such as labor markets, government policy, and globalization.[53] Oddly enough, even though a variety of observers have offered critical perspectives on *Shark Tank* (though sometimes the critiques are

American Dreams,
American Nightmares

The havoc the Great Recession wreaked on the lives of Americans places *Shark Tank* and our fascination with entrepreneurs in the starkest light. The first episode of *Shark Tank* appeared in early August 2009, soon after General Motors filed for bankruptcy in June and not long before the unemployment rate hit 10 percent for the first time in a quarter of a century in October. Looking back, we can see that the Great Recession intensified interest in issues of inequality, insecurity, fractured communities, and political dysfunction. Then the 2016 election encouraged journalists and social scientists to more urgently examine deep fissures in American life as they wrote for even more eager audiences.

On September 14, 2018, ten years minus one day after the storied financial firm Lehman Brothers failed, the Pulitzer Prize–winning *New York Times* columnist David Leonhardt cast his eyes over the economy then and now. He wrote that, despite the rosy picture painted by official statistics charting the recovery of the stock and labor markets, as well as the economy as measured by the GDP, the essential problems that triggered the recession were hardly resolved; indeed, he noted that "the financial crisis remains the most influential event of the 21st century." In its wake, the near collapse of the world's financial systems had "left millions of people—many of whom were already anxious about the economy—feeling more anxious, if not downright angry" and thus "helped create a threat to Western liberal democracy" that had been unimaginable a decade earlier. Looking past the positive economic figures some journalists and many politicians offered up, Leonhardt drew conclusions from very different data.

Earlier in the postwar period, many among the working poor and middle class had enjoyed greater increases in their take-home pay than the rich—increases that were so robust that their standard of living was set to double every thirty years. Around 1970 the trend began to reverse itself so dramatically that by around 2015, a tiny portion of society now saw the most significant growth in wealth and income. Moreover, while the stock market had recovered dramatically by 2018, the net worth of tens of millions of households remained below 2007 levels, as did the incomes of many families. Official unemployment figures might have dropped dramatically, but they did not account for the significant number of people who were no longer looking for jobs, in large part because they could not find any that paid decent wages and offered benefits as well. Although Leonhardt recognized that there was no way to return to what had existed earlier, he nonetheless believed that policy changes could dramatically improve the lives of most Americans. His policy wish list, he said, "would start with a tax code that does less to favor the affluent, a better-functioning education system, more bargaining power for workers and less tolerance for corporate consolidation."[1]

Self-help literature, TED Talks, TV shows, movies, and popular as well as academic books all help us understand what *Shark Tank* tries to accomplish and skillfully avoids. They operate at a time when the emphasis is on the power of markets, entrepreneurship, and self-determination. Placing these varied expressions in conversation with one another in the contexts of life in America in the years after the Great Recession helps contextualize what viewers see in *Shark Tank*. Divergent views of American life compete for attention as ways of understanding and explaining the program's meaning. The show trades in conflicting visions of pathways to success and uses a variety of stories as examples of what is possible. Explaining *Shark Tank* is challenging because the episodes are so rife with contradictions, which both amateur and professional observers have explored in suggestive but often contradictory ways. In the end, though, the episodes entertain more than they educate, and they do both in ways that reveal why people struggle to understand the meanings of the American dream in the wake of the Great Recession.

Mark Burnett, the Sharks themselves, and *Shark Tank* episodes offer a picture of the American economy characterized by striving entrepreneurs who aspire to achieve the American dream in a free-market, individualistic world filled with opportunity. If, however, we turn our attention to best-selling books, scholarly writings, and widely followed media outlets, we come upon a very different picture. True, much of the often over-the-top inspirational literature resembles the celebratory hosannas of Napoleon Hill's 1937 *Think and Grow Rich* and Norman Vincent Peale's 1952 *The Power of Positive Thinking*. Yet while some popular books on entrepreneurship straddle the border between the inspirational and the practical, others offer specific advice on how to launch a startup and achieve success by deploying social media, lowering customer acquisitions costs, and developing perfect investor pitches. Informed by data and often sober in their conclusions, writers outside the field of entrepreneurship call into question the assumptions behind *Shark Tank*'s presentation of the way that American entrepreneurship works. Then there are those who post on social media in distinctive and highly personal ways. Especially striking is the contrast between the picture of American life that the reality TV show (and most of the media coverage of *Shark Tank*) offers and what social scientists and journalists portray—in which insecurity, inequality, and the collapse of community life play crucial roles.

Albeit not without ironic contradictions, *Shark Tank* and the Sharks offer visions of ambitious entrepreneurs chasing after the American dream, often successfully. In this supposedly meritocratic world, the Sharks urge the pitchers—who see themselves as somewhere on the road from rags to riches—to rely on hard work rather than luck, natural talent rather than formal academic training, innovation and experimentation rather than tradition, themselves rather than others (and especially not on help from the federal government). The key skills and attributes continuously invoked are the ability to sell, comfort with risk-taking, perseverance, and determination—all of which are deployed in a dog-eat-dog Darwinian world where learning from failures leads to successes. Marketing—of the self as well as the product, on the set where episodes are filmed as well as out in the real world—prevails in an economy supposedly built on fair and responsive markets.

In the risk-filled world of openly competitive markets that *Shark Tank* presents, events and factors in the wider world are not very often in view. To be sure, especially in the show's first few years, when discussion of the Great Recession was hard to avoid, the power of the business cycle to dash hopes was very much on the minds of some pitchers, and when appropriate, Sharks ask whether the federal government has granted a patent on a product.[2] But they less often inquire about trade policy, corporate subsidies, regulations, or taxes, and other major forces outside the tank that seldom make sustained appearances on screen. The show displays little evidence of the power of international markets, and globalization is represented as mainly involving the tension between manufacturing at home to save American jobs and manufacturing abroad to drive down costs. Immigration is part of the stories of talented Sharks and contestants, but it's not portrayed as involving border-crossings that might threaten the well-being of Americans. Technological innovations appear not as a threat to jobs or a force auguring massive disruption but as investment opportunities and aids in selling, principally through social media. Reflecting their commitment to self-reliance, Sharks often, on air and in what they write, advise pitchers to follow their lead and avoid organizations, especially business schools (even though they offer MBAs and business training), banks (even though they lend money to businesses), and large corporations (which Sharks say stifle initiative, even though many corporations encourage innovation).

The tank in which the Sharks swim stands in contrast to Silicon Valley's world of venture capital and Wall Street's world of private equity. The differences have hardly escaped the notice of savvy observers. Under the headline "The Vile and Un-American Reality of *Shark Tank*," a 2016 blog post by tech and business writer Frank Moraes contrasted the reality TV show with the reality of venture or angel investing capital. Most of the Sharks, he said, were dealmakers, not entrepreneurs—people "who used other people's ideas to enrich themselves." The show presented the Sharks as "gods," members of a "Council of Nine on Mount Olympus" who listened to the begging of their subjects. Moraes observed that the way the Sharks struck deals on-screen did not resemble the way venture capitalists made deals. First, the Sharks made offers before carrying out their due diligence, without access to management teams and adequate data. Second, the average deal in the real world involved surrendering 15 percent equity, but in *Shark Tank*'s pretend world, that figure was close to 40 percent. "So the show screws the actual entrepreneurs," he said, forcing them to make a decision immediately and shaming them with an implicit accusation: "How dare you question the combined wisdom of the sharks!" "More show than reality," *Shark Tank* was "vile" because it illustrated "what's wrong with America."[3]

Also in 2016, when Paul Graham, cofounder of the accelerator Y Combinator, tweeted an implicit criticism of *Shark Tank*—"Startups: Instead of appearing on Shark Tank, spend that energy fixing whatever makes your product so unappealing you think you need to"—Mark Cuban and Chris Sacca, an angel investor from Silicon Valley and occasionally a guest Shark, responded. Deploying his sharp wit, Cuban turned the tables on Graham by calling out "the sense of entitlement and arrogance" conveyed by startup founders who joined Y Combinator, but apparently not by the Sharks. Sacca emphasized that even if a pitcher didn't get a deal on *Shark Tank*, simply appearing on the show provided exposure to millions of viewers.[4]

The pitchers on *Shark Tank* are typically people with ample ambition but whose goals are more modest than those of entrepreneurs who appear before investors in Silicon Valley or Lower Manhattan, or at professional pitch competitions. Whether they come on the *Shark Tank* set in Culver City, California, alone or with others, they are often embedded in networks of friends and family. Although there are some adults who are near or at the age of Social Security eligibility, most contestants range in age from their teens to their forties. They are from regionally diverse backgrounds, though the producers seem to prefer people from cosmopolitan cities and comfortable suburbs. Although the producers and Sharks themselves remain leery of people with MBAs, there are plenty of highly educated pitchers, who stand in sharp contrast with the plainspoken, down-home folks from picturesque locations who occasionally appear. There are a fair number of down-and-out pitchers, even some whom the Great Recession and hard luck have forced to live in their cars or with friends and family. More common, however, are people who have been able to invest hundreds of thousands of dollars of their own money, or that of friends and family.

The identities of pitchers underscore how unrepresentative is the world *Shark Tank* pictures, and the show often handles dimensions of diversity in problematic ways. Women don't appear on the show in proportion to their numbers in the general population. Even more striking is how seldom Asian Americans and African Americans take the stage, and almost no Latinx men or women appear as pitchers. Alas, I know of no data on the participation of immigrants or their children, but my guess is that such figures would pale in comparison to the relatively high numbers of immigrants and their children who participate in startups—recall that immigrants or their children founded almost half of all Fortune 500 corporations. Thus, by most metrics, contestants on *Shark Tank* hardly represent either America or American entrepreneurship. They are disproportionately white, native-born, and male. Whether intentionally or not, the show pays lip service to a cosmopolitan world but gives little attention to sectors of the American population that are actually entrepreneurial.[5]

As writers, inspirational speakers, and cast members, the Sharks offer a full range of practical advice, but in the end it is their invocation of the American dream that they hope resonates. "If it's real for them," asked promotional material for the show in late 2018, "why couldn't it be real for you?"[6] Burnett provided the most sustained expression. "To me," he said, "the American Dream means anything is possible. Any individual willing to work, develop their natural talents, and persevere when the going gets tough can see their goals realized. No other place on earth offers such an opportunity as the United States of America."[7] In most instances the evocations of the American dream by Burnett and the Sharks have proved more tantalizing than specific, couched in brief, vague clichés. Though they have used the term hundreds if not thousands of times, it is typically an empty, floating, or vague signifier. Sometimes the Sharks use it when emphasizing materialistic goals. More often they use it when offering hosannas to finding opportunity, achieving the rags-to-riches story, owning your own business, gaining financial freedom, deploying self-sacrifice and hard work to overcome the odds or achieve second chances, building families, and enjoying the fruits of individual self-determination.

Of course, the term *American dream* has had various meanings, depending in large measure on the temper of the times, the social location of dreamers, and the perspectives of those speaking. Among them are religious freedom, rebirth in a new land, upward social mobility, equality, personal fulfillment, and homeownership.[8] There is considerable evidence that, despite the many critics who see the American dream as a problematic myth in a society beset by inequality and rigidity, what matters most to Americans is not material success or social mobility but a satisfying family life, a good education, and the freedom to choose where to live. It may well be that most Americans continue to see the nation as a land of opportunity where ingenuity and hard work bring modest steps on the road to success.[9]

It turns out that watching reality TV shows (including *Shark Tank*) that emphasize the rags-to-riches dream increases the extent to which viewers have confidence in its promise, perhaps because these shows reinforce what they already believed. According to the work of the political science and communications scholar Eunji Kim on audiences of TV programs like *Shark Tank*, among those for whom watching such shows enhanced their faith in economic and social mobility were the employed, Republicans, young people, more optimistic people, those with higher incomes, and those with immigrant parents, as well as those who believe self-determination is more important than government support. What fostered or reinforced faith in mobility and even legitimated disparities of wealth was a show's focus on ordinary people, its offer of substantial rewards, and its emphasis on hard work and merit. If in an earlier Gilded Age Americans read Horatio Alger's novels, today they can turn on their television sets and surf a seemingly unending number of channels that offer entertaining and inspiring rags-to-riches stories.[10]

What Burnett and the Sharks have articulated is somewhat less explicitly materialistic but nonetheless more secular than many iterations of the American dream. They rarely evoke the notion of America as a city on a hill, serving as a beacon to the rest of the world. What they celebrate exists more in here-and-now situations than as a utopian hope. The TV show rarely emphasizes the prospect of homeownership, relies more on individual achievement than on communal possibilities, and mentions earthly accomplishments rather that the role of divine power.

The possibility of achieving the American dream through entrepreneurship has changed over time, in part because of the ups and down of the business cycle, the rising and falling appeal of employment in large corporate entities, the waxing and waning of the power of egalitarianism and elitism, the erosion of the importance of trade unions, and the growing prevalence of self-employment in a world where jobs in larger organizations have lost their attractiveness. In these contexts, the version of the American dream *Shark Tank* offers often contains serious contradictions, including the tension between self-determination and reliance on wealthy strategic partners, to say nothing of the importance of social and cultural capital.[11] What makes the *Shark Tank* version of the American dream so interesting and perhaps unprecedented is the vision of the investor as both judge and savior. The stereotypical American aspirant still achieves success by hard work, luck, guts, and imagination. However, now, in a world where financialization is so powerful, the Sharks serve as both gatekeepers to and funders of the American dream.

The contradiction between the celebration of the self-made individual and the reliance on the rich and powerful is an impulse fully in view on the show. The Sharks talk of self-sacrifice as something especially important early on, when an entrepreneur is living simply and working 24-7. Just as the bootblack in Horatio Alger's *Ragged Dick* (1868) needed a wealthy benefactor, so too, under very different conditions, does a pitcher on *Shark Tank* have to rely on a rich Shark for expertise, financing, and connections. The Sharks may emphasize grit and resilience as important character traits, but their status as celebrities evokes self-celebration and self-expression.[12] What rules on *Shark Tank* is personality more than product, chance more than hard work, celebrity more than gritty entrepreneurship.[13] Celebrities promise success in a world where inequality and insecurity reign. Just when many citizens feel the American dream is more difficult to achieve, celebrities with dramatic stories of their own ascent offer reassurance that it is still possible for anyone to achieve the wealth and fame of the Sharks.[14] On-screen, the Sharks project the importance of individualism, but off-screen they are organization men and women who deploy professional expertise and institutional heft. Myths, like the many variants of the American dream, are powerful precisely because they involve such contradictions. In face of a rapidly changing and often confusing world, invocations of the American dream offer more comfort than resolution.

The Sharks and the pitchers who ambitiously approach them are not necessarily disingenuous in their embrace of some version of the American dream. There is no need to suspect that the Sharks are not true believers when they frame their life stories the way they do. As television personalities speaking to audience members, they may well believe what they are saying even if they do not reveal all that they believe in. Yet we should be suspicious about their professed commitment to self-made individualism, given how much we know about both the power of the social and economic structures that shape lives (theirs included) and the importance of government-sponsored research, cultural traditions, and networks of family, friends, and associates.[15]

We can understand *Shark Tank*'s power by locating it historically. Both social scientists and ordinary citizens see the period from the mid-1930s to the late 1960s as a time when many Americans lived under imperfect but generally improving conditions. In what is known as the Keynesian system or the New Deal order, strong labor unions, corporations committed to the public good, and a federal government bent on improving the lives of citizens together helped create a more egalitarian society and sustain widely shared prosperity. Communities often functioned effectively, giving citizens access to abundant and supportive social connections; at the local level there was widespread participation in a variety of religious and civic organizations that were critical in promoting people's satisfaction with their lives; and nationally, bipartisan cooperation helped underwrite some degree of political peace. At a time when the white male breadwinner was ascendant, not everyone flourished—not African Americans, Latinxs, or, largely, women. Nonetheless, in the memories of millions of Americans and in the writings of a much smaller number, these years serve as a starting point from which the nation has tragically departed.[16] Later changes, including those introduced by the Great Recession, dramatically undercut the social and economic well-being of millions and created the conditions that would later exacerbate political tensions in ways that threatened constitutional and democratic norms. The economic collapse and the government's rescue of major banks and corporations but not ordinary Americans raised questions about the legitimacy of political and economic elites and the institutions they represented.[17]

Today, social scientists and journalists offer a dramatically bleaker picture of American life than what viewers see on *Shark Tank*.[18] They focus on a series of changes that have overtaken the nation since the 1970s, precisely the same time when entrepreneurship came into prominence.[19] Half of American children today live in poverty for at least one year. Almost half of American households don't have $400 in cash to cover an emergency expense. The median amount of money people aged fifty-five to sixty-four have in a retirement account is $120,000, which is hardly enough for most people to live on in the decades of retirement even if they receive Social Security. The United States has the highest incarceration rate in the world, a figure that took off in the late 1970s. Latinxs make up almost 20 percent and African Americans almost 40 percent of those incarcerated.[20] Slightly more than one in three Americans do not expect their children to be better off than their parents. From 2000 to 2015, the average poverty rate was higher than it was from 1970 to 1985. Almost one in five American men in their prime working years do not have full-time jobs. In 2012 the approximately 160,000 households in the top 0.1 percent commanded 22 percent of the nation's wealth, a figure that had grown from 10 percent in the early 1960s. In contrast, the wealth of the people in the lowest 90 percent declined significantly after 1985. From 1976 to today, the wealthiest 1 percent received 56 percent of the benefits from economic growth. In these years and after, the incomes of tens of millions of middle-class Americans, those living between poverty and wealth, stagnated or declined.

Suicide, drug addiction, environmental degradation, family disruption, and loss of steady, well-paying jobs with benefits have left communities in tragic disarray.[21] Some people in coastal cities have benefited from the growth in high-paying jobs in the finance and tech sectors. Yet at a time when there is a robust market for mansions and McMansions, tens of millions of Americans struggle to keep a decent roof over their heads. This includes not only those who are literally homeless but those who are in danger of being evicted, subject to unaffordable rent increases, threatened with foreclosure, or commuting four hours a day or more because they can't afford a home closer to their job.[22] The benefits of educational opportunities are also unevenly distributed—not only in elementary schools but also in colleges and universities. As many as 20 percent of students do not complete high school in four years. There are also high dropout rates for college students—and a hefty proportion of those who do graduate get jobs that do not require the education on which they spent so much time and money. About 44 million Americans owe a total of $1.5 trillion in student loan debt. Budget deficits—created in part by tax policies that favor the wealthy—threaten Social Security, Medicare, and Medicaid, on which so many Americans rely. What makes it difficult for the nation to begin to solve these problems is that the political system is fractured, reflecting deep social and ideological divisions in the nation.

A number of forces have hollowed out the middle class and greatly weakened the health of the working class. Trade unions, which once provided access to middle-class incomes, have come under sustained attack, often by alliances of business, government, and well-funded advocacy groups. What frequently takes the place of collective action by employees is collective action by employers.[23] Local, state, and federal government jobs, historically central to social mobility, have also come under attack. The growth in the gig economy, which is characterized by flexible and uncertain patterns of employment, has further reduced the number of stable, well-paying jobs with benefits. Some celebrate the success of companies like Uber, Airbnb, TaskRabbit, and WeWork as evidence of the empowering of entrepreneurs, but critics point out that an erosion of protections for workers and an increase in uncertainty has accompanied that success.[24] Growing inequality and attendant threats to social mobility (both within a generation and intergenerationally) have both driven and resulted from these changes. Just as influential has been the force of growing insecurity as tens of millions of people have experienced greater risk—most notably in health care, employment, housing, and retirement.[25] The impact of all these changes has fallen most heavily on African Americans, Latinxs, and members of the white working class—notably, even life expectancy has declined for rural and working-class Americans. In the end it is tragically problematic that so many Americans cling to a belief in social mobility precisely at a time when, compared with what has been true historically in America and is still true in much of Western Europe, real rates of social mobility are so compromised.[26]

We live in a new Gilded Age. The very wealthy lead lives well out of reach of the rest. Moreover, they have come to wield an outsize amount of power through a variety of means, including exerting influence in politics, economics, and philanthropy. Very wealthy Americans use philanthropy and other means to preserve the very systems that helped make them wealthy, and they do so in ways that impede social progress rather than, as they often claim, advance it. Those who gather at Davos and elsewhere use buzzwords such as *artificial intelligence, sustainable capitalism, philanthrocapitalism*, and of course *entrepreneurship* to promote innovation, but they fail to call into question the very forces that have both helped created their wealth and made life difficult for so many others.[27]

Powerful forces—globalization, immigration, technology, public policy—have driven these transformative changes, which resulted in the triumph of powerful winners over vastly more numerous losers.[28] Globalization, spurred by free trade and new technologies, has fundamentally reshaped labor, consumer, and capital markets. Immigration has benefited the fortunate but often adversely affected the work opportunities of others. Outsourcing services and importing goods from abroad increased dramatically in the last two decades as deindustrialization took hold. This meant that Americans traded stable, well-paying jobs for inexpensive consumer goods. And as a force that has made more tenuous the hold millions of people have on decent living standards, advances in technology have come with high social costs—ones whose impact will continue.

If those on the Right problematically see immigrants as the main economic threat, those on the Left emphasize new technologies taking jobs away from American workers. Several studies of the impact of robotics, automation, and artificial intelligence predict looming challenges to jobs from technology. Although for the time being sluggish productivity growth has slowed these changes, new technologies pose a threat not only to the 3.5 million cashiers and 1.8 million truck drivers but also to white-collar professionals.[29] Congressional gridlock and wrong turns in American politics have made it impossible for government to deal effectively with this threat. Deregulation, begun during the presidency of Jimmy Carter and intensified in the 1980s during the presidency of Ronald Reagan, when the Chicago school of economics gained traction, has eroded protections for workers and consumers. Another important factor in the shifts in the American economy since the 1970s was the change from the Keynesian emphasis on demand to an emphasis on supply, as supported by the writings of George Gilder and Arthur Laffer. With antitrust initiatives weak and even, until recently, off the table, the power of monopolies and oligopolies has increased, often at the expense of small businesses and startups.[30]

Today, in the second decade of the twenty-first century, the nation is witnessing the slowest rate of formation of new companies since at least the 1970s.[31] Despite what the popularity of *Shark Tank* and the media's focus on gig economy suggest, in the new century steady and significant corporate employment has remained strong. Small-scale businesses may create abundant numbers of new jobs, but many of them are precarious or short-lived.

Much of what I have written above relies on the work of left-leaning scholars and journalists. However, some conservative writers, though offering different causal explanations and different solutions, also emphasize the devastation wreaked on millions of Americans since the 1960s. In 2012, four years before the election of Donald Trump, in *Coming Apart: The State of White America, 1960–2010*, political scientist Charles Murray painted a dire picture of an America characterized by a chasm between what he called the "new upper class" and the "new lower class." The former, he said, live comfortably in wealthy enclaves where they remain ignorant of the other America. Focusing not on race but on class, Murray pictured the new lower class devastated by the breakdown of family life, the erosion of industriousness among men, the spread of crime and violence, the absence of religious commitments, and the collapse of social capital. These trends, he concluded gloomily, "signify damage to the heart" of American life because "many of the best and most exceptional qualities of American culture cannot survive unless they are reversed."

In 1984, while a fellow at the Manhattan Institute, a conservative think tank, Murray had authored *Losing Ground: American Social Policy, 1950–1980*, in which he argued that social welfare policies increased rather than decreased poverty because they relied on destructive incentives. Now, in *Coming Apart*, without advocating specific remedies, he called for a "Civic Great Awakening." With a "political agenda" centered on pro-life advocacy, tax revolts, and media criticism, this movement would "reinstate the principle of equality of opportunity versus the continuing attempt of the disciples of the Third Great Awakening to extend the principle of equality of condition." This "awakening" would happen if America's elites would "once again fall in love with what makes America different," envisioning, he wrote in the book's final sentence, "the American prospect for what it has been: a different way for people to live together, unique among the nations of the earth, and immeasurably precious."[32]

What explains the disjuncture between the world envisioned on *Shark Tank* and the views of contemporary American life offered by journalists and social scientists? *Shark Tank* draws some of its appeal from how amply it provides solace and advice to people who feel they can no longer hope for substantial help from a government-sponsored safety net, even if they do rely on such aid. Instead, in a world of free-market individualism, Americans are told they must rely on self-determination, grit, ambition, and hard work. For many people, their lives are thus enterprising ones. Again and again, Burnett and the Sharks emphasize self-governance, the promise of individual liberation through entrepreneurship, and the fulfillment of the American dream in a world governed by powerful though largely invisible external forces.[33]

Yet some on the Left insist that programs like *Shark Tank* cleverly prevent viewers from seeing a much more problematic reality. These critics insist that, among other forces, mass media transforms active citizens into passive viewers in ways that prevent them from seeing how powerful social, political, and economic forces and their advocates are manipulating them. This involves, such critics argue, lulling viewers into various somnambulant states that prevent them from understanding how shows like *Shark Tank* use distracting entertainment to reframe reality. This makes it difficult if not impossible for citizens to think critically about the relationships between what they see on-screen and the challenges they face in their own lives. Instead of protesting inequities, viewers turns to fantasies of escape from confining conditions and aspire to become wealthy like the Sharks.[34]

A different interpretation sees the relationships between purveyors and consumers of mass culture as more reciprocal, its power as potentially utopian.[35] Its advocates emphasize pleasures that TV shows, for example, offer in the face of the dystopian circumstances in which audience members find themselves. This approach enables us to balance the conceptual power of neoliberalism with an understanding of how people on the ground see their own lives and express their longings. Reconciling *Shark Tank* with the social and economic conditions that prevail in the early twenty-first century involves comprehending the ways that reality TV helps people learn how to rely on self-determination. Reality TV appeals because it addresses everyday challenges and losses by offering viewers an aspirational, escapist, or utopian prospect. Faced with scarcity, popular cultural productions such as *Shark Tank* enable people to imagine a capacity to act and to understand what they see on-screen as part of communal experiences. Consuming television can provide short-term answers to the problems of the imperfect society we live in.

What would it mean to apply such an approach to *Shark Tank*? Faced with economic and social challenges, contestants and viewers can envision abundance and more equal opportunity. If they cannot find satisfactory work, they can imagine a world where work is like play. *Shark Tank* is aspirational, letting fans imagine intense and dramatic experiences. Living as many of them do in a world that fragments their lives and leaves them isolated, *Shark Tank* may help them envision what it might be like to live in a community with access to some form of cooperative action, whether in the form of help from the Sharks or as members of imagined communities on screen, online, and even in person.

We've seen throughout this book the influence of figures such as Horatio Alger, Napoleon Hill, and Norman Vincent Peale. Those who invoke them do so to reconcile the real and the ideal, which in the case of *Shark Tank* involves the gap between a dangerous world and reassurances that an individual can transcend or conquer it. All such resolutions rest on some kind of divergence that is essential to the approach's power. For some of the elect, skill, hard work, or just plain luck make it possible to achieve the seemingly impossible, just as Mark Burnett, Barbara Corcoran, Robert Herjavec, and Daymond John did. The fact that there are such examples makes it credible that the viewer can also make it. The historian Daniel T. Rodgers put it cogently when I asked him to explain the appeal of the television show's vision in such troubled times: "Take a small piece of reality, pump up its magical powers in your mind, hug close its reassurances, let it sweep away the pains you live with—isn't that the way fantasies and fantasy shows work?"[36]

Not surprisingly, all these explanations help us through the thicket of messy reality. It is hardly coincidental that *Shark Tank* was launched when the effects of the Great Recession were being widely felt. Moreover, there is plenty of evidence in the episodes themselves and in the reactions to them that an emphasis on self-governance can prevent people from taking effective political action. In the hands of some observers, both neoliberalism and the idea that powerful forces block people from effectively piercing reality can too easily rely on concepts that intellectuals and scholars impose on complicated reality from above. Yet it does strike me that more cautiously stressing the importance of aspirational and perhaps utopian visions can help explain how a show like *Shark Tank* provides hope for viewers living in difficult times, and its possibilities and limitations. Entrepreneurship rests on a powerful set of ideas and is all the more alluring precisely because of its mythological power.

Despite the exaggerated rhetoric that surrounds the concept of the American dream, most Americans might be satisfied with relatively modest gains—seeing a child graduate from college, the first in the family to do so, or paying off a mortgage. Moreover, it is important to remember, if my survey of audience reactions is correct, that most viewers experience *Shark Tank* as pleasurable entertainment. They luxuriate in gossip about personalities, products, and pitches rather than rely on the show to educate them about how to become successful entrepreneurs. They choose this show as one of many forms of entertainment that they enjoy. It is also possible that behind such reactions operate powerful forces that prompt them to limit their political consciousnss by viewing the show as circuslike entertainment.

The seemingly unbounded celebration of the entrepreneur on *Shark Tank* reflects both a rejection of the presumably soulless character of the organization man and the cultural and even spiritual belief in the transcendent qualities of the entrepreneur. In a talk he gave at New York University's Stern School of Business in early 2019, Mark Cuban contrasted the world of the old-style organization man with the world he believed those in his audience faced. A long time ago, he said, MBA students felt pressure to pursue careers at large corporations such as General Motors or IBM and then retire comfortably on an ample pension. "Those days are gone," he observed. "You're a free agent. And you're always going to be a free agent on the market.... What have you got to lose?"[37]

In the first four months of 2019, I audited two courses at the University of Southern California's Marshall School of Business, which prompted me to ponder the new entrepreneurial economy. Once a week I listened in as Noam Wasserman taught Founder's Dilemmas and watched Christina Lubinski teach Entrepreneurial Imagination: Past, Present and Future. As I traveled on the Los Angeles Metro system, I had a lot of time to think about the contrasts between the secure world I had inhabited as a college professor, what I saw out the window en route to the University of Southern California, and the worlds of the students in these two classes, most of whom already had business experience and were now pursuing MBA degrees. I thought about how my career as a salaried man was the higher-education equivalent of the older career trajectory Cuban described. Researching and writing this book, and then auditing two courses on entrepreneurship, introduced me to a very different perspective. Through American entrepreneurship generally and *Shark Tank* specifically, I began to understand what the new economic order looks like.

The post–World War II social and economic order was powerful and comprehensive, though hardly perfect—especially for disenfranchised workers, sexual outliers, women, Latinxs, and African Americans. Similarly, the entrepreneurial order that gained traction in the 1970s and even

In Los Angeles County there are more than 50,000 homeless people, many of whom sleep on the streets at night. This picture shows a tent city in downtown L.A.; the tallest skyscraper in the background, exactly one mile away, is the U.S. Bank Building, which houses Lloyd Greif's investment banking firm. The University of Southern California, three and a half miles from that skyscraper, is the home of the Lloyd Greif Center for Entrepreneurial Studies in the Marshall School of Business. Chon Kit Leong / Alamy Stock Photo.

with its problematic aspects was fully visible in the new century, has an important logic of its own. In the clichéd, entertainment version of the economy seen on *Shark Tank* and, more important, in the lives of myriad entrepreneurs, especially the more successful ones, the present seems exciting and the future promising. There is risk and uncertainty, to be sure, for serial entrepreneurs in a rapidly changing world. However, for the more fortunate this is offset by excitement, creativity, opportunity—rewards both material and otherwise. The inauguration of Barack Obama as president in January 2009 took place three years after the publication of his book *The Audacity of Hope: Thoughts on Reclaiming the American Dream*. The Great Recession continued to threaten the nation when the first episode of *Shark Tank* aired seven months later. In politics and in entrepreneurship, sometimes hope fails, but sometimes it wins.

In the end, there are many ways to understand *Shark Tank*'s resonance. It may well provide viewers with the tools to envision, aspire to, and even achieve their dreams—or at least indulge in them, fruitfully or not. For millions of people it is capacious, pleasurable, anesthetizing, compelling entertainment. Yet it also takes strength from cultural traditions that reverberate in difficult times, most powerfully in new media. *Shark Tank* specifically and the multitudinous expressions of entrepreneurship more generally remain problematic in their wondrous celebration of an exciting and transformative future. Their promises of hope all too often remain hollow in a world that needs more healing than risk.

Acknowledgments

On *Shark Tank*, aspiring entrepreneurs seek from wealthy investors not only strategic partnerships but also funding in exchange for some equity. In contrast, when I asked others for help, I could promise in return only my gratitude—expressed to them in person and now in print.

To read what I was writing, I first turned to Helen L. Horowitz, who gave multiple drafts careful readings that improved what I wrote on both micro and macro levels. Once again, Lynn Dumenil and Judy Smith proved how wonderful they are as writing buddies and editors. Jim Hoopes contributed the unusual combination of his acuity as an editor, his insights as a historian of American capitalism, and his sustained firsthand familiarity with entrepreneurship education and practices. Ken Lipartito saved me from making mistakes, broadened the scope of my attention, and enriched what I was trying to do. Larry Glickman gave the entire manuscript a careful and probing reading that pushed me to connect the dots and write more critically. Two anonymous readers—one for another press and one for the University of North Carolina Press—provided some pertinent warnings and suggestions. I am deeply grateful to Pamela Walker Laird, an official reader and an unofficial adviser, for bringing her abundant skills as a business historian and more generally as a thoughtful colleague to help make this a better book. Dan Rodgers brought his probing intelligence to bear on issues I was struggling to resolve in chapter 9, helping me figure my way out of some intellectual dead ends. Having read several chapters, Nan Enstad helped me think through some sticky and critical issues and did so in probing and transformative ways. At a critical moment and in crucial ways, John Demos helped me understand why I write the way I do.

Other scholars helped me in more particular ways, among them Joel Best, Emma Bloomfield, Christian Christiansen, Susan Douglas, Tom Eisenmann, Larry Friedman, Bill Gartner, Louis Hyman, Brian Kingsley Krumm, Donald Kurtatko, Jeff Melnick, Chad Newsom, Tom Nicholas, Ellen O'Connor, Laurie Ouellette, Dana Polan, Jeffrey Pollack, Liz Pryor, James Shapiro, Elliott Stoller, Karl Vesper, Angelino Viceisza, Steve Viscelli, and Benjamin C. Waterhouse. Carol Bleier and Barbara Burstin but especially Eric Lidji and Joel Tarr helped me locate Mark Cuban in Pittsburgh historically. Then there were friends who sent me news of the Sharks and responded to my queries, including Tim Breen, Bettina Friedl, Herwig Friedl, David Gordon, Gwen Jensen, Len Katz, Jay Pasachoff, Monroe Price, Carol Rigolot, Amanda Seligman, Carl Smith, and Jane Smith.

Footnotes refer to some who have watched even more episodes of *Shark Tank* than have I and talked with me about what they saw. Among the high school students are Anushka Nair, Alizah Nauman, Mikey Paine, and Piram Singh. Courtney Bigony, Jamie Grischkan, Andrew Katz, Jake Katz, Jeffrey Katz, Chelsea Margolies, Rob O'Reilly, Susan Riecken, Tom Vo, and Sean Zoka shared their impressions with me. Jennifer Estlin helped me understand *Shark Tank, the Musical*. People who chose to remain anonymous (whom I call "someone experienced in entrepreneurship"; a "serial entrepreneur"; a "private investor"; and an "experienced television executive") greatly helped me understand how people with extensive experience in their fields critically view what happens on *Shark Tank*.

Many are those who helped me understand the institutional contexts of American entrepreneurship. Alisha Slye, formerly executive director of Blackstone LaunchPad, informed me about that project, and Dr. Wendy E. F. Torrance told me about the Ewing Marion Kauffman Foundation. Alisha put me in touch with Paul Major and Marc Nager of the Telluride Foundation. Cameron Ford informed me about entrepreneurship efforts at the University of Central Florida and then connected me with other useful informants, including Phil Dumas. Tami Raaker introduced me to students at Foothill High School in Pleasanton, California. Dr. Lisa-Marie Burns of Washington High School in Fremont, California, guided me into and through the world of high school business education and competitions. John Fistolera helped me understand DECA's support of high school entrepreneurs. Ted Rogers drew on his career in private equity to describe how pitches were made in that world.

Even though I'm retired from teaching, academic institutions and the people in them remain crucial to my research and writing. Smith College provided funds that supported my research. Among those who made comprehensible what goes on at Babson College are Candida Brush, Fritz Fleischmann, Jim Hoopes, Debi Kleiman, Jeff Melnick, Heidi Neck, and Stephen Spinelli.

The Founder Central initiative at the Lloyd Greif Center for Entrepreneurial Studies at University of Southern California's Marshall School of Business played an outsize role in helping me understand the new territory I entered with this project. How I got there seemed accidental. Early on, I used Google to identify key books in the field of entrepreneurship. That led me to Noam Wasserman, now the dean at the Sy Syms School of Business at Yeshiva University but then at USC. His commanding knowledge and abundant generosity helped me fathom key aspects of the world of entrepreneurship. I learned from him through emails, over lunch in Brookline, Massachusetts, and in the classroom in California where I watched with admiration as he taught his course Founder's Dilemmas in the spring semester of 2019. Noam introduced me to Christina Lubinski, who was visiting USC from the Copenhagen School of Business. Auditing her course Entrepreneurial Imagination: Past, Present, and Future deepened my knowledge. Christina introduced me to Christoph Viebig, who helped me understand platform enterprises. Both Christina and Christoph helped me sharpen my analysis in a chapter they read. Christina also connected me with Dan Wadhwani, and they invited me to talk about my work in late October 2019 at the Historical Entrepreneurship Research Symposium at the Greif Center. There I learned from and connected with scholars, including many non-historians, who are doing path-breaking work that connects disparate fields. Then Wadhwani, having read drafts of four chapters, deployed his extraordinary command of the areas where history and entrepreneurship meet in ways that profoundly enhanced what I wrote.

I could not have researched and written this book without the help of libraries and librarians. Emily Miles of the Horn Library at Babson College and Heather Oswald of Special Collections at Harvard Business School guided me to what I needed in their holdings. The libraries of Occidental College, Harvard College, and Smith College gave me access to so much of what I needed. The public libraries of Pasadena, California, and Cambridge, Massachusetts, provided access to how-to books and other widely read texts. In the winter months the Huntington Library provided a home away from home. Its Spring Seminar, originated by Malcolm Rohrbaugh and carried on by Carol Rigolot, provided an ideal venue for presenting my research. At a meeting in late March 2019, many members responded to my talk in ways that wonderfully inform this book—including Hal Baron, Tim Breen, John Demos, Lilia De Katzew, David Gordon, Helen L. Horowitz, Ellen Landau, Howard Landau, Sharon Strom, and Howard Weinbrot.

Since people directly involved with *Shark Tank* would not respond to my inquiries, I turned elsewhere. David Abel, Lynn Dumenil, Judy Milestone, and Michael Rivera put me in touch with knowledgeable insiders. When I was just beginning on this project, Liz Bronstein served as my guide to unfamiliar territory. Susan Baronoff patiently explained how episodes of reality TV programs are edited. Among others, Noah Pollack and David Eilenberg graciously helped me understand the world of reality TV.

For legal concerns, I have relied on Andrew J. Ungberg in the Manhattan office of Frankfurt Kurnit Klein & Selz PC and on legal advice provided by the University of North Carolina Press. With some illustrations, I benefited from the help of Suzie Tibor. Lucky me to have this book published by the University of North Carolina Press. Mary Carley Caviness and Catherine Robin Hodorowicz skillfully handled the manuscript until Erin Granville finally guided the project from typescript to published book—and she did so with extraordinary tact, skill, and intelligence. Dino A. Battista and his colleagues worked with me to think about how to enhance the book's impact. From the very beginning Mark Simpson-Vos understood what I was doing. His faith in this project sustained me. Over time, he helped me find my voice as he taught me how to revise a manuscript so that the resulting book was more ambitious, careful, analytic, and capacious. At moments I found myself using words he inserted in his marginal notes; at other times, I was stunned by his ability to see issues, large and small, that I missed. His faith and his editorial work reminded me how much editors have made my professional life possible—something I have tried to capture in the book's dedication.

Notes

PREFACE

1. Michael Pettit, review of *Happier?*, by Daniel Horowitz, *Journal of the History of the Behavioral Sciences* 54 (Autumn 2018): 315–16.

INTRODUCTION

1. Many episodes of *Shark Tank* are available on YouTube, and all of them are available on Hulu. Wikipedia offers a full list of episodes, complete with dates, episodes, cast, pitches, and results: https://en.wikipedia.org/wiki/List_of_Shark_Tank_episodes. Sometimes when I refer in these notes to material posted on popular sites, such as TED Talks, Facebook posts, tweets, Instagram posts, podcasts, or material on institutional websites, I do not provide links.

2. Gale Robinson, "Shark Tank: How Is xCraft Drones Doing Today?," TVOvermind, December 12, 2017, https://www.tvovermind.com/shark-tank-xcraft-drones-today.

3. Ben Russell, "XCraft after *Shark Tank*—Recent Updates for 2017," Gazette Review, June 19, 2016, https://gazettereview.com/2016/06/xcraft-after-shark-tank-update.

4. Bobby Paschall, "ReadeREST after Shark Tank," Gazette Review, December 13, 2016, https://gazettereview.com/2016/03/readerest-shark-tank-recent-update.

5. Jason Lynch, "How the Reality TV King Created 11 Popular Shows and Counting," *Adweek*, April 19, 2015, https://www.adweek.com/tv-video/how-reality-tv-king-created-11-popular-shows-and-counting-164157.

6. Burnett's selection of Trump as the star of *The Apprentice* helped lead Trump to the White House. Burnett had contributed to Barack Obama's campaigns but resisted pressure in late 2016 to release potentially damaging clips from *The Apprentice* that had ended up on the cutting-room floor. During the fall campaign he criticized Trump when he remarked, "My wife and I reject the hatred, division, and misogyny that has been a very unfortunate part of his campaign." Cynthia Littleton, "Mark Burnett: 'I Have Never Been a Supporter of Donald Trump's Candidacy,'" *Variety*, October 12, 2016; Brian Naylor, "Trump Touts Apprentice Ratings, Tells Prayer Breakfast: 'Pray for Arnold,'" NPR, February 2, 2017, http://www.npr.org/2017/02/02/513052930/trump-touts-apprentice-ratings-tells-prayer-breakfast-pray-for-arnold. According to *New Yorker* reporter Patrick Radden Keefe and those he interviewed, once Trump was president Burnett performed a delicate dance to avoid harming his own brand. Patrick Radden Keefe, "Winning:

How Mark Burnett, the King of Reality Television, Helped Turn a Floundering D-Lister into President Trump," *New Yorker*, January 7, 2019, 30–45.

7. The peak and then decline in ratings resulted in a discussion of how long it would remain on the air: in a 2018 blog post, Rob Merlino speculated on the reasons for its decline, including Cuban's politics; the show's shift to Sunday evenings, where it competes with NFL games; and a flood of rebroadcasts on CNBC. Rob Merlino, "Will There Be a *Shark Tank* Season Ten?," *Shark Tank Blog*, March 7, 2018, http://www.sharktankblog.com/will-there-be-a-shark-tank-season-ten.

8. R. Daniel Wadhwani, "Death and Rebirth of the Entrepreneurial Hero" (presentation, Business History Conference, Cartagena, Colombia, March 16, 2019). Any list of other factors driving the increased attention to entrepreneurship would include the Rockefeller Foundation's support of the Harvard Research Center in Entrepreneurial History, which was founded in 1948 and sponsored the publication of the scholarly journal *Explorations in Entrepreneurial History*. It would also include, more generally, the impact of Cold War modernization theory.

9. Among earlier critiques were William H. Whyte, *The Organization Man* (New York: Simon and Schuster, 1956); Vance Packard, *The Status Seekers* (New York: McKay, 1959); and John Keats, *Crack in the Picture Window* (Boston, Mass.: Houghton Mifflin, 1956), which were all followed by more ideological renderings such as Charles Reich, *The Greening of America* (New York: Random House, 1969); and Herbert Marcuse, *One-Dimensional Man* (Boston, Mass.: Beacon, 1964).

10. For historical scholarship on the rise of conservative economics, see Binyamin Applebaum, *The Economists' Hour: False Prophets, Free Markets, and the Fracture of Society* (Boston, Mass.: Little, Brown, 2019); Angus Burgin, *The Great Persuasion: Reinventing Free Markets since the Great Depression* (Cambridge, Mass.: Harvard University Press, 2012); Kim Phillips-Fein, *Invisible Hands: The Making of the Conservative Movement from the New Deal to Reagan* (New York: W. W. Norton, 2009).

11. Ronald Reagan, "Remarks and a Question-and-Answer Session with Members of the Chamber of Commerce in Mooresville, Indiana," June 19, 1985, Ronald Reagan Presidential Library and Museum, https://www.reaganlibrary.gov/research/speeches/61985a.

12. Christian Olaf Christiansen, *Progressive Business: An Intellectual History of the Role of Business in American Society* (New York: Oxford University Press, 2015), 182. Alan Greenspan and Adrian Woolridge's *Capitalism in America: A History* (New York: Penguin Press, 2018) provides a useful discussion of the rise of entrepreneurship and worries about threats to its vitality. Among the other useful writings are Sven Beckert, "History of American Capitalism," in *American History Now*, ed. Eric Foner and Lisa McGirr (Philadelphia: Temple University Press, 2011), 314–35; "Interchange: The History of Capitalism," *Journal of American History* 101 (September 2014): 503–36; Louis Hyman, "Why Write the History of Capitalism?" (blog post), *Symposium Magazine*, July 8, 2013, http://www.symposium-magazine.com/why-write-the-history-of-capitalism-louis-hyman/; "History of Capitalism Initiative," ILR School, Cornell University, http://hoc.ilr.cornell.edu/home; Kenneth Lipartito, "Reassembling the Economic: New Departures in Historical Materialism," *American Historical Review* 121 (February 2016): 101–39;

James Hoopes, *Corporate Dreams: Big Business in American Democracy from the Great Depression to the Great Recession* (New Brunswick, N.J.: Rutgers University Press, 2011); Richard R. John and Kim Phillips-Fein, *Capital Gains: Business and Politics in Twentieth-Century America* (Philadelphia: University of Pennsylvania Press, 2017); and Sven Beckert and Christine Desan, eds., *American Capitalism: New Histories* (New York: Columbia University Press, 2018).

13. Anthony Sampson, *Company Man: The Rise and Fall of Corporate Life* (London, UK: HarperCollins, 1995), x–xi, 15, 122, 133, 168–71, 186–88.

14. Barry Bluestone and Bennett Harrison, *The Great U-Turn: Corporate Restructuring and the Polarizing of America* (New York: Basic, 1988); Judith Stein, *Pivotal Decade: How the United States Traded Factories for Finance in the Seventies* (New Haven, Conn.: Yale University Press, 2011). For a history of the late twentieth century that provides background on the emergence of an entrepreneurial world, see Daniel T. Rodgers, *Age of Fracture* (Cambridge, Mass.: Harvard University Press, 2011).

15. Sampson, *Company Man*, 169–70.

16. Joseph A. Schumpeter, *Capitalism, Socialism, and Democracy* (New York: Harper, 1942), 83, 156.

17. "Entrepreneurial history," wrote two historians perceptively, is "*the study of the creative processes that propel economic change.*" See R. Daniel Wadhwani and Christina Lubinski, "Reinventing Entrepreneurial History," *Business History Review* 91 (Winter 2017): 767. See also R. Daniel Wadhwani, "How Entrepreneurship Forgot Capitalism: Entrepreneurship Teaching and Research in Business Schools," *Society* 49 (May 2012): 223–29. In preparation for a late October 2019 conference at the Marshall School of Business at the University of Southern California, titled Historical Entrepreneurship Research Symposium, Wadhwani and Lubinski highlighted material on historical entrepreneurship and presented an original, annotated bibliography for this emerging field. The meeting brought together scholars from many disciplines whose work pointed me toward fresh and exciting scholarship, including special issues of history in management and organizational studies journals, and exemplary books that demonstrate how to write historically in ways that complicate and broaden how we think about business—including Stephen Cummings et al., *A New History of Management* (New York: Cambridge University Press, 2017); Ellen S. O'Connor, *Creating New Knowledge in Management: Appropriating the Field's Lost Foundations* (Stanford, Calif.: Stanford Business Books, 2012); and Hans Landström and Franz Lohrke, *Historical Foundations of Entrepreneurship Research* (Northampton, Mass.: Edward Elgar, 2010).

18. Scott Shane and Sankaran Venkataraman, "The Promise of Entrepreneurship as a Field of Research," *Academy of Management Review* 25 (January 2000): 218.

19. Wadhwani, "Death and Rebirth."

20. K. H. Vesper and W. B. Gartner, "Measuring Progress in Entrepreneurship Education," *Journal of Business Venturing* 12 (September 1997): 406, quoted in Heidi M. Neck, Patricia G. Greene, and Claudia G. Brush, *Teaching Entrepreneurship: A Practice-Based Approach* (Northampton, Mass.: Edward Elgar, 2014), 3. In

a November 5, 2018, email to the author, Karl Vesper talked of the somewhat impressionistic evidence on which they relied to come to this conclusion.

21. Wadhwani and Lubinski, "Reinventing Entrepreneurial History," 773. See also Geoffrey Jones and R. Daniel Wadhwani, "Entrepreneurship," in *The Oxford Handbook of Business History*, ed. Geoffrey Jones and Jonathan Zeitlin (New York: Oxford University Press, 2007), 501–28. Raymond Boyle and Lisa W. Kelly explore changing images of entrepreneurs on television in *The Television Entrepreneurs: Social Change and Public Understanding of Business* (Burlington, Vt.: Ashgate, 2012), 14–22, 72–85.

22. See figure 11.2 in Angus Burgin, "The Reinvention of Entrepreneurship," in *American Labyrinth: Intellectual History for Complicated Times*, ed. Raymond Haberski Jr. and Andrew Hartman (Ithaca, N.Y.: Cornell University Press, 2018), 175.

23. Nandini Rajagopalan and Elissa Grossman, letter to participants in Historical Entrepreneurship Research Symposium, copy in author's possession.

24. Jerome A. Katz, "The Chronology and Intellectual Trajectory of American Entrepreneurship Education, 1976–1999," *Journal of Business Venturing* 18 (March 2003): 284.

25. Donald F. Kuratko, "The Emergence of Entrepreneurship Education: Development, Trends, and Challenges," *Entrepreneurship Theory and Practice* 29 (September 2005): 578. A historical narrative is provided in Neck, Greene, and Brush, *Teaching Entrepreneurship*, 1–17. Not until late 1981 did Harvard Business School begin to make significant commitments to the field of entrepreneurship in its curriculum. See Howard W. Stevenson and Teresa M. Amabile, "Entrepreneurial Management: In Pursuit of Opportunity," in *The Intellectual Venture Capitalist: John H. McArthur and the Work of the Harvard Business School, 1980–1995*, ed. Thomas K. McCraw and Jeffrey L. Cruikshank (Boston, Mass.: Harvard Business School Press, 1999), 133–62. In his article "The Small Business Myth" and in work on his current project titled "The Small Business Mystique: Big Dreams and Last Resorts at the End of the American Century," Benjamin C. Waterhouse focuses on this topic in many ways that parallel what I write about the mystique of the entrepreneur. See Benjamin C. Waterhouse, "The Small Business Myth," Aeon, November 8, 2017, https://aeon.co/essays/what-does-small-business-really-contribute -to-economic-growth.

26. Lawrence B. Glickman, *Free Enterprise: An American History* (New Haven, Conn.: Yale University Press, 2019). The rise of discussions of the entrepreneur also came after the waning of the left-liberal vision of a postcapitalist order described in Howard Brick, *Transcending Capitalism: Visions of a New Society in Modern American Thought* (Ithaca, N.Y.: Cornell University Press, 2006). In *Transaction Man: The Rise of the Deal and the Decline of the American Dream* (New York: Farrar, Straus and Giroux, 2019), Nicholas Lemann charts a three-stage transformation that also helps explain the rise of the entrepreneur: the first stage was the New Deal order; the second, the takeover of the nation by finance beginning in the 1970s; and the third, Silicon Valley's combination of disruption and reknitting of the social fabric through social media.

27. James Poniewozik writes of how other reality television shows provide poor

people a vision of something they aspire to in *Audience of One: Donald Trump, Television, and the Fracturing of America* (New York: Liveright, 2019), 119.

28. Michel Foucault, *The Birth of Biopolitics: Lectures at the Collège de France, 1978–1979*, ed. Michel Senellart, trans. Graham Burchell (New York: Palgrave Macmillan, 2008), 218, 219, 226.

29. David Harvey, *A Brief History of Neoliberalism* (New York: Oxford University Press, 2005), 2.

30. For probing essays on neoliberalism, see Daniel T. Rodgers, "The Uses and Abuses of 'Neoliberalism,'" *Dissent*, Winter 2018, 78–87; Kim Phillips-Fein, "The History of Neoliberalism," in *Shaped by the State: Toward a New Political History of the Twentieth Century*, ed. Brent Cebul, Lily Geismer, and Mason B. Williams (Chicago, Ill.: University of Chicago Press, 2018), 347–62; Bruce J. Schulman, "Post-1968 U.S. History: Neo-consensus History for the Age of Polarization," *Reviews in American History* 47 (September 2019): 479–99; and Bruce Robbins, "Everything Is Not Neoliberalism," *American Literary History* 31 (Winter 2019): 840–49. On the connections between neoliberalism, reality TV, and celebrity culture, see Laurie Ouellette, "'Take Responsibility for Yourself': *Judge Judy* and the Neoliberal Citizen," in *Reality TV: Remaking Television Culture*, ed. Susan Murray and Laurie Ouellette (New York: New York University Press, 2004), 231–50; Guy Redden, "Is Reality TV Neoliberal?," *Television & New Media* 19 (July 1, 2018): 319–44; Marwan M. Kraidy, "Reality Television from *Big Brother* to the Arab Uprisings: Neoliberal, Liberal, and Geopolitical Considerations," in *A Companion to Reality Television*, ed. Laurie Ouellette (Malden, Mass.: Wiley, 2014), 541–56; Alison Hearn, "Producing 'Reality': Branded Content, Branded Selves, Precarious Futures," in Ouellette, *A Companion to Reality Television*, 437–55; John Hay, "Unaided Virtues: The (Neo)-Liberalization of Domestic Space," *Television & New Media* 1 (February 2000): 53–73; David Grazian, "Neoliberalism and the Realities of Reality Television," *Contexts* 9 (Spring 2010): 68–71; Paul Gilroy, "'. . . We Got to Get Over Before We Go Under . . .': Fragments for a History of Black Vernacular Neoliberalism," *New Formations* 80–81 (Winter 2013): 23–38; Adrienne Shaw, introduction to *The Politics of Reality Television: Global Perspectives*, ed. Marwan M. Kraidy and Katherine Sender (New York: Routledge, 2011), 61; Katherine Sender, "Migrating Genres, Travelling Participants, Shifting Theories," in Kraidy and Sender, *Politics of Reality Television*, 4–5; Nick Couldry and Jo Littler, "The Work of Work: Reality TV and the Negotiation of Neo-liberal Labour in *The Apprentice*," in *Rethinking Documentary: New Perspectives and Practices*, ed. Thomas Austin and Wilma de Jong (London, UK: Open University Press, 2008), 258–67; and Jessalyn Marie Keller, "Fiercely Real? Tyra Banks and the Making of New Media Celebrity," *Feminist Media Studies* 14 (February 2014): 1047–64. More generally, Janice Peck, *The Age of Oprah: Cultural Icon for the Neoliberal Era* (Boulder, Colo.: Paradigm, 2008); Harvey, *Brief History of Neoliberalism*; and Wendy Brown, *Undoing the Demos: Neoliberalism's Stealth Revolution* (Brooklyn, N.Y.: Zone, 2015) are essential reading. No discussion of neoliberalism is possible without an understanding of Foucault's concept of governmentality: see Graham Burchell, Colin Gordon, and Peter Miller, eds., *The Foucault Effect: Studies in Governmentality, with Two Lectures by and an Interview with Michel Foucault* (Chicago,

Ill.: University of Chicago Press, 1991). A vivid description of key elements of the neoliberal order may be found in Jill Lepore, *These Truths: A History of the United States* (New York: W. W. Norton, 2018), 733–38.

31. For the full story of these changes, see Tom Nicholas, *VC: An American History* (Cambridge, Mass.: Harvard University Press, 2019).

32. Matt Mansfield, "Startup Statistics: The Numbers You Need to Know," *Small Business Trends*, December 26, 2018, https://smallbiztrends.com/2016/11 /startup-statistics-small-business.html; "Small Business or Big Business: Which Really Creates the Most Jobs?" *Factor Finders*, https://www.factorfinders.com /small-business-job-creation-vs-big.

33. Boyle and Kelly, *Television Entrepreneurs*, 51.

34. On these changes in the television industry, see Chad Raphael, "The Political Economic Origins of Reali-TV," in Murray and Ouellette, *Reality TV*, 119–26; Ted Magder, "The End of TV 101: Reality Programs, Formats, and the New Business of Television," in Murray and Ouellette, *Reality TV*, 137–56; Su Holmes and Deborah Jermyn, eds., *Understanding Reality Television* (New York: Routledge, 2004); Laurie Ouellette and Susan Murray, introduction to Murray and Ouellette, *Reality TV*, 7. Although she doesn't mention *Shark Tank*, Katie Kilkenny discusses the challenges a similar show faces as audience numbers shrink and producers demand more of creative workers with less compensation in "Reality TV's Story Producers Face Decreasing Wages, Tougher Working Conditions," *Hollywood Reporter*, September 18, 2019.

35. For the debate over the "reality" of reality TV, see Annette Hill, *Restyling Factual TV: Audiences and News, Documentaries and Reality Genres* (New York: Routledge, 2007), and Mark Andrejevic, "Real-izing Exploitation" in Kraidy and Sender, *Politics of Reality Television*, 18–30.

36. C. Littleton, "Dialogue with Producer Mark Burnett," *Hollywood Reporter*, May 26, 2004.

37. Laurie Ouellette, introduction to Ouellette, *Companion to Reality Television*, 2.

38. Shelley Levitt, "What the Sharks Have Learned After a Decade in the Tank," *Success*, February 6, 2018, https://www.success.com/what-the-sharks-have-lear ned-after-a-decade-in-the-tank/.

39. An experienced television executive whose name is withheld by mutual agreement, conversation with author, January 14, 2019.

40. Andrew Ross Sorkin, "The Echoes of Lehman in Our Time of Distrust," *New York Times*, September 11, 2018.

41. In the context of the Great Recession, the producers learned that viewers wanted not meanness but inspiring stories and useful information, as well as roads to the American dream they could understand: Noah Pollack, "*Shark Tank*—Corie Henson and David Eilenberg," *Exec/Producer with Noah Pollack*, podcast, September 20, 2018, https://player.fm/series/execproducer-with-noah -pollack-2378550/shark-tank-corie-henson-david-eilenberg; David Eilenberg (chief creative officer, ITV America), telephone discussion with author, February 11, 2019.

42. Margaret O'Mara, *The Code: Silicon Valley and the Remaking of America* (New York: Penguin, 2019); Nicholas, *VC*, 108–9, 132–46, 173–82, 315–19. Mariana Mazzucato counters the widely accepted division between an unimaginative state and an innovative private sector as she emphasizes the reciprocal relationships between the two and the role governments have played in economic development in *Entrepreneurial State*, rev. ed. (London, UK: Anthem, 2015), and *The Value of Everything: Making and Taking in the Global Economy* (London, UK: Allen Lane, 2016).

43. I have drawn on the abundant literature on reality TV, although in some important ways the questions I ask differ from those posed by scholars in the field. Among the best places to begin are several edited books that offer overviews of the field: Ouellette, *Companion to Reality Television*; Murray and Ouellette, *Reality TV*; and Laurie Ouellette and John Hay, *Better Living through Reality TV: Television and Postwelfare Citizenship* (Malden, Mass.: Blackwell, 2008). Other useful books are Miranda J. Banks, Bridget Conor, and Vicki Mayer, eds., *Production Studies, the Sequel! Cultural Studies of Global Media Industries* (New York: Routledge, 2009); Boyle and Kelly, *Television Entrepreneurs*; John Thornton Caldwell, *Production Culture: Industrial Reflexivity and Critical Practice in Film and Television* (Durham, N.C.: Duke University Press, 2008); Holmes and Jermyn, *Understanding Reality Television*; Kraidy and Sender, *Politics of Reality Television*; Anna McCarthy, *The Citizen Machine: Governing by Television in 1950s America* (New York: New Press, 2010); Toby Miller, *Cultural Citizenship: Cosmopolitanism, Consumerism, and Television in a Neoliberal Age* (Philadelphia: Temple University Press, 2007); Dana Polan, *Julia Child's "The French Chef"* (Durham, N.C.: Duke University Press, 2011); Diane Negra and Yvonne Tasker, eds., *Gendering the Recession: Media and Culture in an Age of Austerity* (Durham, N.C.: Duke University Press, 2014); Beverley Skeggs and Helen Wood, *Reacting to Reality Television: Performance, Audience and Value* (New York: Routledge, 2012); Julie Anne Taddeo and Ken Dvorak, eds., *The Tube Has Spoken: Reality TV and History* (Lexington: University Press of Kentucky, 2010). For an exploration of the relationship between Donald Trump and reality television, see Poniewozik, *Audience of One*, xxii, 106–41. To follow up-to-date discussions, see the website In Media Res and the journal *Television & New Media*. There are several avenues others have explored with *Shark Tank* and with reality TV more generally that I have not pursued, most notably global, comparative dimensions. For one study that offers a comparative perspective, see Dan Senor, *Start-Up Nation: The Story of Israel's Economic Miracle* (New York: Twelve, 2009). There are also some scholarly articles, many of which focus on education, entrepreneurship, and demographic identity. See, for example, Jeffrey M. Pollack, Matthew W. Rutherford, and Brian G. Nagy, "Preparedness and Cognitive Legitimacy as Antecedents of New Venture Funding in Televised Business Pitches," *Entrepreneurship Theory and Practice* 36 (September 2012): 915–39.

44. Mark Cuban, email to author, January 9, 2019.

45. Dan Fuchs, email to author, December 27, 2018; Caroline Mendoza, email to author, March 28, 2019.

46. Susan Baronoff, conversation with author, February 24, 2019.

47. An experienced television executive, conversation with author, January 14, 2019.

48. Poniewozik, *Audience of One*, 107.

49. John Carreyrou, *Bad Blood: Secrets and Lies in a Silicon Valley Startup* (New York: Knopf, 2018), 30, 101.

CHAPTER 1

1. Ken Langone, *I Love Capitalism! An American Story* (New York: Penguin, 2018), x, 41. Pamela Walker Laird, by emphasizing the importance of social capital, offers a trenchant and important challenge to the myth of the self-made individual in *Pull: Networking and Success since Benjamin Franklin* (Cambridge, Mass.: Harvard University Press, 2006) and "How Business Historians Can Save the World—from the Fallacy of Self-Made Success," *Business History Review* 59 (November 2017): 1201–17.

2. Langone, *Capitalism*, 251.

3. Tom Nicholas emphasizes the importance of the federal government for venture capitalism in his book *VC: An American History* (Cambridge, Mass.: Harvard University Press, 2019). For works on how luck and the connections between the state and business development challenge the myth of the self-made person, see Brian Miller and Mike Lapham, *The Self-Made Myth: And the Truth about How Government Helps Individuals and Businesses Succeed* (San Francisco, Calif.: Berrett-Koehler, 2012); and Robert H. Frank, *Success and Luck: Good Fortune and the Myth of Meritocracy* (Princeton, N.J.: Princeton University Press, 2016).

4. Philippe Sommer, letter to author, February 19, 2019. For books whose titles alone give a sense of the genre's hyped claims, see Gary Vaynerchuk, *Crushing It! How Great Entrepreneurs Build Their Business and Influence—and How You Can Too* (New York: HarperCollins, 2018); and Jay Samit, *Disrupt You! Master Personal Transformation, Seize Opportunity, and Thrive in the Era of Endless Innovation* (New York: Flatiron, 2015).

5. Among other sources, this chapter draws on Mark Burnett with Martin Dugard, *Survivor, the Ultimate Game: The Official Companion Book to the CBS Television Show* (New York: TV Books, 2000); Mark Burnett, *Survivor II, the Field Guide: The Official Companion to the CBS Television Show* (New York: TV Books, 2001); Mark Burnett, *Dare to Succeed: How to Survive and Thrive in the Game of Life* (New York: Hyperion, 2001); Mark Burnett, *Jump In! Even If You Don't Know How to Swim* (New York: Ballantine, 2005); Daymond John with Daniel Paisner, *The Power of Broke: How Empty Pockets, a Tight Budget, and a Hunger for Success Can Become Your Greatest Competitive Advantage* (New York: Crown Business, 2015); Michael Parrish DuDell, *Shark Tank: Jump Start Your Business: How to Launch and Grow a Business from Concept to Cash* (New York: Hyperion, 2013); Patrick Radden Keefe, "Winning: How Mark Burnett, the King of Reality Television, Helped Turn a Floundering D-Lister into President Trump," *New Yorker*, January 7, 2019, 30–45. With *Survivor II* and *Dare to Succeed*, Dugard's name did not appear on the title page, but in the acknowledgments Burnett made clear his reliance on him.

6. Burnett, *Dare to Succeed*, 1–2.

7. John, *Power of Broke*, 240.

8. Burnett, *Dare to Succeed*, 3.

9. Burnett, 21–22. Burton Borman (1928–2012) was a prominent corporate executive, art collector, and mentor to young entrepreneurs.

10. Burnett, 3–4.

11. Burnett, 23.

12. Burnett, *Survivor II*, 146.

13. Burnett, *Dare to Succeed*, 52.

14. Noah Pollack, media producer and executive and host of the podcast *Exec/ Producer with Noah Pollack*, telephone conversation with author, January 16, 2019.

15. Burnett, *Dare to Succeed*, 128. With *Survivor*, Burnett amplified what he had done with *Raid Gauloises* in developing what he claimed was a new business model for financing television programs. He spent a considerable amount of time finding sponsors and going from network to network to sell his show. He then arranged to share the profits with the network. These complicated arrangements helped shift production costs from the network to the sponsors, in effect having the advertisers pay to have access to a television audience. At the same time, he kept the intellectual property rights to the format.

16. Burnett, *Survivor II*, 146.

17. Burnett, *Survivor, the Ultimate Game*, 10.

18. Keat Murray, "Surviving *Survivor*: Reading Mark Burnett's *Field Guide* and De-naturalizing Social Darwinism as Entertainment," *Journal of American and Comparative Cultures* 24 (Fall/Winter 2001): 44.

19. Burnett, *Jump In!*, 185–87. On key aspects of reality TV's methods, see Alison Hearn, "Producing 'Reality': Branded Content, Branded Selves, Precarious Futures," in *A Companion to Reality Television*, ed. Laurie Ouellette (Malden, Mass.: Wiley, 2014), 441; Ted Magder, "The End of TV 101: Reality Programs, Formats, and the New Business of Television," in *Reality TV: Remaking Television Culture*, ed. Susan Murray and Laurie Ouellette (New York: New York University Press, 2004), 140–42; Annette Hill, "Reality TV Experiences: Audiences, Fact, and Fiction," in Ouellette, *Companion to Reality Television*, 118.

20. Among the scholarly considerations of *The Apprentice* are articles in the November 2016 issue of *Television & New Media*; and Laurie Ouellette and James Hay, *Better Living through Reality TV: Television and Postwelfare Citizenship* (Malden, Mass.: Blackwell, 2008), 149–52, 187–88.

21. "Mark Burnett Net Worth," *Celebrity Net Worth*, http://www.celebritynetworth .com/richest-businessmen/producers/mark-burnett-net-worth.

22. Burnett, *Jump In!*, 159.

23. Burnett, *Dare to Succeed*, 26.

24. Donald J. Trump, introduction to Burnett, *Jump In!*, xii.

25. John, *Power of Broke*, 243.

26. Burnett, *Jump In!*, v, 49, 108, 184, 221; John, 247.

27. Burnett, *Dare to Succeed*, 10.

28. Burnett, *Jump In!*, 272.

29. Mark Burnett, foreword to DuDell, *Jump Start Your Business*, viii–ix.

30. Burnett, *Dare to Succeed*, 1, 36.

31. Burnett, *Survivor II*, 144–45.

32. Keefe, "Winning," 33.

33. Dianne Burnett, *Road to Reality: Voted Off the Island! . . . My Journey as a Real-Life Survivor* (Los Angeles, Calif.: Agape Media International, 2012), 3.

34. D. Burnett, 91, 143–44.

35. Keefe, "Winning," 36.

CHAPTER 2

1. Joseph A. Schumpeter, *Capitalism, Socialism, and Democracy* (New York: Harper, 1942), 83, 156.

2. Scott Shane and Sankaran Venkataraman, "The Promise of Entrepreneurship as a Field of Research," *Academy of Management Review* 25 (January 2000): 218.

3. For information on how the show has changed over time, what the Sharks claim to have learned, and their favorite investments, see Shelley Levitt, "What the Sharks Have Learned after a Decade in the Tank," *Success*, February 6, 2018, https://www.success.com/what-the-sharks-have-learned-after-a-decade-in-the -tank/.

4. Kevin Harrington, who developed infomercials and plays a major role on the Home Shopping Network, was a mainstay in the first two seasons; Chris Sacca, a venture capitalist, appeared in several later seasons. In recent seasons, several guest Sharks made appearances, apparently because the producers wanted to have a more diverse cast, since several were women (including Sara Blakely, Bethenny Frankel, and Alli Webb), one was Latinx (Alex Rodriguez), one was African American (Charles Barkley), and two were Brits (Richard Branson and Zambia-born Rohan Oza). Andy Denhart, "*Shark Tank* Is Adding Five Guest Sharks, Including Bethenny Frankel," reality blurred, May 15, 2017, https://www .realityblurred.com/realitytv/2017/05/shark-tank-season-nine-guest-sharks.

In addition to books by individual Sharks, this chapter draws on Kelly Cole, *Conversations with Sharks: Success Stories Shared by the Sharks on ABC's Hit TV Show "Shark Tank,"* rev. ed. (n.p.: Prime Time Marketing and Kelly Cole, 2014); and Michael Parrish DuDell, *Shark Tank: Jump Start Your Business: How to Launch and Grow a Business from Concept to Cash* (New York: Hyperion, 2013). DuDell's website says this is "the official business book" of the show: http://www .michaelparrishdudell.com. In a glossy magazine format, *Inside the Shark Tank* (New York: Hearst, 2019) appeared in connection with season ten.

5. Noah Pollack, "*Shark Tank*—Corie Henson and David Eilenberg," *Exec/Producer with Noah Pollack*, podcast, September 20, 2018, https://player.fm/series /execproducer-with-noah-pollack-2378550/shark-tank-corie-henson-david -eilenberg. On the importance of branding on reality TV, see Alison Hearn, "Producing 'Reality': Branded Content, Branded Selves, and Precarious Futures," in *A Companion to Reality Television*, ed. Laurie Ouellette (Malden, Mass.: Wiley, 2014), 437–55; and June Deery, "Mapping Commercialization in Reality Television," in Ouellette, *Companion to Reality Television*, 11.

6. Raymond Boyle and Lisa W. Kelly, *The Television Entrepreneurs: Social Change and Public Understanding of Business* (Burlington, Vt.: Ashgate, 2012), 55.

7. This relies on the work of Chris Rojek, as presented in Julie A. Wilson, "Reality Television Celebrity: Star Consumption and Self-Production in Media Culture," in Ouellette, *Companion to Reality Television*, 422. On the history of celebrity culture, see Susan J. Douglas and Andrea McDonnell, *Celebrity: A History of Fame* (New York: New York University Press, 2019).

8. Boyle and Kelly, *Television Entrepreneurs*, 55, 83, 101, 148.

9. Corcoran's writings appear in three versions: Barbara Corcoran with Bruce Littlefield, *Use What You've Got and Other Business Lessons I Learned from My Mom* (New York: Penguin, 2003); republished, with most of the same content but with a more explicit discussion of lessons learned, as *If You Don't Have Big Breasts, Put Ribbons on Your Pigtails, and Other Lessons I Learned from My Mom* (New York: Penguin, 2004); and Barbara Corcoran with Bruce Littlefield, *Shark Tales: How I Turned $1,000 into a Billion Dollar Business* (New York: Penguin, 2011), which added "Shark Lessons" to the "Mom Lessons" that had appeared in the earlier versions. For other sources of information on Corcoran, see Penelope Green, "The Real Estate 'Queen' in Her Hive," *New York Times*, September 25, 2005; and William Neuman, "Big Deal: A Gun, a Gallop, and a Goodbye," *New York Times*, October 30, 2005.

10. "Barbara Corcoran's Favorite Mistake: Believing She Was Stupid," *Newsweek*, January 16, 2012. See also Kim Lachance Shandrow, "How Being Dyslexic and 'Lousy in School' Made *Shark Tank* Star Barbara Corcoran a Better Entrepreneur," *Entrepreneur*, September 19, 2014, https://www.entrepreneur.com/article/237669.

11. Corcoran, *Shark Tales*, 5.

12. Carter B. Horsley, "Study Shows Co-op Prices Nearly Quintupled," *New York Times*, August 20, 1981.

13. Corcoran, *Shark Tales*, 87.

14. Some sources call this a second marriage. I can find no reference to a first, but I assume she had married and then divorced Ray Simon.

15. Corcoran, *Shark Tales*, 198, 205.

16. She and her husband later adopted a girl.

17. Corcoran, *Shark Tales*, 227.

18. Corcoran, 4.

19. Corcoran, *Put Ribbons on Your Pigtails*, 6.

20. Corcoran, *Shark Tales*, 15, 63, 152, 156, 196, 232.

21. Corcoran, 231–41.

22. Robert Herjavec with John Lawrence Reynolds, *Driven: How to Succeed in Business and in Life* (Toronto, Canada: HarperCollins, 2010); Robert Herjavec with John Lawrence Reynolds, *The Will to Win: Leading, Competing, Succeeding* (Toronto, Canada: HarperCollins, 2013); Robert Herjavec with John Lawrence Reynolds, *You Don't Have to Be a Shark: Creating Your Own Success* (New York: St. Martin's Press, 2016).

23. Throughout this book, I am unable to distinguish between Canadian and United States dollars because my sources usually fail to do so.

24. Herjavec, *Driven*, 43, 190.

25. Herjavec, *You Don't Have to Be*, 117.

26. Unusually for a Shark, at some point he took three years off to help raise his children so his first wife, Diane Plese, a Canadian-born woman of Croatian ancestry and an optometrist, whom he had married in 1990, could return to work.

27. Deidre Kelly, "The BIG White House," *Globe and Mail*, May 12, 2016.

28. Herjavec, *Will to Win*, 13, 137.

29. Herjavec, *You Don't Have to Be*, 259, 263, 265, 268, 270.

30. Heather Nunn and Anita Biressi, "'Walking in Another's Shoes': Sentimentality and Philanthropy on Reality Television," in Ouellette, *Companion to Reality Television*, 491-92.

31. Herjavec, *You Don't Have to Be*, 268, 270.

32. Herjavec, *Will to Win*, 12-13, 25, 28-30.

33. Herjavec, *Driven*, 29.

34. Daymond John with Daniel Paisner, *The Power of Broke: How Empty Pockets, a Tight Budget, and a Hunger for Success Can Become Your Greatest Competitive Advantage* (New York: Crown Business, 2015), 10, 14.

35. Daymond John with Daniel Paisner, *The Display of Power: How FUBU Changed a World of Fashion, Branding and Lifestyle* (Nashville, Tenn.: Naked Ink, 2007), v, 2. In my discussion of John's career, I am relying on a number of sources, including books by him with Paisner: not only *Power of Broke* and *Display of Power* but also *Rise and Grind: Outperform, Outwork, and Outhustle Your Way to a More Successful and Rewarding Life* (New York: Crown, 2018); and *Brand Within: The Power of Branding from Birth to the Boardroom* (New York: Display of Power Publishing, 2010).

36. John, *Display of Power*, 10, 11, 14. See also Leslie Kaufman, "Trying to Stay True to the Street," *New York Times*, March 14, 1999.

37. *Inside the Shark Tank*, 66.

38. John, *Display of Power*, 35-36.

39. John, *Power of Broke*, 131.

40. Michel Marriott, "Out of the Woods," *New York Times*, November 7, 1993.

41. John, *Display of Power*, 58, 60, 139-40.

42. John, *Power of Broke*, 15.

43. John, *Brand Within*, 110.

44. John, *Display of Power*, 86, 90 (emphasis in original).

45. John, *Power of Broke*, 27.

46. Richard Feloni, "'Shark Tank' Investor Daymond John Landed a Deal That Helped Him Make $30 Million by Taking Out a Newspaper Ad," Business Insider, February 1, 2018, https://markets.businessinsider.com/news/stocks/shark-tank -daymond-john-newspaper-ad-samsung-deal-2018-2-1014839034.

47. John, *Display of Power*, 133, 162.

48. In *Rise and Grind*, John drew on interviews of people from diverse backgrounds, especially African Americans, Latinxs, and immigrants.

49. John, *Display of Power*, 155.

50. John, *Brand Within*, 3, 6, 10.

51. Lisa Bertagnoli, "Neat Trick: Patenting Her Way to Wealth," *Crain's Chicago*

Business, September 26, 2009. Of all the Sharks, Greiner is the one for whom there is the least information available, and it is especially difficult to find out much about her life before 1996.

52. Lori Greiner, *Invent It, Sell It, Bank It! Make Your Million-Dollar Idea into a Reality* (New York: Ballantine, 2014), 42. For information on Greiner, see her website (www.lorigreiner.com) and the Wikipedia entry on her (https://en.wikipedia .org/wiki/Lori_Greiner).

53. Greiner, *Invent It*, v, xxi, 9, 253.

54. "Greiner says she did not take out a loan from her family to start her business but admits she had a plan in place to financially lean on them, if needed": Kim Lachance Shandrow, "*Shark Tank*'s Star Lori Greiner's 4 Money Rules for New Entrepreneurs," *Entrepreneur*, October 15, 2014, https://www.entrepreneur .com/article/238448.

55. Greiner, *Invent It*, 249.

56. For his books, see Kevin O'Leary, *Cold Hard Truth on Business, Money, and Life* (Toronto, Canada: Anchor Canada, 2011); and Kevin O'Leary, *Cold Hard Truth on Men, Women, and Money: 50 Common Money Mistakes and How to Fix Them* (Toronto, Canada: Doubleday Canada, 2012).

57. James Poniewozik emphasizes the importance to reality television of the cruel antihero, a persona O'Leary presents on *Shark Tank*, in *Audience of One: Donald Trump, Television, and the Fracturing of America* (New York: Liveright, 2019), 114.

58. O'Leary, *Men, Women, and Money*, 250; *Business, Money, and Life*, 247.

59. O'Leary, *Business, Money, and Life*, 12, 27.

60. O'Leary, 25.

61. O'Leary, 4, 41–42.

62. O'Leary, 62, 67.

63. O'Leary, 76, 83.

64. O'Leary, 88.

65. O'Leary, 102, 110, 115.

66. Unlike the other Sharks, Cuban does not have a book that combines extensive stories about his life with advice. Nonetheless, much information is available in Mark Cuban, *How to Win at the Sport of Business: If I Can Do It, You Can Do It* (New York: Diversion, 2011); Mark Cuban, *Top 15 Secrets to Success in Life and Business: The Sportsmanship of Business* (n.p.: EntrepreneurshipFacts.com, 2016); David Dagen, *Mark Cuban: The Life and Success Stories of a Shark Billionaire* (n.p.: EntrepreneurshipFacts.com, 2017); Mark Cuban, foreword to Gary Shapiro, *The Comeback: How Innovation Will Restore the American Dream* (New York: Beaufort, 2011), ix–xi; and Mark Cuban, Shaan Patel, and Ian McCue, *Kid Start-Up: How You Can Be an Entrepreneur* (New York: Diversion Books, 2018), on whose back cover Cuban is called "self-made."

67. Brad Townsend, "Norton Cuban 'Absolutely Lives for His Sons,' Including Mavericks Owner, Whom He Taught to 'Live Young Every Day,'" *Dallas Morning News*, July 12, 2018, https://sportsday.dallasnews.com/dallas-mavericks/mav ericks/2018/07/12/norton-cuban-taught-mavericks-owner-son-mark-live-young -every-day-died-age-92.

68. Wikipedia, on which I often rely, says these new locations were in a working-class Jewish neighborhood, and the *Dallas Morning News* story cited above describes Norton Cuban as "a working-class man"; however, I identify Cuban's family of origin during Mark's youth as middle class because Norton was a business owner and by the time Cuban was a preteen the family lived in houses that were clearly middle class. In discussing Cuban's background I am relying on Eric S. Lidji, email to author, February 20, 2019; Barbara S. Burstin, email to author, February 9, 2019; and Joel Tarr, emails to author, January 10–15, 2019. On Cuban in Mount Lebanon, see J. W. Stehle, "Modern Mogul," *Mt. Lebanon Magazine*, March 24, 2014. One of the Squirrel Hill residences was just under a mile from the Tree of Life Congregation, the site of the 2018 massacre of eleven Jews by a white supremacist.

69. For example, a *New York Times* article revealed that Cuban owns eight residences (including a 24,000-square-foot home in the Preston Hollow section of Dallas), two private jets, and a yacht. See Paul Sullivan, "How Mark Cuban Hangs Onto His Money," *New York Times*, February 19, 2017.

70. Dagen, *Mark Cuban*, 6.

71. Cuban, *How to Win*, 3.

72. Cuban, 7, 10.

73. Verne Kopytoff, "5 Worst Internet Acquisitions of All Time," *Fortune*, May 21, 2013.

74. Sullivan, "How Mark Cuban."

75. Pollack, "*Shark Tank*—Corie Henson and David Eilenberg"; the quotes are from all three.

76. Boyle and Kelly, *Television Entrepreneurs*, 55. For a study of the kinds of behavior that bring success to entrepreneurs, including actions by pitchers on one season of *Shark Tank*, see Jeffrey M. Pollack, Matthew W. Rutherford, and Brian G. Nagy, "Preparedness and Cognitive Legitimacy as Antecedents of New Venture Funding in Televised Business Pitches," *Entrepreneurship: Theory and Practice* 36 (September 2012): 915–39.

77. John, *Brand Within*, 239.

78. Greiner, *Invent It*, xxii–xxiii.

79. Natalie Robehmed, "5 Lessons for Female Entrepreneurs from *Shark Tank*'s Lori Greiner," *Forbes*, July 24, 2012.

80. John, *Brand Within*, 239, 240.

81. Greiner, *Invent It*, 9.

82. John, *Brand Within*, 240.

83. Will Yakowicz, "Mark Cuban Made *Shark Tank* Change Its Contracts," *Inc.*, October 20, 2013, https://www.inc.com/will-yakowicz/mark-cuban-forces-shark-tank-to-remove-equity-clause.html.

84. Pollack, "*Shark Tank*—Corie Henson and David Eilenberg."

85. Kirsten Acuna, "Sony Emails Reveal Mark Cuban's Anger over 'Shark Tank' Compensation Talks: 'Beyond an Insult,'" Business Insider, December 12, 2014, http://www.businessinsider.com/shark-tank-mark-cuban-salary-2014-12.

86. John, *Brand Within*, 7.

87. John, 7.

88. Barbara Corcoran, foreword to Fredrik Eklund with Bruce Littlefield, *The Sell: The Secrets of Selling Anything to Anyone* (New York: Penguin Random House, 2015), xi (emphasis in original).

89. Corcoran, *Use What You've Got*, 65.

90. John, *Display of Power*, 70, 130–32. Especially in the titles of his books, John often used the word *power*, which he did not explicitly link to Black Power, although the connection is not out of the question. Implicitly invoking Martin Luther King Jr., John dedicated *The Power of Broke* to the Jewish venture capitalist David Freschman, who "never saw the color of a man's skin but focused only on the integrity of a man's heart": John, *Power of Broke*, v.

91. John, *Rise and Grind*, 18.

92. Cuban, *How to Win*, 15, 21, 30.

93. Greiner, *Invent It*, xvii–xix.

94. Herjavec, *Driven*, 79, 165.

95. Herjavec, *You Don't Have to Be*, 93.

96. Herjavec, *Driven*, 10, 173.

97. Corcoran, John, and O'Leary are dyslexic. For evidence of its relevance, see Chris Warren, "In the Business World, the Frustrating Disorder Dyslexia Can Actually Be a Prime Asset," 2008, http://dyslexia.yale.edu/DYS_secretsuccess .html (no longer available).

98. Herjavec, *Will to Win*, 68; John, *Brand Within*, 133.

99. Douglas and McDonnell, *Celebrity*, 2, 3, 4, 5, 230–34, 259–65.

100. Joshua Gamson, *Claims to Fame: Celebrity in Contemporary America* (Berkeley: University of California Press, 1994), 168, 172.

101. O'Leary, *Business, Money, and Life*, 218.

102. *The Last Word with Lawrence O'Donnell*, "How Barbara Corcoran Beat Trump," reported by Lawrence O'Donnell, aired October 25, 2016, on MSNBC, http://www.msnbc.com/the-last-word/watch/how-barbara-corcoran-beat -trump-793692739961.

103. Paige Lavender, "Barbara Corcoran Says Donald Trump Talked about Her Breast Size When She Was Pregnant," Huffington Post, October 27, 2016, http:// www.huffingtonpost.com/entry/barbara-corcoran-donald-trump_us_58129823 e4b064e1b4b188b5.

104. To follow Cuban's politics, including his relationship with Trump, see Kim Bellware, "Mark Cuban Has a Guess as to Why Trump Whacked Him Out of Nowhere," Huffington Post, February 12, 2017, http://www.huffingtonpost.com/entry /donald-trump-mark-cuban-2020_us_58a0b2dfe4b03df370d7567e?y6djqoof4qu 050cnmi&.

105. Tyler Durden, "Mark Cuban Explains Why He Changed His Mind about Trump," Zero Hedge, September 15, 2016, http://www.zerohedge.com/news/2016 -09-15/mark-cuban-explains-why-he-changed-his-mind-about-trump; Allan Smith, "Mark Cuban Goes Off on Potential 'Trade War' with Mexico: Trump May Cut Off 'Our Economic Nose to Spite Our Face,'" Business Insider, January 27, 2017, http://www.businessinsider.com/mark-cuban-trade-war-border-tax-mex ico-trump-2017-1; Catherine Clifford, "Mark Cuban Doubles Down: Trump Should Build Robots, Not Roads," CNBC, January 26, 2017, http://www.cnbc.com

/2017/01/26/mark-cuban-doubles-down-trump-should-build-robots-not-roads
.html; David Ferguson, "Mark Cuban Trolls Trump with Hilarious NBA All-Star
'Voter Fraud' Conspiracy," Raw Story, January 26, 2017, https://www.rawstory
.com/2017/01/mark-cuban-trolls-trump-with-hilarious-nba-all-star-voter-fraud
-conspiracy; and Karen Tumulty and John Wagner, "The Trump Effect: Everyone's
Thinking of Running for President," *Washington Post*, January 6, 2017.

106. John, *Display of Power*, 35–36.

107. Stephanie Levitz, "'I Am Not Donald Trump': Kevin O'Leary Denies Paral-
lels with Bombastic American," *National Post*, January 14, 2016; Tim Baysinger,
"*Shark Tank* Star Spotlights Immigrant Entrepreneurs in New Web Series for
Inc. Magazine," *Adweek*, April 21, 2016, https://www.adweek.com/tv-video/shark
-tank-star-spotlights-immigrant-entrepreneurs-new-web-series-inc-magazine
-170923/.105.

108. Dan Amira, "Kevin O'Leary Is Unmoved by Your Tears," *New York Times*,
January 17, 2018.

109. O'Leary, *Business, Money, and Life*, 2, 241.

110. Cuban, foreword to *Comeback*, x–xi.

111. For examples, see Stephen Gandel, "TV's *Shark Tank* Guru: In Real Life, No
Business Whiz," *Time*, September 10, 2009; and Renae Merle, "Mark Cuban Takes
His Grudge to the Supreme Court," *Washington Post*, March 16, 2016.

112. Bruce Livesey and Tim Kiladze, "Kevin O'Leary's Not a Billionaire: He Just
Plays One on TV," *Globe and Mail*, September 28, 2012.

113. See O'Leary, *Men, Women, and Money*, 208; Mark Burnett, *Jump In! Even If
You Don't Know How to Swim* (New York: Ballantine Books, 2005), 129; Daymond
John, *Display of Power*, 157; Ky Trang Ho, "*Shark Tank*'s Robert Herjavec Pursu-
ing Disruptors—Big and Small—to Change Cancer Care," *Forbes*, July 30, 2016;
Lynne Hybels, "Let There Be Light for Syrian and Iraqi Refugees," *Lynne Hybels*
(blog), December 12, 2014, https://www.lynnehybels.com/lets-turn-on-the-light
-for-syrian-and-iraqi-refugees (no longer available); Leslie Kaufman, "Trying to
Stay True to the Street," *New York Times*, March 14, 1999; and "IU Athletics Re-
ceives $5 Million Gift to Establish the Mark Cuban Center for Sports Media and
Technology" (press release), Indiana University, June 5, 2015, http://archive.news
.indiana.edu/releases/iu/2015/06/mark-cuban-center-for-sports-media-and
-technology.shtml.

114. Bethany Moreton, *To Serve God and Wal-Mart: The Making of Christian
Free Enterprise* (Cambridge, Mass.: Harvard University Press, 2009); Nicole
Woolsey Biggart, *Charismatic Capitalism: Direct Selling Organizations in America*
(Chicago, Ill.: University of Chicago Press, 1988).

CHAPTER 3

1. Evan Baehr and Evan Loomis, *Get Backed: The Handbook for Creating Your
Pitch Deck, Raising Money, and Launching the Venture of Your Dreams* (Boston, Mass.: Harvard Business Review Press, 2015), 225. Using Daniel Kahneman,
Thinking, Fast and Slow (New York: Farrar, Straus and Giroux, 2011) enables us to
understand the contrast between the Sharks' instinctive responses on screen and
what happens in venues like the one I observed.

2. On the role of product placement and the extension of shows into additional media, see Ted Magder, "The End of TV 101: Reality Programs, Formats, and the New Business of Television," in *Reality TV: Remaking Television Culture*, ed. Susan Murray and Laurie Ouellette (New York: New York University Press, 2004), 148–51.

3. Mark Andrejevic, "When Everyone Had Their Own Reality Show," in *A Companion to Reality Television*, ed. Laurie Ouellette (Malden, Mass.: Wiley, 2014), 49.

4. This analysis relies on a comparison of *Shark Tank* episodes over time, from very first in early August 2009 to more recent ones such as "Toy Mail," from early 2017.

5. David Eilenberg, telephone conversation with author, February 11, 2019.

6. For example, in the first season, the pitch for Ava the Elephant, a medicine dispenser for children, was characterized by a diffidence and uncertainty that disappeared in later seasons.

7. Susan Baronoff, conversation with author, February 22, 2019.

8. Mark Cuban, "Shark Fight," in *Inside the Shark Tank* (New York: Hearst, 2018), 28.

9. Annette Hill explores the relationship between emotions and authenticity in reality television more generally in "Reality TV Experiences: Audiences, Fact, and Fiction," in Ouellette, *Companion to Reality Television*, 123.

10. On the reconfiguration of the set for the ninth season, see Andy Denhart, "Why *Shark Tank* Changes Its Sharks' Seats and Set," reality blurred, February 18, 2018, https://www.realityblurred.com/realitytv/2018/02/shark-tank-cast-set-changes. On the contestants paying for their own setup, see "A 'Shark Tank' Entrepreneur Gives the Inside Scoop and Tips for Making Your Dream Pitch," *Inc.*, December 6, 2018, https://www.inc.com/entrepreneurs-organization/the-story-behind-festive-shark-tank-deal-barbara-corcoran-stole.html. Scholars of reality television emphasize that the work of contestants may often be seen as unpaid labor. In the case of *Shark Tank*, pitchers can garner publicity, expertise, and funding in exchange for the work they do and the expenses they lay out, although those who prepare and do not appear, as well as many of those who do appear, are engaged in unreimbursed work. For a discussion of the dynamics of labor on television programs, see Andrew Ross, "Reality Television and the Political Economy of Amateurism," in Ouellette, *Companion to Reality Television*, 32–33.

11. Richard Feloni, " 'Shark Tank' Investor Robert Herjavec Says the Sharks Are 'Cold, Hungry, and Miserable' during Shoots," Business Insider, November 4, 2015, https://www.businessinsider.com.au/what-the-shark-tank-shooting-schedule-is-like-2015-11. Crowdfunding, an internet-reliant way for entrepreneurs to raise money, differs as a source of funding from *Shark Tank* and venture capitalism.

12. Kelly Cole, *Conversations with Sharks: Success Stories Shared by the Sharks on ABC's Hit TV Show "Shark Tank,"* rev. ed. (n.p.: Prime Time Marketing and Kelly Cole, 2014), 18–20.

13. Ky Trang Ho, "18 Entrepreneurs on the Rise Rejected by Shark Tank," *Forbes*, July 2, 2016. For statistics from the beginning of season ten, see Joan Oleck, " 'Shark Tank' Stars Dissect Their Show's Popularity on the Eve of Its Tenth

Season," *Entrepreneur*, September 25, 2019. For a company that promises to consider producing "Your Shark Tank Idea," see http://portal.ideabuyer.com/shark -tank-idea-application/. For season ten, approximately 1,000 applicants made it to the second round of applications; of those, 158 had their pitches filmed, but only 88 pitches were aired: Gary Levin, "'Shark Tank': All Your Burning Questions, Answered," *USA Today*, January 4, 2019.

14. Cole, *Conversations with Sharks*, 112.

15. Lori Greiner, *Invent It, Sell It, Bank It! Make Your Million-Dollar Idea into a Reality* (New York: Ballantine, 2014), 135–37.

16. Greiner, 135–37.

17. Michael Parrish DuDell, *Shark Tank: Jump Start Your Business: How to Launch and Grow a Business from Concept to Cash* (New York: Hyperion, 2013), 168.

18. DuDell, 252–54.

19. Richard Feloni, "Why These Karaoke Founders Turned Down 4 Offers of $1.5 Million on 'Shark Tank,'" Business Insider, November 3, 2014, https://www .businessinsider.com.au/singtrix-karaoke-on-shark-tank-2014-11.

20. Cole, *Conversations with Sharks*, 57. In *Rise and Grind: Outperform, Outwork, and Outhustle Your Way to a More Successful and Rewarding Life* (New York: Currency, 2018), 183–85, Daymond John says they shoot in two nine-day sessions, usually one session in June and one in September. Filming occurs on soundstage 25; though on screen it seems the size of a conference room, one observer characterized it as a "cavernous hangar of a building." See Nancy Nichols, "Inside the *Shark Tank* with Mark Cuban," *D Magazine*, March 2014.

21. Feloni, "Investor Robert Herjavec Says"; Richard Feloni, "14 Behind-the-Scenes Secrets You Didn't Know about 'Shark Tank,'" Business Insider, November 3, 2015, https://www.businessinsider.com/shark-tank-behind-the-scenes-sec rets-2015-10; Levin, "Burning Questions."

22. Feloni, "Investor Robert Herjavec Says." For information on how producers use earpieces to prompt Sharks, see Stephen LaConte, "35 'Shark Tank' Secrets That Will Fuck You Up a Little," BuzzFeed, January 16, 2018, https://www.buzzfeed .com/stephenlaconte/insane-behind-the-scenes-secrets-about-the-making-of.

23. Feloni, "Investor Robert Herjavec Says."

24. Greiner, *Invent It*, xiv, xx.

25. Feloni, "Investor Robert Herjavec Says."

26. Cole, *Conversations with Sharks*, 119.

27. Someone experienced in entrepreneurship whose name is withheld by mutual agreement, emails to author, February 19, 2019, and October 2, 2019.

28. Feloni, "Investor Robert Herjavec Says"; for a similar description from Herjavec, see *Inside the Shark Tank*, 56.

29. Raymond Boyle and Lisa W. Kelly, *The Television Entrepreneurs: Social Change and Public Understanding of Business* (Burlington, Vt.: Ashgate, 2012), 51 (emphasis in original).

30. Feloni, "Investor Robert Herjavec Says."

31. Patrick Radden Keefe, "Winning: How Mark Burnett, the King of Reality

Television, Helped Turn a Floundering D-Lister into President Trump," *New Yorker*, January 7, 2019, 34.

32. Robert Herjavec with John Lawrence Reynolds, *The Will to Win: Leading, Competing, Succeeding* (Toronto, Canada: HarperCollins, 2013), 156–57.

33. In discussing the editing process, I am relying principally on my exchanges with Susan Baronoff, February 22–24, 2019. See also Feloni, "Investor Robert Herjavec Says," and LaConte, "35 'Shark Tank' Secrets."

34. Feloni, "Investor Robert Herjavec Says."

35. Feloni.

36. *Inside the Shark Tank* featured pitches by young entrepreneurs on pages 42–45.

37. For an example of a good product but problematic pitcher, see Kirk Taylor, "LifeBelt Robert Allison Shark Tank Update," *Shark Tank Blog*, April 17, 2012, https://www.sharktankblog.com/lifebelt-robert-allison-shark-tank-update. See also John, *Brand Within*, 243.

38. "Does Shark Tank Have a Woman Problem?" (blog post), National Women's Business Council, October 22, 2015, https://www.nwbc.gov/2015/10/22/does-shark-tank-have-a-woman-problem.

39. For discussions of the representations of gender on reality television more generally, see Rachel E. Dubrofsky, "*The Bachelorette*'s Postfeminist Therapy: Transforming Women for Love," in Ouellette, *Companion to Reality Television*, 191–207; and Andrea L. Press, "Fractured Feminism: Articulations of Feminism, Sex, and Class by Reality TV Viewers," in Ouellette, *Companion to Reality Television*, 208–28. In "The Gender Principle," *Inside the Shark Tank*, 82, Kevin O'Leary notes that almost 90 percent of what his portfolio has earned comes from *Shark Tank* companies run by women.

40. Rob Merlino, "Hold Your Haunches," *Shark Tank Blog*, April 14, 2014, https://www.sharktankblog.com/hold-your-haunches-update.

41. Steve Kahn, "Hold Your Haunches Update: What Happened after Shark Tank," Gazette Review, June 16, 2016, https://gazettereview.com/2016/06/hold-your-haunches-update-shark-tank.

42. "Does Shark Tank Have a Woman Problem?." At times, Greiner engaged in a certain double standard on gender, claiming to be gender neutral at the same time that she occasionally played the feminist card. See, for example, Greiner, *Invent It*, 7–8.

43. Another key example is Mo's Bows, which aired in season five on April 25, 2014. John agreed to mentor eleven-year-old African American Moziah Bridges for free because he saw much of himself in the young clothing entrepreneur. See also Daymond John with Daniel Paisner, *The Power of Broke: How Empty Pockets, a Tight Budget, and a Hunger for Success Can Become Your Greatest Competitive Advantage* (New York: Crown Business, 2015), 142–43. On the deployment of race in cultural productions, see Linda Williams, *Playing the Race Card: Melodramas of Black and White from Uncle Tom to O. J. Simpson* (Princeton, N.J.: Princeton University Press, 2001). See also Catherine R. Squires, "The Conundrum of Race and Reality Television," in Ouellette, *Companion to Reality Television*, 264–82;

and Hunter Hargraves Squires, "Tan TV: Reality Television's Postracial Delusion," in Ouellette, 293–305. These authors explore the issue of whether reality TV programs offer a postracial world shaped by neoliberalism.

44. "Billy Blanks Jr.," Dance It Out, http://www.meettheblanks.com/about-us /billy-blanks-jr/.

45. Andy Debolt, "Billy Blanks Jr. Dance with Me—after Shark Tank Update," Gazette Review, March 24, 2016, https://gazettereview.com/2016/03/billy-blanks -jr-dance-shark-tank-update.

46. Debolt, "Billy Blanks Jr."

47. Leslie Kaufman, "Trying to Stay True to the Street," *New York Times*, March 14, 1999.

48. John, *Brand Within*, 139–40 (emphasis in original).

49. David Sicilia, "Swimming with Sharks in the Great Recession," TV Worth Watching, January 19, 2012, http://www.tvworthwatching.com/post/Swimming -with-Sharks-in-the-Great-Recession.aspx.

50. Paige Turner, "Invis-A-Rack Update—the Shark Tank Company Now in 2017," Gazette Review, May 15, 2016, https://gazettereview.com/2016/05/invis -rack-update-see-happened-shark-tank. Another instance of the gap between cosmopolitan Sharks and a seemingly out-of-the-mainstream pitcher appeared with Tree T-Pee, but this time the pitcher was less a struggling small-town entrepreneur and more a successful rural one. As with Invis-A-Rack, the segment exposed the gap between the twentieth-century dynamic capitalism that the cosmopolitan Sharks represented and a more modest yet admirably traditional approach to business.

CHAPTER 4

1. For *Shark Tank* examples of social entrepreneurship products, see Mission Belt (season four, aired April 26, 2013) and Grace and Lace (season five, aired November 22, 2013).

2. Steve Dawson, "Hungry Harvest Update—What Happened after Shark Tank," Gazette Review, December 5, 2016, https://gazettereview.com/2016/07 /hungry-harvest-update-after-shark-tank; Evan Lutz, "Why Mark Cuban Was Wrong about My Business," CNBC, April 4, 2017, https://www.cnbc.com/2017 /04/06/why-mark-cuban-was-wrong-about-my-business.html; Ashley Nickle, "'Ugly' Produce Delivery Service Hungry Harvest Continues to Grow," *The Packer*, June 6, 2018, https://www.thepacker.com/article/ugly-produce-delivery -service-hungry-harvest-continues-grow.

3. Alyssa Ralston, "Wake N Bacon Now: The After *Shark Tank* Update," Gazette Review, December 5, 2016, https://gazettereview.com/2015/12/wake-n-bacon -now-shark-tank-update.

4. Rob Merlino, "Sullivan Generator Follow Up," *Shark Tank Blog*, April 24, 2012, https://www.sharktankblog.com/mark-sullivan-generator-follow-up/.

5. For a summary of the story and its aftermath, see Alyssa Ralston, "The Sullivan Generator Update—How They're Doing after *Shark Tank*," Gazette Review, December 5, 2016, http://gazettereview.com/2016/04/sullivan-generator-update -theyre-shark-tank.

6. Alyssa Ralston, "Cougar Limited Update—What Happened after *Shark Tank*," Gazette Review, December 5, 2016, https://gazettereview.com/2016/09/cougar-limited-shark-tank-update. Although I've focused on these three products, many viewers found the Ionic Ear to be the worst offering.

7. Steve Dawson, "Q-Flex Update—What Happened after *Shark Tank* 2017," Gazette Review, January 3, 2018, https://gazettereview.com/2016/06/q-flex-update-after-shark-tank.

8. Dawson, "Q-Flex Update." Vanessa Van Edwards, founder of the human behavior research lab Science of the People, looked at all the episodes in the first seven seasons of *Shark Tank* to determine why some pitches succeeded and others failed. Stepping out of the tank to talk to a friend or associate, crying on air, and having a demographic resemblance to a Shark helped more often than they hurt. Problems conveying the math of a business were deal breakers; what helped most was entering the tank in a way that conveyed agreeableness, using body language or a powerful voice to convey confidence, having Sharks interact physically with a product, presenting a compelling story, especially an inspirational one, and having a humorous, unique, or even bizarre aspect of the pitch. See Vanessa Van Edwards, "10 Secrets to the Perfect Shark Tank Pitch," Science of People, n.d., https://www.scienceofpeople.com/the-10-secrets-to-the-perfect-shark-tank-pitch.

9. Steven Kahn, "Scholly Update—What Happened after *Shark Tank*," Gazette Review, December 5, 2016, http://gazettereview.com/2016/09/scholly-update-happened-shark-tank. The response to the pitch for Cycloramic during season five also amply illustrates the complicated and skillful dynamics of bidding.

10. Among the successful products for which I could not obtain sufficient information are Tower Paddle Boards, Bottle Breacher, and Red Dress Boutique.

11. Dominic Powell, "The Story of Scrub Daddy: How This Sponge Business Became the Most Successful Shark Tank Company Ever," SmartCompany, January 31, 2019, https://www.smartcompany.com.au/entrepreneurs/influencers-profiles/scrub-daddy-sponge-shark-tank-success/.

12. *Inside the Shark Tank* (New York: Hearst, 2018), 60–63, 94–95.

13. Luke Christou, "Scrub Daddy Net Worth: Scraping Grit, Grime, Dirt (and Profit), Compelo, June 23, 2017, https://www.ns-businesshub.com/popular/scrub-daddy-net-worth/. One article estimates that the company that owns Scrub Daddy is worth $170 million; see Aili Nahas, "The Stories Behind *Shark Tank*'s Most Successful Products Ever! And What They're Worth Now!" *People*, November 25, 2018, https://people.com/tv/shark-tank-success-stories/. If so, and if Greiner still owns 20 percent, her share would be valued at $34 million. However, there is too little information publicly available to be sure of the accuracy of such estimates.

14. For information on DECA, the organization that hosts the Career Development Conferences, see "International Career Development Conference," DECA, n.d., https://www.deca.org/about/. For the story of how a high school student went from a DECA competition to an appearance on *Shark Tank*, see Janelle Arrighi, "From Last Place DECA Project to Pitching on *Shark Tank*," *DECA Direct*, January 19, 2018, http://www.decadirect.org/2018/01/19/last-place-deca-project

-pitching-shark-tank. For more information on the studies by L. Balachandra that emphasized that character, trustworthiness, coachability, and an improvisational style are more important than passion, see "How Venture Capitalists Really Assess a Pitch," *Harvard Business Review*, May–June 2017, 25–28.

15. "About DECA," DECA, n.d., https://www.deca.org/about.

16. DECA, "Entrepreneurship Series Events, Participant Instructions," program for Northern California Career Development Conference, 2018, copy in author's possession.

17. For the history of DECA, I am relying on John Fistolera, telephone conversation with author, January 19, 2018.

18. Anushka Nair and Alizah Nauman, conversation with author, January 27, 2019.

19. Piram Singh, conversation with author, February 17, 2019.

20. Michael Paine, conversation with author, February 10, 2019; Michael Paine and Justin Morgan, *Success HS*, podcast, https://anchor.fm/success-hs.

21. For the script, see flash.sonypictures.com/video/movies/thesocialnetwork /awards/thesocialnetwork_screenplay.pdf.

CHAPTER 5

1. Ben Horowitz, *The Hard Thing about Hard Things: Building a Business When There Are No Easy Answers* (New York: HarperCollins, 2014), 243.

2. In selecting which TED Talks to focus on, I relied on the lists of the most popular ones that a Google search led me to. Only Simon Sinek's "How Great Leaders Inspire Action" appeared on all of them. Bill T. Gross, "The Single Biggest Reason Why Startups Succeed," which aired in March 2015, was also wildly popular.

3. Simon Sinek, *Start with Why: How Great Leaders Inspire Everyone to Take Action* (New York: Penguin, 2009), x, 216, 219; Adam Fridman, "3 Ways Simon Sinek's 'Why?' Changed My Life," *Inc.*, August 17, 2015.

4. Carlos Brandon notes a similar parallel between Sinek's influence and his timing in "The Effects of the Great Recession on Millennial Economic Behavior," *Moderno* (blog), April 5, 2017, https://moderno.blog/2017/04/05/the-effects-of -the-great-recession-on-millennial-economic-behavior.

5. Nicole Weaver, "'Shark Tank' Failures: 10 Products That Didn't Make It," Showbiz Cheat Sheet, June 6, 2018, https://www.cheatsheet.com/entertainment /shark-tank-failures-products-didnt-make.html. One list of ten *Shark Tank* products that failed offers a mixed bag of reasons for failures, including deals falling through because of misunderstandings, disputed contracts, fights between pitchers, or failures to meet contingencies, or because the pitcher had appeared on the show only for the sake of publicity.

6. Dan Schwabel, "*Shark Tank* Roundtable—Their Best and Worst Deals," *Forbes*, June 4, 2012.

7. Nick Cobb, "Toygaroo Update: How They're Doing Now after *Shark Tank*," Gazette Review, December 5, 2016, http://gazettereview.com/2016/03/toygaroo -update-how-theyre-doing-now-after-shark-tank; Rob Merlino, "Toygaroo Up-

date from Former CTO," *Shark Tank Blog,* May 9, 2012, http://sharktankblog.com /toygaroo-bankruptcy-update-from-former-cto.

8. Schwabel, "*Shark Tank* Roundtable."

9. Alyssa Ralston, "The Smart Baker Update—See What Happened after *Shark Tank*," Gazette Review, December 5, 2016, http://gazettereview.com/2016/02 /the-smart-baker-update-after-shark-tank; Elizabeth Hollingsworth, "Lessons Learned: Baking Site Says No to *Shark Tank*," Practical Ecommerce, February 11, 2015, http://www.practicalecommerce.com/Lessons-Learned-Baking-Site-Says -No-to-Shark-Tank.

10. Steve Dawson, "'How Do You Roll' Update—What Happened after *Shark Tank*," Gazette Review, December 5, 2016, http://gazettereview.com/2016/09/roll -update-happened-shark-tank; Joe Caruso, "ABC's *Shark Tank* Sushi Franchise Fiasco," Franchise-Info, February 26, 2017, http://www.franchise-info.ca/supply _chain/2017/02/abcs-shark-tank-sushi-franchise-fiasco.html.

11. Kiah McBride, "How Lip Bar Founder Melissa Butler Went from 'Shark Tank' Rejection to Shelves of Major Retailers," xoNecole, March 11, 2019, http://xonecole .com/how-the-lip-bar-founder-went-from-shark-tank-rejection-to-a-400000 -brand. For a similar venture that the Sharks also turned down yet had some measure of success, see Steve Dawson, "Hammer & Nails Update—What Happened after Shark Tank," Gazette Review, December 5, 2016, http://gazettereview .com/2016/06/hammer-nails-update-happened-shark-tank.

12. Ali Montag, "How This 32-Year-Old 'Shark Tank' Reject Got Her Lipsticks on the Shelves at Target," CNBC, July 30, 2018, https://www.cnbc.com/2018/07 /30/how-shark-tank-reject-the-lip-bar-got-to-be-sold-at-target.html. Other examples of companies with considerable success despite no deal with Sharks are CellHelmet, a protective cover for smartphones backed by an insurance plan that pays to repair or replace the phone if it's damaged while in its case, and Rocketbook, a spiral notebook whose jottings are scanned, sent to the cloud, and then erased when placed in a microwave.

13. Other examples of products whose creators turned down offers on air and then went on to achieve success are Proof Eyewear, eco-friendly eyeglasses; Xero Shoes, which enable people to run almost as if barefoot; and CoatChex, a high-tech system for checking coats at bars and restaurants. Echo Valley Meats almost fits this category, but in the pitcher's second appearance on the show, a deal was struck.

14. Eric Siemers, "Why an Oregon Winemaker Is OK with Being the 'Most Hated' Pitchman to Appear on 'Shark Tank,'" *Portland Business Journal,* April 10, 2015. Voyage-Air Guitar is an example of prey that got away in its first appearance, but it was later captured by a Shark.

15. Ali Montag and Sarah Berger, "Amazon Bought 'Shark Tank' Reject Last Year," CNBC, February 22, 2019, https://www.cnbc.com/2018/02/27/amazon -buys-ring-a-former-shark-tank-reject.html.

16. Ali Montag, "Kevin O'Leary: Ring Won't Be the Last 'Shark Tank' Business to Sell for $1 Billion," CNBC, February 28, 2018, https://www.cnbc.com/2018/02 /28/kevin-oleary-amazons-ring-deal-wont-be-the-last-for-shark-tank.html.

17. In some instances, the ultimate proof of a successful investment comes when a company a Shark invests in is later purchased by a big corporation; this has happened several times, including when Shutterfly purchased GrooveBook in 2014. See Sarah Perez, "*Shark Tank*–Backed GrooveBook Acquired by Shutterfly for $14.5 Million," TechCrunch, November 17, 2014, https://techcrunch.com/2014 /11/17/shark-tank-backed-groovebook-acquired-by-shutterfly-for-14-5-million.

18. This analysis relies on an examination of twelve of the nineteen episodes of *Beyond the Tank* that aired: episodes 1–3 in season 1 and episodes 4, 6–8, 10, 12–14, and 16 in season 2.

19. Julie Goldman also had a successful second chance after she failed to close an on-air deal for Original Runner Company but later came to terms with Corcoran.

20. Pitchers often present in pairs: parent-child, husband-wife, or siblings. They even more frequently speak of family legacy, of passing on to future generations not just a company but a set of values and beliefs. For a good example of an invocation of family legacy, see the presentation for Hamboards, a company that manufactured skateboards, which spoke of the hopes of a mother and father for their five sons and one grandchild.

21. A mid-April 2017 episode announced that the barbecue company's revenues had reached $16 million and that John had brokered a deal with the fast-food restaurants Hardee's and Carl's Jr. to use Bubba's products at 3,000 locations. See Catherine Clifford, "How Daymond John's 'Biggest Deal Ever' on 'Shark Tank' Went from $154,000 to $16 million in Sales in Three Years," CNBC, April 15, 2017, https://www.cnbc.com/2017/04/15/shark-tank-hosts-biggest-deal -everwent-from-154000-to-16-million-in-sales-in-3-years.html.

22. One example is how Mensch on a Bench addressed the common experience that intermarriage underscored the importance of educating children about religious traditions in a diverse society where intermarriage is common.

23. In the updates on *Beyond the Tank*, the viewer often sees a Lone Ranger Shark greeting a newly successful entrepreneur. For examples, see the updates for TurboPup (February 5, 2016), Pipsnacks (March 13, 2015), Squatty Potty (May 8, 2015), and PiperWai (February 26, 2016).

24. Kevin O'Leary, "The *Shark Tank* Effect," in *Inside the Shark Tank* (New York: Hearst, 2018).

25. A somewhat similar case occurred when John brought Lisa Lloyd into his company as an entrepreneur-in-residence in the episode that aired January 29, 2010.

26. Richard Feloni, "14 Behind-the-Scene Secrets You Don't Know about 'Shark Tank,'" Business Insider, November 11, 2015, http://www.businessinsider.com /shark-tank-behind-the-scenes-secrets-2015-10.

27. Robert Herjavec with John Lawrence Reynolds, *Driven: How to Succeed in Business and in Life* (Toronto, Canada: HarperCollins, 2010), 109, 139. For what can happen after an agreement is struck on screen, see Sean Daly, "Deal Interrupted: On 'Shark Tank,' a Lot Can Happen after the Handshake," *New York Post*, January 30, 2013. See also Robert Herjavec with John Lawrence Reynolds, *The Will to Win: Leading, Competing, Succeeding* (Toronto, Canada: HarperCollins, 2013),

205–6. For a not-very-revealing picture of what it is like to work with O'Leary, see Vivian Giang and Alison Griswold, "What It's Like Working with the Meanest Investor on 'Shark Tank,'" Business Insider, November 25, 2013, http://www.businessinsider.com/what-its-like-working-with-kevin-oleary-on-shark-tank-2013-11.

28. David K. Williams, "Lori Greiner, *Shark Tank* Star and Queen of QVC, on a Great Asset: A Partner in Her Spouse," *Forbes*, September 22, 2012. Lori Greiner briefly discusses her husband's role in *Invent It, Sell It, Bank It! Make Your Million-Dollar Idea into a Reality* (New York: Ballantine, 2014), xiv.

29. Daymond John with Daniel Paisner, *The Power of Broke: How Empty Pockets, a Tight Budget, and a Hunger for Success Can Become Your Greatest Competitive Advantage* (New York: Crown Business, 2016), 257.

30. In addition to what I discuss here, there are sites that aggregate and sell products seen on the shows, especially All Shark Tank Products (https://allsharktankproducts.com), the official such site.

31. Susan J. Douglas and Andrea McDonnell, *Celebrity: A History of Fame* (New York: New York University Press, 2019), 2; Eric Guthey, Timothy Clark, and Brad Jackson, *Demystifying Business Celebrity* (New York: Routledge, 2009), 3–5. See also Joshua Gamson, *Claims to Fame: Celebrity in Contemporary America* (Berkeley: University of California Press, 1994), 58, 104–5.

32. Alison Hearn, "Producing 'Reality': Branded Content, Branded Selves, and Precarious Futures," in *A Companion to Reality Television*, ed. Laurie Ouellette (Malden, Mass.: Wiley, 2014), 438. See also June Deery, "Mapping Commercialization in Reality Television," in Ouellette, *Companion to Reality Television*, 18.

33. Lori Greiner, "I'll Make You MILLIONS: Road to Millions," LoriGreiner.com, http://www.lorigreiner.com/success.html. The products page of Greiner's website reveals just how many product lines she's involved in: http://www.lorigreiner.com/products.html.

34. Aly Weisman, "A Grueling 22-Hour Workday in the Life of a QVC Host & 'Shark Tank' Judge," Business Insider, April 23, 2012, https://www.businessinsider.com/day-in-the-life-shark-tank-judge-and-qvc-host-lori-greiner-2012-4.

35. "Speaking," RobertHerjavec.com, https://www.robertherjavec.com/speaking/.

36. "Speaking," BarbaraCorcoran.com, http://www.barbaracorcoran.com/speaking.

37. "Forefront Venture Partners," AngelList, https://angel.co/forefront-venture-partners; "Portfolio," Forefront Venture Partners, http://www.forefrontvp.com/portfolio.

38. "About," KevinOLeary.com, https://www.kevinoleary.com/about/.

39. "Speaking," DaymondJohn.com, https://daymondjohn.com/pages/speaking; "Consulting," DaymondJohn.com, https://daymondjohn.com/pages/consulting.

40. "Daymond John's Shark Branding: Social Media Internship," job posting, SmartRecruiters, https://jobs.smartrecruiters.com/SharkBranding1/89550262-social-media-internship.

41. Daymond John with Daniel Paisner, *Rise and Grind: Outperform, Outwork,*

and Outhustle Your Way to a More Successful and Rewarding Life (New York: Currency, 2018), 298. For a useful article on John's expanding empire, see Richard Feloni, "'Shark Tank' Investor Daymond John Is Building an Entrepreneur Hub in a 14-Story New York High-Rise," Business Insider, March 24, 2017, http://www .businessinsider.com/shark-tank-daymond-john-blueprint-co-2017-3.

42. www.markcubancompanies.com.

43. Michael J. Roberts and Nicole Tempest, "ONSET Ventures," HBS No. 898154-PDF-ENG (Cambridge, Mass.: Harvard Business Publishing, 1998).

44. Kevin O'Leary, *Cold Hard Truth on Business, Money, and Life* (Toronto, Canada: Anchor Canada, 2011), 43, 46, 245–47.

CHAPTER 6

1. On the original ABC broadcasts, advertisements are typically for national, family-oriented brands such as Target, Toyota, Taco Bell, Geico, and Ashley Home Furnishings. In contrast, until recent years, the ads on CNBC rebroadcasts were either for other CNBC shows or for business-oriented brands such as American Express, Dell, and Capital One. See John Cassillo, "*Shark Tank* Attention Scores Bite Hard," TV[R]EV, September 5, 2017, https://tvrev.com/shark-tank-reruns -make-killing-smart-cmos-taking-advantage. By 2019, however, the advertisers on CNBC reruns were roughly similar to those on the original broadcasts, although CNBC also relied on ads from personal money management companies such as Acorns.

2. On the relationship between original shows and other media, see Henry Jenkins, *Convergence Culture: Where Old and New Media Collide* (New York: New York University Press, 2006), 243. In *The Television Entrepreneurs: Social Change and Public Understanding of Business* (Burlington, Vt.: Ashgate, 2012), 101, 109–12, Raymond Boyle and Lisa W. Kelly, focusing on the British version of *Shark Tank*, talk of how viewers both believe that the shows are authentic and understand that, because of choices producers make, what airs is hardly an accurate depiction of the realities of the business world. For an empirical investigation of audience response, albeit for shows very different from *Shark Tank*, see Steven Reiss and James Wiltz, "Why People Watch Reality TV," *Media Psychology* 6 (November 2004): 363–78.

3. For examples, see David Gelles, "Selling High-End Socks by Giving Them Away," *New York Times*, March 19, 2016; and Steve Israel, "Steve Israel: Confessions of a Congressman," *New York Times*, January 8, 2016.

4. Kevin Brass, "The Money Game: Secrets of Surviving the 'Shark Tank'— Judges and Contestants Lay Out What It Takes to Win on the Entrepreneurial Reality Show," *Wall Street Journal*, August 25, 2014.

5. Bruce Nolop, "Do Companies Spend Too Much Time Searching for Groundbreaking Innovations?," *Wall Street Journal*, September 17, 2013.

6. "Venture Capitalist Makes Case against 'Shark Tank'; Show Sacrifices Investment Lessons for Entertainment," *The Accelerators* (blog), *Wall Street Journal*, September 17, 2014, https://www.wsj.com/articles/venture-capitalist-makes-case -against-shark-tank-1410996729.

7. Jaime Lowe, "Letter of Recommendation: 'Shark Tank,'" *New York Times*

Magazine, September 28, 2017. For a rare substantial critique in a nonbusiness online publication, see Ann Derrick Gaillot, "*Shark Tank* and the Myth of Capitalist Benevolence: How the Reality TV Show Pushes the Idea That Only Certain People Can Succeed," The Outline, October 6, 2017, https://theoutline.com/post/2374/shark-tank-and-the-myth-of-capitalist-benevolence.

8. Lee Habeeb, "All-American Sharks," *National Review*, November 5, 2013.

9. For several years, *Forbes* presented recaps of episodes. For an example of the magazine's coverage, see Alejandro Cremades, "They Were Rejected on *Shark Tank* and Today Are Making Millions," *Forbes*, April 20, 2019.

10. See, as an example, Emily Conklin, "8 Quotes from *Shark Tank*'s Lori Greiner That Will Make You Proud to Be an Entrepreneur," *Entrepreneur*, December 19, 2017.

11. Emily Canal, "We Fact-Checked Seven Season of *Shark Tank* Deals. Here Are the Results," *Forbes*, October 21, 2016. For another analysis of the data, see Emily Canal, "Why Is Mark Cuban the Greatest Shark in the Tank? He Strikes after the Camera Stops Rolling," *Forbes*, October 21, 2016; and Emily Canal, "Which 'Shark Tank' Star Invests the Most Money? We Break Down $63 Million in Deals," *Forbes*, October 25, 2016. For another gathering of statistics on the show's results, in this case for the first six seasons, see Ewan Maalerud, "*Shark Tank* Analytics with SAP Analytics Cloud" (blog post), SAP Analytics Cloud, https://www.sapanalytics.cloud/resources-shark-tank-analytics. Other examples of reporting on results are Bill Murphy Jr., "These Entrepreneurs Were on 'Shark Tank': Here's the Giant Problem They Say the Show Created for Them Afterward," *Inc.*, April 28, 2019; and Tracy Leigh Hazzard, "How Swimming with Sharks Can Tank Your Business," *Inc.*, December 6, 2018. In "'Shark Tank' Isn't Entrepreneurship — and That's Dangerous for New Businesses Everywhere," *Inc.*, April 18, 2019, Brian Hamilton criticized the show for misrepresenting how funding actually occurs.

12. Emily Canal, "Yes, There Is a *Shark Tank* Bump," *Inc.*, October 2018, 34–35. She also noted that though many more men appeared, women fared somewhat better. In addition, Cuban and John had the most dramatic successes, and Mr. Wonderful's weak record would offer "fodder for on-air trash talk." For scholarly articles that focus on gender in episodes, see Hila Keren, "Women in the *Shark Tank*: Entrepreneurship and Feminism in a Neoliberal Age," *Columbia Journal of Gender and Law* 34 (2016): 75–123; Mandy Wheadon and Nathalie Duval-Couetil, "The Gendering of Entrepreneurship on Reality Television," *Journal of Small Business Management* 57 (2019) 1676–97; and Sharon Poczter and Melanie Shapsis, "Know Your Worth: Angel Financing of Female Entrepreneurial Ventures," SSRN, May 19, 2016, http://dx.doi.org/10.2139/ssrn.2782266.

13. Zachary Crockett, "*Shark Tank* Deep Dive: A Data Analysis of All Ten Seasons," Hustle, May 19, 2019, https://thehustle.co/shark-tank-data-analysis-10-seasons.

14. Graham Winfrey, "4 Reasons 'Shark Tank' Is the New 'American Idol,'" *Inc.*, July 31, 2015.

15. Huffington Post, a widely followed left-leaning site, is unusual in that, more than any other general interest outlet, it focuses extensively on women entrepreneurs and publishes thoughtful articles critiquing the show for its lack of diversity.

For some of its notable articles, see Angélica Pérez-Litwin, "The Case of the Missing Latina/o Shark," Huffington Post, May 17, 2015, https://www.huffingtonpost .com/angelica-perezlitwin-phd/the-case-of-the-missing-latinao-shark_b _6867158.html; Wombi Rose, "3 Things That Shocked Me about *Shark Tank*," Huffington Post, December 16, 2016, https://www.huffingtonpost.com/wombi-rose-/3 -things-that-shocked-me-_b_8819480.html; and Robert F. Brands, "Prime Time Innovation: Why Audiences Can't Get Enough of 'Shark Tank' and Other Entrepreneurial Reality TV Shows," Huffington Post, September 25, 2016, https://www .huffingtonpost.com/robert-f-brands/prime-time-innovation-why_b_8196042 .html. Vox's search engine makes it difficult to locate articles on *Shark Tank*. BuzzFeed brings up about seventeen stories going back to November 2017, and for the most part they offer the usual BuzzFeed-style "secrets" and lists. The Daily Beast also has relatively few stories on *Shark Tank*, and an unusually high proportion of them are on the connections between the show and American politics. Also of note is Gazette Review, discussed in another chapter, which has offered perhaps as many as 700 articles on *Shark Tank*, almost all of which either summarize what transpired on the show or provide updates on pitched products. One website, reality blurred, belies its title by offering the usual combination of gossip, lists, and promotional material.

16. One exception to the rule of simply reporting, providing lists, and offering gee-whiz enthusiasm is the data-driven work of Jishai Evers, reported on in Richard Feloni, "A 'Shark Tank' Fan Analyzed Every Episode to Determine Who Gets the Investors' Money," Business Insider, January 31, 2015, https://www .businessinsider.in/A-Shark-Tank-fan-analyzed-every-episode-to-determine -who-gets-the-investors-money/articleshow/46073316.cms.

17. Alison Griswold, "Former 'Shark Tank' Contestant: If You Want to Raise Money, Don't Go on the Show," Business Insider, March 12, 2014,https://www .businessinsider.in/Former-Shark-Tank-Contestant-If-You-Want-To-Raise -Money-Dont-Go-On-The-Show/articleshow/31905725.cms. A milder example of a critical assessment in a business publication, in this case one that appears online and in print, is Ami Kassar, "The *Shark Tank* Myth Is Alive and Well," *Inc.*, May 14, 2017. In this article, Kassar criticizes entrepreneurs who waste their time pursuing famous investors, like those on *Shark Tank*. Another business publication, *Success*, claims it is the "only magazine that focuses on people who take full responsibility for their own development and income" and that its "readers understand that the world has changed and the classic employer-to-employee relationship has changed from a patriarchal to a transactional one." "Our Mission," *Success*, https://www.success.com/about/. Both the print magazine and the website feature scores of inspirational and how-to articles on *Shark Tank*.

18. In addition to the media outlets named earlier, there are several important ones that specifically cover the entertainment industry, including *Variety, Hollywood News Daily*, the *Hollywood Reporter*, and Cynopsis, whose principal focal points are changes in business and personnel. Also part of the seemingly bottomless pit of online responses to *Shark Tank* are articles on Yahoo! Finance, most of which resemble (and draw on) others cited. This discussion relies on an analy-

sis of Facebook, YouTube, Tumblr, Twitter, Instagram, and other sites specifically mentioned. *Shark Tank*'s blog (https://www.sharktankblog.com/) and the *Shark Tank* wiki (http://sharktank.wikia.com/wiki/The_Shark_Tank) are not very useful to me. The liveliest discussions are found in the Primetimer forums (http://forums.primetimer.com/forum/299-shark-tank). The Shark Tank Fan Club on Facebook (https://www.facebook.com/thesharktankfanclub), which mainly promoted the show and commercial products, seems to have been short-lived. As far as I can determine, the Shark Tank Fan Site (http://sharktankfansite.com) is no longer operating. The Facebook group Shark Tank Fans (https://www.facebook .com/pg/SharkTankFanpage) seems to post mostly ads for Sharks and products that resulted from deals on the show. The Straight Dope message board on *Shark Tank* (https://boards.straightdope.com/sdmb/showthread.php?t=826581) appears to have lasted less than two weeks in May 2017. The *Shark Tank* message board on Investors Hangout (https://investorshangout.com/Shark-Tank-87627), established in February 2013, hasn't had a new post since October 2017; with one exception, all of the posts are identified as coming from the moderator, and they principally feature information that pitchers provided on their products. In addition to all these discussion forums, there are at least two more short-lived ones: HotBlogs and FanLib.

19. One other evocation of the American dream came from "Amarsir" on the Primetimer forums. "I'd love it if they could stop putting ads for the show inside the show itself. 'Shark Tank helps make the American Dream a reality.' Yes, I know thank you. That's why I'm watching. You can stop telling me how great you are and go about the actual show."

20. There are some things producers can learn from tracking website discussions: for example, on what nights viewers wish ABC would air shows, what set designs they prefer, whether there should be fewer episodes that feature products of questionable value, and whether viewers prefer to see fewer guest Sharks. The production company relies on a number of strategies more sophisticated than my excavation of online comments to gauge audience responses. Those involved with this show and similar ones are skeptical about the correlation between social media activity and success, though Twitter may be more useful than other sites. Nielsen provides a relatively blunt instrument that lets producers infer why audience members change channels. Producers often dismiss data, however, and trust their gut, but they remain jealous of the data gathered by Netflix. Research departments at Sony and/or ABC might well rely on the responses of focus groups whose members watch a show and use a dial to indicate what they like and dislike. This enables producers to gauge the intensity of the appeal of a Shark, pitch, or product. However, producers may also rely less on sophisticated surveys because getting information on audiences can be expensive and "poses a potential threat to decision-making professionals, since it eliminates their claim to be able to 'feel' public tastes." Joshua Gamson, *Claims to Fame: Celebrity in Contemporary America* (Berkeley: University of California Press, 1994), 118.

21. See also three blogs—*In the Shark Tank* (www.inthesharktank.com), *Blog Shark Tank* (www.blogsharktank.com), and *Shark Tank Blog* (www.sharktankblog

.com). The news page on ABC's *Shark Tank* site (http://abc.go.com/shows/shark
-tank/news), while not a blog proper, posts occasional announcements and recaps.

22. I rely here on the podcast episode that focuses on season nine, episode
eleven, with cohosts Pierce Marrs and Steven Hayes. *The Catalyst John Show:
Entrepreneurs Wanted* was a somewhat similar podcast about *Shark Tank* that encouraged listeners to follow their dreams, which seem more modest than many
held out on the TV show. In several episodes, the hosts refer to the Bible and
books by Dale Carnegie and Norman Vincent Peale as their favorites, in ways
that reflect the power of religious inspiration rarely mentioned on *Shark Tank*.
Two episodes—season six, episodes seven and eight—are good examples of the
podcast's format: in the first two-thirds of the show, the host and a guest chat informally for thirty-plus minutes about a *Shark Tank* episode in a way that combines random digressions and lots of critiques of products, pitches, and Sharks'
responses; in the last third of the show, they offer somewhat general advice on
entrepreneurship followed by discussion of their favorite movies, vacation spots,
and scripture verses. The show ends with something the host wants to promote.
Among the other podcasts that review *Shark Tank* episodes, mostly uncritically,
are *The Chum: A "Shark Tank" Breakdown* and *"Shark Tank" Podcast with TJ Hale*.

23. Gimlet also features the podcast *StartUp*, which offers investigative journalism about the world of venture capitalism and whose episodes implicitly
counter *Shark Tank*. One list of podcasts similar to *Shark Tank* includes *Startup*
and *The Pitch*, but others on the list—*How I Built This, 20 Minute VC, Side Show
Hustle, Open for Business, Art of the Kickstart*—offer more general advice on
entrepreneurship. Mikki Stith, "Love *Shark Tank*? Check Out These 7 *Shark Tank*
Podcasts," Enventys Partners, June 14, 2017, https://enventyspartners.com/blog
/love-shark-tank-check-out-these-7-shark-tank-podcasts.

24. Sara Ashley O'Brien, "*Shark Tank*–like Podcast Aims to Get Diverse Founders Funded," CNN, November 1, 2017, https://money.cnn.com/2017/11/01/technol
ogy/culture/the-pitch-podcast/index.html.

25. In September 2017, Alexander, blocked by ABC from unauthorized use of
its brand, canceled *Shark Tank Breakdown* and launched a new show with a different but related format.

26. Four years after the parody of *Shark Tank* appeared on *SNL*, *Shark Tank,
the Musical* debuted at the Annoyance Theatre, an improv comedy theater in Chicago. I happened to be in that city at the time, and friends (Carl and Jane Smith)
made it possible for me to see a performance. Not as polished as *Jerry Springer,
the Opera*, it nonetheless captured the spirit of the TV show. The two people who
wrote the show, Jennifer Estlin and Greg Ott, pitched the idea of expanding it into
a touring company to *Shark Tank*'s production company, but it was rejected because lawyers wanted to protect the brand.

27. Another *SNL* parody of *Shark Tank* appeared on March 2, 2019. For another
parody that ably captures the approaches of Sharks, see Nutlock, "Shark Tank Parody—Dolphin Tank," YouTube video, 4:55, August 6, 2014, https://www.youtube
.com/watch?v=ZabH_gLJEKM. Among the other parodies are an Asian Indian
one: SnG Comedy, "What If | Shark Tank Was in India | Season 2 Ep 4 | Shark Tank

Parody," YouTube video, 7:28, October 26, 2016, https://www.youtube.com/watch ?v=M5MgedWZUFw. For a program called *Loan Shark Tank*, which imitated and made fun of *Shark Tank*, see Andy McDonald, " 'Loan Shark Tank' Is the Reality Show for People with No Other Option," Huffington Post, February 16, 2016, https://www.huffingtonpost.com/entry/loan-shark-tank-is-the-reality-show-for -people-with-no-other-option_us_56c35ea0e4b0b40245c8043a. In season six, on October 24, 2014, *Shark Tank* itself presented a self-parody when Jimmy Kimmel pitched custom-made pants for horses that his mother supposedly fabricated in her basement. Cuban also offered a spoof where he played variations of himself: Devon Joseph and Graham Flanagan, "Mark Cuban Just Sent Us This Hilarious *Shark Tank* Spoof That Replaces All the Judges with Clones of Himself," Business Insider, June 15, 2015, http://www.businessinsider.com/mark -cuban-shark-tank-spoof-charity-2015-7. In early 2018, university administrators used a *Shark Tank*–like exercise to explore budget priorities: Fernanda Zamudio-Suaréz, "Hypothetical 'Shark Tank' Session Sets Off Real Worries at U. of Baltimore," *Chronicle of Higher Education*, January 29, 2018. For news of a *Shark Tank* for nonprofits, see Sheela Nimishakavi, "Philanthropic *Shark Tank* with a Twist," *Boston Globe*, November 15, 2017. Another example of a cleverly packaged imitator is the annual Piranha Pond Pitch Party, hosted by the South Coast Entrepreneurs Collaborative (https://sneef.wildapricot.org/event-3463495).

28. Allison Hagan, "No Kidding: At Age 12, He's Running a Business," *Boston Globe*, September 19, 2018.

29. James Covert, "Tech Titans Bring Specialized Classes to Inner-City Schools," *New York Post*, April 13, 2016. The College and Career Academy Support Network at the University of California, Berkeley, relies on a guide developed by a high school teacher. In addition to encouraging participation in school competitions, parents of children as young as eight have begun to send their offspring to summer camps that they hope will inspire them to become entrepreneurs. See Brendan O'Connor, "Capitalism Camp for Kids," *New York Times*, May 22, 2019.

30. Emily Liebtag, "Performance Assessment in Different Learning Environments," Getting Smart, January 2, 2017, http://www.gettingsmart.com/2017/01/per formance-assessment-different-learning-environments.

31. Megan Guza, "Pittsburgh-Area Teens Make 'Shark Tank'–Style Pitches to Improve Schools," *Tribune-Review* (Pa.), October 27, 2016, https://archive.triblive .com/local/pittsburgh-allegheny/pittsburgh-area-teens-make-shark-tank-style -pitches-to-improve-schools/.

32. "Great Schools Are Good Business," www.americasucceeds.org.

33. Dan Kadlec, "*Shark Tank* for Kids: This Game Delivers the American Dream," *Money*, May 26, 2015.

34. "Deac Tank Competition—Featuring *Shark Tank* Stars!," Wake Forest University, March 21, 2017, http://events.wfu.edu/event/deac_tank_competition _-_featuring_shark_tank_stars#.WdTbHFuPLX6.

35. "Penn State Sophomore Entrepreneur Wins Grand Price in 'Shark Tank'–Style Competition," StateCollege.com, May 11, 2017, http://www.statecollege.com /news/local-news/penn-state-sophomore-entrepreneur-wins-grand-prize-in -shark-tankstyle-competition,1472288.

36. https://futurefounders.com/news-article/future-founders-announces-24 -semi-finalists-for-u-pitch-college-elevator-pitch-competition-featuring-shark -tanks-daymond-john (no longer available).

37. "NYS Business Plan Competition," Farmingdale State College, February 2019, http://www.farmingdale.edu/business/ny-business-plan-competition/in dex.shtml.

38. Allison Spooner, "Making It in GR: Pitch Competitions Put Entrepreneurs in the Spotlight," Rapid Growth, November 17, 2016, http://www.rapidgrowthmedia .com/features/111716-Making-it-in-Grand-Rapids-pitch-competitions.aspx.

39. Henry Jenkins, "Transmedia Storytelling 101," *Confessions of an Aca-Fan* (blog), March 21, 2007, http://henryjenkins.org/2007/03/transmedia_storytelling _101.html.

40. Jenkins, *Convergence Culture*, 257. Among Jenkins's most relevant works are, in addition to *Convergence Culture*, Henry Jenkins, *Textual Poachers: Television Fans and Participatory Culture*, 20th anniversary ed. (New York: Routledge, 2013); and Henry Jenkins, Mizuko Itoo, and danah boyd, *Participatory Culture in a Networked Era: A Conversation on Young, Learning, Commerce and Politics* (Malden, Mass.: Polity, 2016).

41. Stuart Hall, "Encoding, Decoding," in *The Cultural Studies Reader*, ed. Simon During (London, UK: Routledge, 1993), 90–103.

42. For a sampling of scholarship on audiences and reality TV, see Annette Hill, *Restyling Factual TV: Audiences and News, Documentary and Reality Genres* (New York: Routledge 2007); Laurie Ouellette and Susan Murray, introduction to *Reality TV: Remaking Television Culture*, ed. Susan Murray and Laurie Ouellette (New York: New York University Press, 2004), 13–14; Justin Lewis, "The Meaning of Real Life," in Murray and Ouellette, *Reality TV*, 288–302; Pamela Wilson, "Jamming *Big Brother*: Webcasting Audience Intervention, and Narrative Activism," in Murray and Ouellette, 323–43; Annette Hill, *Reality TV: Audiences and Popular Factual Television* (New York: Routledge, 2005); Derek Foster, "'Jump in the Pool': The Competitive Culture of *Survivor* Fans Networks," in *Understanding Reality Television*, ed. Su Holmes and Deborah Jermyn (New York: Routledge, 2004), 270–89; Joshua Green and Henry Jenkins, "The Moral Economy of Web 2.0: Audience Research and Convergence Culture," in *Media Industries: History, Theory and Method*, ed. Jennifer Holt and Alisa Perren (Malden, Mass.: Wiley-Blackwell, 2009), 213–25; and Robin L. Nabi, Erica N. Biely, Sara J. Morgan, and Carmen R. Stitt, "Reality-Based Television Programming and the Psychology of Its Appeal," *Media Psychology* 5 (November 2003): 303–30. More so than many in the field, Mark Andrejevic is skeptical about how much reality TV empowers audience members; see Mark Andrejevic, *Reality TV: The Work of Being Watched* (Lanham, Md.: Rowman and Littlefield, 2004). Raymond Boyle and Lisa W. Kelly offer carefully researched data on the response of British audiences to a wide variety of business-related shows in *Television Entrepreneurs*, especially pages 89–149. On the work of audience members and others as unpaid labor, see Mark Andrejevic, "Real-izing Exploitation," in *The Politics of Reality Television: Global Perspectives*, ed. Marwan M. Kraidy and Katherine Sender (New York: Routledge, 2011), 18–30.

43. John Fiske, "The Cultural Economy of Fandom," in *The Adoring Audience: Fan Culture and Popular Media*, ed. Lisa A. Lewis (New York: Routledge, 1992), 30, 37.

44. For a richly suggestive analysis of audience reactions that emphasizes the tension between authenticity and artifice, see Gamson, *Claims to Fame*, 141–71.

45. Annette Hill, "Reality TV Experiences: Audiences, Fact, and Fiction," in *A Companion to Reality Television*, ed. Laurie Ouellette (Malden, Mass.: Wiley, 2014), 117. Hill relies in part on B. Joseph Pine II and James H. Gilmore, *The Experience Economy: Work Is Theatre and Every Business a Stage* (Boston, Mass.: Harvard Business Review Press, 1999).

46. For a critical assessment of the Australian version of *Shark Tank*, see Alexandra Cain, "Why I Hate *Shark Tank*," *Sydney Morning Herald*, March 26, 2015.

47. Gamson, *Claims to Fame*, 92, 93, 95.

48. James Poniewozik, *Audience of One: Donald Trump, Television, and the Fracturing of America* (New York: Liveright, 2019), 131.

CHAPTER 7

1. Among the most prominent and well-established textbooks on entrepreneurship are Donald F. Kuratko and Richard M. Hodgetts, *Entrepreneurship: Theory, Process, and Practice*, 6th ed. (Mason, Ohio: Thomson South-Western, 2004); and Robert D. Hisrich, Michael P. Peters, and Dean A. Shepherd, *Entrepreneurship*, 8th ed. (New York: McGraw-Hill, 2010).

2. Kuratko and Hodgetts, *Entrepreneurship*, xiii, 3.

3. "Our Mission," Center for Entrepreneurial Leadership, University of Central Florida, https://cel.ucf.edu/about/our-mission/.

4. "Entrepreneurship," Conway Innovation and Entrepreneurship Center, Smith College, https://www.smith.edu/academics/conway-center/entrepreneurship.

5. Grace Chen, "Calling All Entrepreneurs! How Community Colleges Can Help You Start Your Business" (blog post), Community College Review, August 7, 2018, https://www.communitycollegereview.com/blog/calling-all-entrepreneurs-how-community-colleges-can-help-you-start-your-business. For an ambitious program that aspires to make innovation and entrepreneurship central focal points of an entire university, see the Tsai Center for Innovative Thinking at Yale: https://www.city.yale.edu/about.

6. Other sources that support investments in enterprises are the National Venture Capital Association and the Angel Capital Association.

7. "Our Story," GAN, https://www.gan.co/who/our-story/.

8. "About," d.school, Stanford University, https://dschool.stanford.edu/about.

9. Erica Swallow, "5 Foundations Supporting Social Good Entrepreneurship," Mashable, October 27, 2011, https://mashable.com/2011/10/27/online-social-entrepreneurship-foundations/#nYkDsNPnKEqE. The focus on major foundations whose reach is national should not detract attention from the many local ones. An important example is the Telluride Foundation in Colorado, an ambitious and imaginative organization that is building an entrepreneurial ecosystem in a sparsely populated area far from coastal tech centers; its goal is to strengthen

communities by developing companies that provide well-paying jobs. I am grateful to Paul Major and Marc Nager for an informative conversation on October 23, 2018.

10. This section draws on the home page of Blackstone LaunchPad, https://www.blackstonelaunchpad.org, which deploys language similar to that used by other Blackstone operations.

11. Alisha Slye, "Entrepreneurship: Job Training for the Future," pamphlet in author's possession.

12. Wendy E. F. Torrance, *Entrepreneurial Campuses: Action, Impact, and Lessons Learned from the Kauffman Campus Initiative*, Ewing Marion Kauffman Foundation, August 2013, https://www.kauffman.org/-/media/kauffman_org/re search-reports-and-covers/2013/08/entrepreneurialcampusesessay.pdf.

13. "Entrepreneurship," Ewing Marion Kauffman Foundation, https://www.kauffman.org/what-we-do/entrepreneurship.

14. Charles Leadbeater, *The Rise of the Social Entrepreneur* (London, UK: Demos, 1997), 1–3. Christian Olaf Christiansen traces the long history out of which social entrepreneurship emerges in *Progressive Business: An Intellectual History of the Role of Business in American Society* (New York: Oxford University Press, 2015). See also Heidi M. Neck, Christopher P. Neck, and Emma L. Murray, *Entrepreneurship: The Practice and Mindset* (Los Angeles, Calif.: Sage, 2018), 88–116; and Joshua Clark Davis, *From Head Shops to Whole Foods: The Rise and Fall of Activist Entrepreneurship* (New York: Columbia University Press, 2017).

15. Swallow, "5 Foundations."

16. "Young Entrepreneurs Conference" (Facebook events post), Babson College, https://www.facebook.com/events/babson-college/young-entrepreneurs -conference/433441663818049/.

17. Flyer for this talk, copy in author's possession.

18. "Mission Statement," Babson College, https://www.babson.edu/about/at-a -glance/mission-statement/.

19. For a discussion of Babson's career, see Walter A. Friedman, *Fortune Tellers: The Story of America's First Economic Forecasters* (Princeton, N.J.: Princeton University Press, 2014), 12–50.

20. John R. Mulkern, *Continuity and Change: Babson College, 1919 to 1994* (Babson Park, Mass.: Trustees of Babson College, 1995), 41. In his authoritative history of the field, Jerome A. Katz pays remarkably little attention to Babson College and Jeffry Timmons; see Jerome A. Katz, "The Chronology and Intellectual Trajectory of American Entrepreneurship Education, 1876 to 1999," *Journal of Business Venturing* 18 (2003): 283–300.

21. "Babson's History," Babson College, https://www.babson.edu/about/news -events/babson-centennial/babsons-history/.

22. "Entrepreneurship at Babson College: Curricular and Co-Curricular Programs," August 2018 official Babson College document in author's possession, also lists a series of innovations in the ensuing years. In 1992 the MBA curriculum shifted its first-year focus to "entrepreneurial management in a global economy": Mulkern, *Continuity and Change*, 210.

23. Fritz Fleischmann, "Entrepreneurship as a Way of Life" (keynote address,

Kongress: Studieren—Forschen—Gründen, German Ministry of Economics and Technology, Berlin, Germany, October 1, 2008), 3. See also Fritz Fleischmann, "What Is Entrepreneurial Thinking: Ten Theses and Provocations," in *Handbuch Entrepreneurship*, ed. Günter Faltin (Wiesbaden, Germany: Springer Gabler, 2018).

24. "Prince Mohammad Bin Salman College of Business Entrepreneurship," Babson Global, https://babsonglobal.org/2016/02/10/philanthropreneurship-for um-london/.

25. "Jamal Khashoggi: All You Need to Know about Saudi Journalist's Death," BBC News, June 19, 2019, https://www.bbc.com/news/world-europe-45812399.

26. Jeffry A. Timmons and Stephen Spinelli Jr., dedication in *New Venture Creation: Entrepreneurship for the 21st Century*, 7th ed. (Boston, Mass.: McGraw-Hill/Irwin, 2007).

27. In this discussion I am relying on Jeffry A. Timmons, Leonard E. Smollen, and Alexander L. M. Dingee, *New Venture Creation: A Guide to Small Business Development* (Homewood, Ill.: Richard D. Irwin, 1977). It is possible there is an earlier edition, but if so I was unable to locate it.

28. Many sources, including the Wikipedia entry on Timmons, offer up this quote, which they say is in Jeffry A. Timmons, *The Entrepreneurial Mind* (Andover, Mass.: Brick House, 1989); though I have not been able to locate it there, I have followed other sources in attributing it to that text. Interestingly, this quote does appear in Jeffry A. Timmons, "America's Entrepreneurial Revolution: The Demise of Brontosaurus Capitalism," pamphlet, Box of Publications for Babson College Center for Entrepreneurship Studies, Babson College Library, Wellesley, Mass.

29. "Entrepreneurship at Babson College," 2.

30. William D. Bygrave, "The Entrepreneurial Process," in *The Portable MBA in Entrepreneurship*, 4th ed., ed. William D. Bygrave and Andrew Zacharakis (New York: Wiley, 2010), 1–2.

31. Neck, Neck, and Murray, *Entrepreneurship*, 5, 15, 22.

32. "Entrepreneurship at Babson College," 3.

33. Bernie Marcus and Arthur Blank with Bob Andelman, *Built from Scratch: How a Couple of Regular Guys Grew the Home Depot from Nothing to $30 Billion* (New York: Random House, 1999), xvii.

34. Statistics provide another way of measuring Babson's success. According to data the federal government recently made available, ten years after graduation the median income of Babson students who had received federal aid was $96,000, compared with $60,800 for Wellesley students and $65,000 for Amherst students. The three colleges had roughly similar graduation rates, though Babson's was a bit lower. Its average, actual tuition was $34,000 per year, while Wellesley's was $21,506 and Amherst's $22,036. The typical student loan debt of Babson graduates, at $26,000, was at least twice that of Wellesley and Amherst graduates. The SAT scores of Babson's students were appreciably lower than those of students at Wellesley and Amherst. In terms of demographics, Babson had a dramatically higher percentage of international students than either Wellesley or Amherst; compared with Wellesley, it had a much lower percentage of Asian Americans; and compared with Amherst, it has a somewhat lower percentage of Hispanics

and a dramatically lower percentage of African Americans. See the relevant material in College Scorecard, U.S. Department of Education, collegescorecard.ed .gov. PayScale, which ranks institutions by what their graduates earn, places Babson at near the top of national institutions in terms of alumni midcareer earnings. "PayScale's 2019–20 College Salary Report," PayScale, https://www.payscale.com /college-salary-report. See also the entry on Babson in Robert Franek, *Colleges That Create Futures: 50 Schools That Launch Careers by Going Beyond the Classroom*, 2nd ed. (New York: Princeton Review, 2017), 19–25.

35. Siminoff's story is featured in *Inside the Shark Tank* (New York: Hearst, 2018), 58–59.

36. Jamie Siminoff, "From Entrepreneur to Shark: How 'Shark Tank' Helped Shape My American Dream," *Entrepreneur*, October 5, 2018, https://www.entre preneur.com/article/321187.

CHAPTER 8

1. For an insightful discussion of the series, see Andrew Marantz, "How 'Silicon Valley' Nails Silicon Valley," *New Yorker*, June 9, 2016.

2. In "Cultures of Culture: Academics, Practitioners and the Pragmatics of Normative Control," *Administrative Science Quarterly* 33 (March 1988): 24–60, Stephen R. Barley, Gordon W. Meyer, and Debra C. Gash explore how, for a decade, beginning in the mid-1970s, practitioners and academics who wrote about organizational behavior responded in distinctive ways to what their peers had claimed.

3. In addition to books cited elsewhere, interested readers can look at Gary Vaynerchuk, *#AskGaryVee: One Entrepreneur's Take on Leadership, Social Media, and Self-Awareness* (New York: HarperCollins, 2016); John Doerr, *Measure What Matters: How Google, Bono, and the Gates Foundation Rock the World with OKRs* (New York: Penguin, 2017); Guy Kawasaki, *The Art of the Start 2.0: The Time-Tested, Battle-Hardened Guide for Anyone Starting Anything*, rev. and expanded ed. (New York: Penguin, 2015); Steven R. Covey, *The 7 Habits of Highly Effective People: Powerful Lessons in Personal Change* (New York: Simon and Schuster, 1989); and books from Harvard Business School, including Evan Baehr and Evan Loomis, *Get Backed: Craft Your Story, Build the Perfect Pitch Deck, Launch the Venture of Your Dreams* (Boston, Mass.: Harvard Business Review Press, 2015); and *The Harvard Business Review Entrepreneur's Handbook: Everything You Need to Launch and Grow Your New Business* (Boston, Mass.: Harvard Business Review Press, 2018).

4. For a summary of the scope of the field of entrepreneurship that is especially useful in tracking how scholarly approaches have changed, see Heidi M. Neck, Patricia G. Greene, and Claudia G. Brush, *Teaching Entrepreneurship: A Practice-Based Approach* (Northampton, Mass.: Edward Elgar, 2014), 1–17. For an important history of the field, see Jerome A. Katz, "The Chronology and Intellectual Trajectory of American Entrepreneurship Education, 1876 to 1999," *Journal of Business Venturing* 18 (2003): 283–300.

5. Joseph A. Schumpeter, *Capitalism, Socialism, and Democracy* (New York:

Harper, 1942), 82–83, 156. Nan Enstad offers an important critique of Schumpeter's work and of those he influenced in "Debunking the Capitalist Cowboy," *Boston Review*, March 21, 2019. For Schumpeter's life, see Thomas K. McCraw, *Prophet of Innovation: Joseph Schumpeter and Creative Destruction* (Cambridge, Mass.: Harvard University Press, 2007). See also William J. Baumol, "Entrepreneurship: Productive, Unproductive, and Destructive," *Journal of Political Economy* 98 (October 1990): 893–921.

6. Angus Burgin, "The Reinvention of Entrepreneurship," in *American Labyrinth: Intellectual History for Complicated Times*, ed. Raymond Haberski Jr. and Andrew Hartman (Ithaca, N.Y.: Cornell University Press, 2018), 174.

7. Compare the two charts in Burgin, 164 and 175.

8. R. Daniel Wadhwani and Christina Lubinski offer a careful analysis of the history of entrepreneurship as a scholarly subject in "Reinventing Entrepreneurial History," *Business History Review* 91 (Winter 2017): 767–799. Wadhwani is working on the history of the transition from organization man to entrepreneur. For some suggestions about what an intellectual history of entrepreneurship would involve, see Hans Landström, "Pioneers in Entrepreneurship Research," in *Crossroads of Entrepreneurship*, ed. Guido Corbetta, Morton Huse, and Davide Ravasi (New York: Springer, 2004), 13–31. Louis Galambos, "The Entrepreneurial Culture and Bureaucracy in Twentieth-Century America," draft paper, January 2, 2020, copy in author's possession, provides a commanding and thoughtful examination of the historical contrasts between bureaucratic and entrepreneurial approaches.

9. Howard H. Stevenson and J. Carlos Jarillo, "A Paradigm of Entrepreneurship: Entrepreneurial Management," *Strategic Management Journal* 11 (Summer 1990): 23. A key document is Howard H. Stevenson, "Why Entrepreneurship Has Won!" (plenary address, United States Association for Small Business and Entrepreneurship conference, San Antonio, Texas, February 17, 2000), http://www.unm .edu/~asalazar/Kauffman/Entrep_research/e_won.pdf. For a thoughtful elaboration on Stevenson's definition of *entrepreneurship*, on which I have drawn here, see Thomas R. Eisenmann, "Entrepreneurship: A Working Definition," *Harvard Business Review*, January 10, 2013.

10. Scholars interested in entrepreneurship have produced abundant literature on key issues that shape investments in startups, including by angel investors, though much of it is not easily accessible to general audiences: see articles in periodicals such as the *Academy of Management Review, Organization Studies, Strategic Entrepreneurship Journal*, and *Entrepreneurship Theory and Practice*. In addition, there are some articles in journals like these that focus specifically on *Shark Tank* or its equivalents in other countries, with a particular emphasis on pitching. See Scott A. Jeffrey, Moren Lévesque, and Andrew Maxwell, "The Noncompensatory Relationship between Risk and Return in Business Angel Investing Decision Making," *Venture Capital* 18 (April 2016): 189–209; Scott A. Jeffrey, Moren Lévesque, and Andrew Maxwell, "Business Angel Early Stage Decision Making," *Journal of Business Venturing* 26 (March 2011): 212–25; and Brian K. Krumm, "Fostering Innovation and Entrepreneurship: *Shark Tank* Shouldn't Be

the Model," *Arkansas Law Review* 70 (2017): 553–608. Baylee Smith and Angelino Viceisza link material from *Shark Tank* episodes with data from sources such as the Small Business Administration and the U.S. Patent and Trademark Office in order to measure the show's impact: see Baylee Smith and Angelino Viceisza, "Bite Me! ABC's *Shark Tank* as a Path to Entrepreneurship," *Small Business Economics* 32 (May 2017): 463–79; and a National Science Foundation grant for 2017–19 to Viveisza on "Collaborative Research: Media Influences on Entrepreneurship and Innovation," award number 1664383, https://www.nsf.gov/awardsearch/showAward?AWD_ID=1664383&HistoricalAwards=false.

11. Scott Shane and Sankaran Venkataraman, "The Promise of Entrepreneurship as a Field of Research," *Academy of Management Review* 25 (January 2000): 218.

12. See Israel M. Kirzner, "Entrepreneurial Discovery and the Competitive Market Process: An Austrian Approach," *Journal of Economic Literature* 35 (March 1997): 60–85.

13. Clayton M. Christensen, *The Innovator's Dilemma: When New Technologies Cause Great Firms to Fail* (Boston, Mass.: Harvard Business Review Press, 1997), ix, xii–xiii, xix–xxiii. For a criticism of Christensen's work, see Jill Lepore, "The Disruption Machine: What the Gospel of Innovation Gets Wrong," *New Yorker*, June 23, 2014. Christensen eventually came to believe that terms like *disruptive innovation* were too widely used.

14. The following discussion hardly covers all the relevant and helpful sources. A longer list would include Steve Blank, *The Four Steps to the Epiphany: Successful Strategies for Products That Win*, 2nd ed. (Foster City, Calif.: CafePress, 2006); and Saras D. Sarasvathy et al., *Effectual Entrepreneurship* (Oxford, UK: Routledge, 2011).

15. Tad Friend, "Tomorrow's Advance Man: Marc Andreessen's Plan to Win the Future," *New Yorker*, May 18, 2015.

16. Ben Horowitz, *The Hard Thing about Hard Things: Building a Business When There Are No Easy Answers* (New York: HarperCollins, 2014), ix, 59, 65, 243.

17. Peter Thiel with Blake Masters, *Zero to One: Notes on Startups, or How to Build the Future* (New York: Crown, 2014), 2, 189. For a critique of the individualistic myth, see Martin Ruef, *The Entrepreneurial Group: Social Identities, Relations, and Collective Action* (Princeton, N.J.: Princeton University Press, 2010).

18. Eric Ries, *The Lean Startup: How Today's Entrepreneurs Use Continuous Innovation to Create Radically Successful Businesses* (New York: Crown, 2011), 2, 8–9. Among the important books in conversation with *Lean Startup* are Steve Blank and Bob Dorf, *The Startup Owner's Manual: The Step-by-Step Guide to Building a Great Company* (Pescadero, Calif.: K and S Ranch, 2012); and Alexander Osterwalder and Yves Pigneur, *Business Model Generation: A Handbook for Visionaries, Game Changers, and Challengers* (Hoboken, N.J.: Wiley, 2010).

19. Brad Feld and Jason Mendelson, *Venture Deals: Be Smarter than Your Lawyer and Venture Capitalist*, 3rd ed. (Hoboken, N.J.: Wiley, 2016), 211.

20. Noam Wasserman, *The Founder's Dilemmas: Anticipating and Avoiding the Pitfalls That Can Sink a Startup* (Princeton, N.J.: Princeton University Press,

2012), 2–4. Wasserman moves into the broader arena of how-to books, especially in terms of decisions about marriage and family, with *Life Is a Startup: What Founders Can Teach Us about Making Choices and Managing Change* (Stanford, Calif.: Stanford University Press, 2019).

21. Wasserman, *Founder's Dilemmas*, 11.

22. Wasserman, 12–19; Barton H. Hamilton, "Does Entrepreneurship Pay? An Empirical Analysis of the Returns to Self-Employment," *Journal of Political Economy* 108 (June 2000): 604–31. Hamilton explores the appeal of nonpecuniary rewards, especially the autonomy of being your own boss, but does not consider other cultural factors, such as the pursuit of the American dream or the allure of celebrity culture.

23. Wasserman, *Founder's Dilemmas*, 371.

24. More in line with strategic thinking than an entrepreneurial vision are Michael E. Porter's two tools: Porter's Five Forces (1979) focuses on understanding the competitive forces a business will encounter, while his Generic Competitive Strategies (1980) explores how a firm can gain advantages over other companies in similar fields. See Michael E. Porter, *Competitive Strategy: Techniques for Analyzing Industries and Competitors* (New York: Free Press, 1998).

25. W. Chan Kim and Renée Mauborgne, *Blue Ocean Strategy: How to Create Market Space and Make the Competition Irrelevant* (Boston, Mass.: Harvard Business School Press, 2005).

26. Scott Shane, *The Illusions of Entrepreneurship: The Costly Myths That Entrepreneurs, Investors, and Policy Makers Live By* (New Haven, Conn.: Yale University Press, 2008), 3–4, 7–8.

27. Dick Lynch, *Connect the Dots . . . to Become an Impact Player* (New York: iUniverse, 2003), 183. Alvin Toffler, *Future Shock* (New York: Random House, 1970), was also among the influential books that helped reshape corporations by advocating antibureaucratic flexibility; see also Louis Hyman, *Temp: How American Work, American Business, and the American Dream Became Temporary* (New York: Viking, 2018), 166–170.

28. Jeffry A. Timmons, "Black Is Beautiful. Is It Bountiful?," *Harvard Business Review* 49 (November/December 1971), 81–84.

29. David C. McClelland and David G. Winter, *Motivating Economic Achievement* (New York: Free Press, 1969), 353. See also David C. McClelland, *The Achieving Society* (New York: D. Van Nostrand, 1961). For the larger context of McClelland's work, see Ellen Herman, *The Romance of American Psychology: Political Culture in the Age of Experts* (Berkeley: University of California Press, 1995), 139–41. For the link between McClelland's work and Black Power, see David D. McClelland, "Black Capitalism," *Think*, July–August, 1969, 6–11; and Samuel L. Woodward, "Black Power and Achievement Motivation," *Clearing House* 44 (October 1969): 72–75.

30. Jeffry A. Timmons, Leonard E. Smollen, and Alexander L. M. Dingee Jr., *New Venture Creation: A Guide to Small Business Development* (Homewood, Ill.: Richard D. Irwin, 1977), ix.

31. Timmons, "Black Is Beautiful," 89, 92 (emphases in original). Timmons's

work coincided with and was influenced by discussions of Black capitalism in the late 1960s at Harvard Business School. In a 2018 pamphlet accompanying an exhibit at Baker Library Special Collections, Harvard Business School, titled *Agents of Change: A Review of Thought Leadership on Race and Black Business Leadership at Harvard Business School*, Laura Morgan Roberts documented Harvard Business School courses and articles in the *Harvard Business Review* that paid some attention to African Americans, especially beginning in 1968. In the rest of his career, Timmons sustained a commitment to developing entrepreneurship among African Americans, including by connecting historically black colleges and universities and Babson: Candida Brush, conversation with author, October 24, 2018.

32. Jeffry A. Timmons, "Entrepreneurial and Leadership Development in an Inner City Ghetto and Rural Depressed Area" (DBA diss., Graduate School of Business Administration, Harvard University, 1970), 17, 301.

33. Timmons, 2, 3, 18, 304. R. Daniel Wadhwani explores an earlier example of how social problems spurred fresh institutional and intellectual approaches in "Poverty's Monument: Social Problems and Organizational Field Emergence in Historical Perspective," *Journal of Management Studies* 55 (May 2018): 545–77.

34. Michael L. Fetters, Patricia G. Greene, and Mark P. Rice, "Babson College," in *The Development of University-Based Entrepreneurship Ecosystems*, ed. John Sibley Butler, Michael L. Fetters, Patricia G. Greene, and Mark P. Rice (Northampton, Mass.: Elgar, 2010), 16. This essay discusses many of the most significant changes at Babson and offers a description of its governing organizational structures.

35. Timmons, Smollen, and Dingee, *New Venture Creation*, 4.

36. Timmons, Smollen, and Dingee, ix, xii, 1, 4, 9, 108.

37. Timmons, Smollen, and Dingee, 5, 7, 108, 198.

38. George Gilder, *Men and Marriage* (Gretna, La.: Pelican, 1986), 108, 139.

39. George Gilder, *Wealth and Poverty* (New York: Basic, 1980).

40. Susan Faludi, *Backlash: The Undeclared War against American Women* (New York: Crown, 1991), 289; for her extensive exploration of Gilder's antifeminism, see pages 283–91.

41. Gilder, *Wealth and Poverty*, 83, 85.

42. George Gilder, *The Spirit of Enterprise* (New York: Simon and Schuster, 1984), 15, 18, 19, 44, 257–58.

43. Gilder, *Wealth and Poverty*, xii. This discussion relies on Henry Allen, "George Gilder and the Capitalists' Creed," *Washington Post*, February 18, 1981; and Ann Crittenden, "George Gilder's Hymn to Getting Rich," *New York Times*, April 26, 1981.

44. Gilder, *Wealth and Poverty*, 56.

45. Crittenden, "George Gilder's Hymn."

46. Rich Karlgaard, "Why Technology Prophet George Gilder Predicts Big Tech's Disruption," *Forbes*, February 9, 2018.

47. Enstad, "Debunking the Capitalist Cowboy."

48. "Kevin O'Leary on Missing Out of Ring on 'Shark Tank,'" CNBC, February

28, 2018, https://www.cnbc.com/video/2018/02/28/kevin-oleary-on-missing-out -on-ring-on-shark-tank.html (emphasis in original).

49. Among the sources on which this summary relies are Sonali K. Shah, Sheryl W. Smith, and E. J. Reedy, *Who Are User Entrepreneurs? Findings on Innovation, Founder Characteristics, and Firm Characteristics*, Kauffman Foundation, February 2012, https://www.law.northwestern.edu/research-faculty/clbe/work ingpapers/documents/Reedy_Who_Are_User_Entrepreneurs.pdf; *HBR's 10 Must Reads on Entrepreneurship and Startups* (Boston, Mass.: Harvard Business Review Press, 2018), especially Diane Mulcahy's 2013 "Six Myths about Venture Capitalists"; *Harvard Business Review on Succeeding as an Entrepreneur* (Boston, Mass.: Harvard Business Review Press, 2011); *Entrepreneur's Handbook*; Noam Wasserman, "Founder-CEO Succession and the Paradox of Entrepreneurial Success," *Organization Science* 14 (March–April 2003): 149–72.

50. Serial entrepreneur whose name is withheld by mutual agreement, email to author, January 25, 2019.

51. Private investor whose name is withheld by mutual agreement, email to author, February 18, 2019. For a critique of the venture capital model, see Erin Griffith, "More Start-Ups Have an Unfamiliar Message for Venture Capitalists: Get Lost," *New York Times*, January 11, 2019. The documentary film *Something Ventured* (2011) captures the history of venture capital in Silicon Valley.

52. Someone experienced in entrepreneurship whose name is withheld by mutual agreement, emails to author, February 19, 2019, and October 2, 2019.

53. For helping me think through these issues, I am greatly indebted to R. Daniel Wadhwani, "How Entrepreneurship Forgot Capitalism: Entrepreneurship Teaching and Research in Business Schools," *Society* 49 (May 2012): 223–29.

CHAPTER 9

1. David Leonhardt, "We're Measuring the Economy All Wrong," *New York Times*, September 14, 2018; David Leonhardt, "Our Broken Economy, in One Simple Chart," *New York Times*, August 7, 2017. For similar coverage, see the articles in the Sunday Business section of the *New York Times* of September 16, 2018.

2. Lori Greiner remarked as late as 2012 that "in a down economy, a time when people are feeling that things are difficult, hopeless, they're worried they might lose their jobs, they tune into *Shark Tank*, and they learn about how to possibly become their own boss": Ami Kassar, "The Queen of QVC Talks about the Risks of Dealing with Sharks," *New York Times*, October 12, 2012.

3. Frank Moraes, "The Vile and Un-American Reality of *Shark Tank*," *Frankly Curious*, January 16, 2016. Moraes relies in part on George Deep, "Comparing 'Shark Tank' to Venture Capital Reality," *Forbes*, October 19, 2013. For other debates about the relative values of *Shark Tank* and other modes of funding, see Brandt Ranj, " 'Entitlement and Arrogance': Billionaire Investors Mark Cuban and Chris Sacca Slam a Well-Known Silicon Valley Venture Capitalist Who Just Bashed 'Shark Tank,' " Business Insider, January 28, 2016, https://www.businessinsider.com /mark-cuban-chris-sacca-and-paul-graham-fight-over-shark-tank-on-twitter

-2016-1/; Andy Denhart, "What Chris Sacca Learned from Being on *Shark Tank*," reality blurred, February 12, 2016, https://www.realityblurred.com/realitytv/2016/02/chris-sacca-shark-tank-interview; and Jaime Lowe, "Letter of Recommendation: 'Shark Tank,'" *New York Times Magazine*, September 28, 2017.

4. Taylor Soper, "Y Combinator Founder Paul Graham Bashes *Shark Tank*; Mark Cuban Fires Back," GeekWire, January 27, 2016, https://www.geekwire.com/2016/y-combinator-founder-paul-graham-bashes-shark-tank-mark-cuban-fires-back.

5. "Does Shark Tank Have a Woman Problem?" (blog post), National Women's Business Council, October 22, 2015, https://www.nwbc.gov/2015/10/22/does-shark-tank-have-a-woman-problem.

6. *Inside the Shark Tank* (New York: Hearst 2019), 4.

7. Mark Burnett, *Dare to Succeed: How to Survive and Thrive in the Game of Life* (New York: Hyperion, 2001), 1. See also Mark Burnett, *Survivor II, the Field Guide: The Official Companion to the CBS Television Show* (New York: TV Books, 2001). For other mentions of the American dream in the Sharks' writings, see Jim Cramer, foreword to *The Brand Within: The Power of Branding From Birth to the Boardroom*, by Daymond John with Daniel Paisner (New York: Display of Power Publishing, 2010), xvi; and Michael Parrish DuDell, *Shark Tank: Jump Start Your Business: How to Launch and Grow a Business from Concept to Cash* (New York: Hyperion, 2013), 104, 260.

8. Jim Cullen, *The American Dream: A Short History of an Idea That Shaped America* (New York: Oxford University Press, 2003); see also Robert J. Shiller, "The Transformation of the 'American Dream,'" *New York Times*, August 8, 2017. Gabriel H. Sanchez discusses how people understand what the American dream means in "This Is What the American Dream Really Means for Americans," BuzzFeed, July 4, 2018, https://www.buzzfeednews.com/article/gabrielsanchez/this-is-what-the-american-dream-really-means-for-americans. For a critique of how emphasis on the American dream makes people feel they are to blame for failing to succeed, see Alissa Quart, "Middle-Class Shame Will Decide Where America Is Headed," *New York Times*, January 5, 2019. Countering the more familiar literature on success mythology is Scott A. Sandage, *Born Losers: A History of Failure in America* (Cambridge, Mass.: Harvard University Press, 2005), which explores the common emphasis on learning from failure during the nineteenth century, one that resonates with how we hear the same reassurance on *Shark Tank*.

9. Samuel J. Abrams, "The American Dream Is Alive and Well," *New York Times*, February 5, 2019; Joel Best, *American Nightmares: Social Problems in an Anxious World* (Berkeley: University of California Press, 2018), 40–42. For a summary of the literature on the relationship between economic inequality and the dream of economic mobility, see Shai Davidai, "Why Do Americans Believe in Economic Mobility? Economic Inequality, External Attributions of Wealth and Poverty, and Belief in Economic Mobility," *Journal of Experimental Social Psychology* 79 (November 2018): 138–48. Davidai argues that awareness of inequality prompts people to lower their expectations of mobility and to give more weight to external factors than to personal traits.

10. In this discussion of how viewers respond to shows like *Shark Tank*, I am relying heavily on Eunji Kim, "Entertaining Beliefs in Economic Mobility" (Ph.D. diss., University of Pennsylvania, 2019). A political science and communications scholar, she concludes that "in this era of choice, entertainment media content is what appeals to citizens, as lowbrow as it may seem; the political consequences, however, are anything but trivial" (13). She also shows that people of color are more optimistic than the average viewer. Although she does not break out data for racial or ethnic subgroups, based on other studies, she assumes that in general Asian Americans are more optimistic than African Americans. For information on Kim's work, visit her website, https://www.eunjikim.pub/.

11. See Chad Newson, "*Shark Tank* and the American Dream," *Flow*, March 23, 2015, http://www.flowjournal.org/2015/03/shark-tank-american-dream; and Pamela Walker Laird, *Pull: Networking and Success since Benjamin Franklin* (Cambridge, Mass.: Harvard University Press, 2006).

12. For a collection of essays on celebrity culture, see Sean Redmond and Su Holmes, eds., *Stardom and Celebrity: A Reader* (Los Angeles, Calif.: Sage, 2007).

13. Cullen, *The American Dream*.

14. Susan J. Douglas and Andrea McDonnell, *Celebrity: A History of Fame* (New York: New York University Press, 2019), 265.

15. For criticism of *Shark Tank* and other shows for giving false hope by emphasizing the American dream, see Emma Frances Bloomfield, "Perpetuating the American Dream through Investment Television," In Media Res, January 12, 2016, http://mediacommons.org/imr/2016/01/06/perpetuating-american-dream-through-investment-television.

16. David Goldfield, *The Gifted Generation: When Government Was Good* (New York: Bloomsbury, 2017); Robert Kuttner, *Can Democracy Survive Capitalism?* (New York: W. W. Norton, 2018); and Marc Levinson, *An Extraordinary Time: The End of the Postwar Boom and the Return of the Ordinary Economy* (New York: Basic Books, 2016) contrast the current situation with an earlier time when American society provided a fair degree of economic security. Jefferson Cowie, *The Great Exception: The New Deal and the Limits of American Politics* (Princeton, N.J.: Princeton University Press, 2016), shows how the decades of reform begun in the Depression were exceptional. Robert Putnam's *Bowling Alone: The Collapse and Revival of American Community* (New York: Simon and Schuster, 2000) provides another point of contrast, painting a picture of robust community engagement that eventually eroded.

17. Adam Tooze, *Crashed: How a Decade of Financial Crises Changed the World* (New York: Viking, 2018); Steven Levitsky and Daniel Ziblatt, *How Democracies Die* (New York: Crown, 2018).

18. Steven Pinker's *Enlightenment Now: The Case for Reason, Science, Humanism, and Progress* (New York: Penguin, 2018) offers an optimistic picture of contemporary life, albeit one that generally avoids issues that on a more granular level shape American lives.

19. Among the books that explore the 1970s as a crucial decade are Judith Stein, *Pivotal Decade: How the United States Traded Factories for Finance in the*

Seventies (New Haven, Conn.: Yale University Press, 2010); and Jefferson Cowie, *Stayin' Alive: The 1970s and the Last Days of the Working Class* (New York: New Press, 2010).

20. Michelle Alexander, *The New Jim Crow: Mass Incarceration in an Age of Colorblindness* (New York: New Press, 2010).

21. Eliza Griswold, *Amity and Prosperity: One Family and the Fracturing of America* (New York: Farrar, Straus and Giroux, 2018); Joan C. Williams, *White Working Class: Overcoming Class Cluelessness in America* (Boston, Mass.: Harvard Business Review Press, 2017); Nancy Isenberg, *White Trash: The 400-Year Untold History of Class in America* (New York: Viking, 2016); J. D. Vance, *Hillbilly Elegy: A Memoir of a Family and Culture in Crisis* (New York: HarperCollins, 2016); Arlie Russell Hochschild, *Strangers in Their Own Land: Anger and Mourning on the American Right* (New York: New Press, 2016); Amy Goldstein, *Janesville: An American Story* (New York: Simon and Schuster, 2017); Robert Putnam, *Our Kids: The American Dream in Crisis* (New York: Simon and Schuster, 2015); George Packer, *The Unwinding: An Inner History of the New America* (New York: Farrar, Straus and Giroux, 2013); Richard G. Wilkinson and Kate Pickett, *The Spirit Level: Why More Equal Societies Almost All Do Better* (London, UK: Allen Lane, 2009); Alissa Quart, *Squeezed: Why Our Families Can't Afford America* (New York: Ecco, 2016); Ganesh Sitaraman, *Crisis of the Middle-Class Constitution: Why Economic Inequality Threatens Our Republic* (New York: Penguin Random House, 2017); Anne Case and Angus Deacon, "Rising Morbidity and Mortality in Midlife among White, Non-Hispanic Americans in the 21st Century," *PNAS* 112 (December 8, 2015): 15078–83; Sarah Smarsh, *Heartland: A Memoir of Working Hard and Being Broke in the Richest Country on Earth* (New York: Scribner, 2018).

22. Matthew Desmond, *Evicted: Poverty and Profit in the American City* (New York: Crown, 2016).

23. Nancy MacLean, *Democracy in Chains: The Deep History of the Radical Right's Stealth Plan for America* (New York: Penguin, 2017); Steven Viscelli, *The Big Rig: Trucking and the Decline of the American Dream* (Berkeley: University of California Press, 2016); Lane Windham, *Knocking on Labor's Door: Union Organizing in the 1970s and the Roots of a New Economic Divide* (Chapel Hill: University of North Carolina Press, 2017).

24. Louis Hyman places the gig economy in long-term and capacious contexts in *Temp: How American Work, American Business, and the American Dream Became Temporary* (New York: Viking, 2018). Alexandrea J. Ravenelle emphasizes the costs of new patterns of labor-capital relationships in *Hustle and Gig: Struggling and Surviving in the Shared Economy* (Berkeley: University of California Press, 2019).

25. A useful starting point for a discussion of inequality is Thomas Piketty, *Capital in the Twenty-First Century* (Cambridge, Mass.: Harvard University Press, 2014). Jacob Hacker's *The Great Risk Shift: The New Economic Insecurity and the Decline of the American Dream*, rev. and expanded ed. (New York: Oxford University Press, 2008), while hardly denying the importance of growing inequality, nonetheless insists that that insecurity poses a more powerful threat.

26. Earl Wysong, Robert Perrucci, and David Wright, *New Class Society: Good-*

bye American Dream?, 4th ed. (Lanham, Md.: Rowman and Littlefield, 2014). On the role of luck, including in shaping our economic fates, see Robert H. Frank, *Success and Luck: Good Fortune and the Myth of Meritocracy* (Princeton, N.J.: Princeton University Press, 2016).

27. Anand Giridhardas, *Winners Take All: The Elite Charade of Changing the World* (New York: Knopf, 2018); Joseph E. Stiglitz, review of same, *New York Times*, August 20, 2018.

28. On the shifting explanations for and political consequences of the Great Recession and its antecedent conditions, see Tooze, *Crashed*, especially pages 449–70 and 564–616.

29. James Manyika et al., *A Future That Works: Automation, Employment, and Productivity*, McKinsey Global Institute, 2017, https://www.mckinsey.com/~/med ia/McKinsey/Featured%20Insights/Digital%20Disruption/Harnessing%20 automation%20for%20a%20future%20that%20works/MGI-A-future-that-works _Full-report.ashx; Mark Muro, Jacob Whiton, and Robert Maxim, "What Jobs Are Affected by AI? Better-Paid, Better-Educated Workers Face the Most Exposure," Brookings, November 20, 2019, https://www.brookings.edu/research/what -jobs-are-affected-by-ai-better-paid-better-educated-workers-face-the-most -exposure/. Jill Lepore explores the debates over the coming impact of new technologies in "The Robot Caravan: Automation, A.I., and the Coming Invasion," *New Yorker*, March 4, 2019, 20–24.

30. Ben Casselman, "A Start-Up Slump Is a Drag on the Economy. Big Business May Be to Blame," *New York Times*, September 20, 2017; David Leonhardt, "The Charts Show How Big Business Is Winning," *New York Times*, June 17, 2018; Lina M. Khan, "Amazon's Antitrust Paradox," *Yale Law Journal* 126 (January 2016): 710–805; Tim Wu, *The Curse of Bigness: Antitrust in the New Gilded Age* (New York: Columbia Global Reports, 2018); Ruchir Sharma, "When Dead Companies Don't Die," *New York Times*, June 15, 2019.

31. Richard Florida, "The Rate of New Business Formation Has Fallen by Almost Half Since 1978," CityLab, May 5, 2014, https://www.citylab.com/life/2014 /05/rate-new-business-formation-has-fallen-almost-half-1978/9026/.

32. Charles Murray, *Coming Apart: The State of White America, 1960–2010* (New York: Crown, 2012), 235, 304, 306. More recently, in *The Once and Future Worker: A Vision for the Renewal of Work in America* (New York: Encounter, 2018), Oren Cass, also a fellow at the Manhattan Institute, criticized economic and political elites on the Left and the Right for prioritizing consumption over production in ways that adversely affect workers, their families, and their communities. Seeking to strengthen working-class families and the position of male breadwinners, Cass called for limiting the immigration of less-skilled immigrants, providing greater support for vocational education, and developing tax, trade, regulatory, and social welfare policies that prioritize productive work for those whom decades of problematic policies have disadvantaged. In his *New York Times* op-eds and in recent books—including *The Social Animal: The Hidden Sources of Love, Character, and Achievement* (New York: Random House, 2011), *The Road to Character* (New York: Random House, 2015), and *The Second Mountain: The Quest for a Moral Life* (New York: Random House, 2019)—David Brooks combines emphases

on character and on community to offer a conservative analysis of contemporary America. For another conservative analysis of the economy in the wake of the Great Recession and growing disparities in wealth, see Tyler Cowen, *Average Is Over: Powering America beyond the Age of the Great Stagnation* (New York; Dutton, 2015).

33. There is a strong parallel between the industrial relationships undergirding the show's production and the ideology the show offers. In the late 1980s, powerful media corporations developed a model that increased their reliance on both nonunion, often economically precarious labor and the uncompensated labor of most contestants. I draw here on Guy Redden, "Is Reality TV Neoliberal?," *Television and New Media* 19 (September 2017): 399–414. For a critique of the concept of neoliberalism, see Daniel Rodgers, "The Uses and Abuses of 'Neoliberalism,'" *Dissent*, Winter 2018, 78, 83, 85. Eric A. Posner and E. Glen Weyl, *Radical Markets: Uprooting Capitalism and Democracy for a Just Society* (Princeton, N.J.: Princeton University Press, 2018), both critiques supposedly free-market economies and offers proposals about how to solve social problems by making economies truly free.

34. For nuanced variations on these themes, see Wysong, Perrucci, and Wright, *New Class Society*, 245, 266–69, 276; Stephen C. Wright and Gregory D. Boese, "Meritocracy and Tokenism," in *International Encyclopedia of the Behavioral Sciences*, 2nd ed., ed. James D. Wright (Elsevier, 2015), 15:239–45; and Andrew L. Stewart and Felicia Pratto, "Social Dominance Orientation," in Wright, *International Encyclopedia*, 22:250–53.

35. This analysis relies especially on Richard Dyer, *Only Entertainment*, 2nd ed. (New York: Routledge, 2002), 19, 20, 22–23, 25, 26, an essay that was originally Richard Dyer, "Entertainment and Utopia," *Movie* 24 (Spring, 1977): 2–13; but also on Heather Nunn and Anita Biressi, "'Walking in Another's Shoes': Sentimentality and Philanthropy on Reality Television," in *A Companion to Reality Television*, ed. Laurie Ouellette (New York: Wiley, 2014), 484. I traced the emergence of this approach in Daniel Horowitz, *Consuming Pleasures: Intellectuals and Popular Culture in the Postwar World* (Philadelphia: University of Pennsylvania Press, 2012).

36. Daniel T. Rodgers, email to author, May 25, 2019.

37. "Fireside Chat, Q&A and 'Stern Tank' with Mark Cuban," Stern School of Business, New York University, January 29, 2019, http://www.stern.nyu.edu/expe rience-stern/news-events/fireside-chat-q-and-stern-tank-with-mark-cuban.

Index

CPSIA information can be obtained
at www.ICGtesting.com
Printed in the USA
LVHW041939011222
734343LV00004B/619